A FABULOUS KINGDOM

A FABULOUS KINGDOM

The Exploration of the Arctic

Charles Officer

Jake Page

SECOND EDITION

OXFORD
UNIVERSITY PRESS

OXFORD
UNIVERSITY PRESS

Oxford University Press, Inc., publishes works that further
Oxford University's objective of excellence
in research, scholarship, and education.

Oxford   New York
Auckland   Cape Town   Dar es Salaam   Hong Kong   Karachi
Kuala Lumpur   Madrid   Melbourne   Mexico City   Nairobi
New Delhi   Shanghai   Taipei   Toronto

With offices in
Argentina   Austria   Brazil   Chile   Czech Republic   France   Greece
Guatemala   Hungary   Italy   Japan   Poland   Portugal   Singapore
South Korea   Switzerland   Thailand   Turkey   Ukraine   Vietnam

Copyright © 2012 by Oxford University Press

Published by Oxford University Press, Inc.
198 Madison Avenue, New York, NY 10016

www.oup.com

Oxford is a registered trademark of Oxford University Press.

Library of Congress Cataloging-in-Publication Data
Officer, Charles B.
A fabulous kingdom : the exploration of the Arctic / Charles Officer, Jake Page. — 2nd ed.
    p.   cm.
Summary: "The second edition of A Fabulous Kingdom will explain the history of the arctic and
describe the current scientific and environmental issues that threaten this fascinating region"—
Provided by publisher.
ISBN 978-0-19-983780-9 (pbk.)
1. Arctic regions—Discovery and exploration. I. Page, Jake. II. Title.
G608.O33   2012
910.911′3—dc23   2011049534

9 8 7 6 5 4 3 2 1

Printed in the United States of America
on acid-free paper

This book is dedicated to the memory of the unsung heroes of Arctic exploration—John Rea, Matthew Henson, Lincoln Ellsworth, and Hubert Wilkins—and to the Inuit people who taught the explorers how to survive in their land.

On our tenth day at sea we expected to see land. There was a message from the Captain after breakfast to say that we were approaching some large icebergs. I felt very excited. There is something magical about those floating crystal jewels. I rushed on deck. . . . Ahead of us two giant bergs, aquamarine streaked with deep turquoise, rose majestically, like two pillars at the entrance of some fabulous kingdom. Emerald-green waves splashed against their bases, sending up showers of tiny sparkling gems. Irregular in shape, the bergs towered high above us. A curving spine surrounded gaping mouths which seemed to call us to them. There was something sinister about their beauty. As we glided tremulously between them, I held my breath, expecting any moment that they would draw together and crush our tiny ship.

—MARIE HERBERT, 1973

CONTENTS

PART FOUR: Climate Change and a Whole New Arctic

THIS IS A BOOK ABOUT THE BRAVE, sometimes foolhardy, sometimes deluded, and sometimes mendacious individuals who have explored the Arctic on behalf of the nations of Europe and North America. It is a story of heroes and in some cases fools; both sorts of men have perished in their attempts to learn what lay to the North, to find the idyllic land of the Hyperboreans that existed beyond the frigid zone, to learn where Ultima Thule was, to find gold or fame, to navigate an open passage through the sea ice from one continent to another, or to stand on the northernmost point on the planet, the North Pole. For centuries it was widely believed that there existed an open polar sea, an ice-free Arctic Ocean, and men sought this out, often with tragic results. The Arctic has always been layered with myths, and this book is also a look at how such myths arise and how they are—sometimes—dispelled.

Some of the names of the Arctic explorers are familiar: John Cabot, Henry Hudson, Robert Peary, Admiral Richard Byrd, and a submarine called *Nautilus*. Other names are more obscure, such as Himlico, a Carthaginian who sailed north in about 500 B.C.; the Zeno brothers, sixteenth-century scam artists of Venice; and Roald Amundsen, perhaps the greatest of all polar explorers.

Besides the quest for straightforward geographical knowledge—what is the lay of the land?—there has been also a quest to understand the nature of this strange place, a quest that in our time we call science. A great deal of science has been done in the Arctic, but perhaps less than in most other places. A great deal more science needs to be done, because the Arctic, for all its ferocious winds, its ice, its cold, and its rawness, is a highly sensitive region. But this is less a book about science than an extended tale of the exploration of the Arctic by Europeans since before the time of Christ. In recent years, numerous books have become available about one or another aspect of Arctic (and Antarctic) exploration. Why, then, another? Without mentioning every expedition, we have sought to put all the major exploratory attempts into a single story, to put them into perspective vis-à-vis each other and some of the non-Arctic historical events—and scientific understandings—that influenced these attempts.

In the long interval during which Europeans have probed the North and speculated about it, there have been three main goals. One, the search for a northeast passage from the North Sea through to the Pacific, was carried out chiefly by the British, the Russians, and the Scandinavians. The second was the search by British and Scandinavians (for the most part) for a northwest passage from the North Atlantic to the waters off Asia. And third was the quest to reach farther and farther north, finally to stand on, fly over, and pass below the ice at the North Pole. This last quest continued up until nearly the end of the twentieth century. Now tourists can—and do—cavort there, on the very top of the Earth. Today, for the most part, we seek instead data about ice packs, frozen seas, melting glaciers, the currents of the oceans, and how the Arctic influences the changing climate of the rest of the world. What we have learned in a half-century are, among other things, the answers to many of the questions explorers have been posing for more than two millennia. And so this book begins with our present knowledge about the nature of the place. We will have the luxury of seeing where miscues were made and understanding how they were made. Also, we will be all the more aware of how stunningly unknown this region was for so long a time, what a cipher it presented to men of temperate climates; and perhaps we will gain an even greater respect for their courage, ingenuity, and sacrifices.

PREFACE TO THE SECOND EDITION

WHEN THIS BOOK FIRST APPEARED (with the title *A Fabulous Kingdom*), its goal was to put the long history of Arctic exploration into a context that included not just geography but scientific understanding of how this unique region works. Referring chiefly to the nineteenth and twentieth centuries, we wrote in the First Edition's Preface that "a great deal of science has been done in the Arctic, but perhaps less than in most other places." That is no longer correct.

By the turn of the present century, it was widely understood that a speeded-up version of a constant feature of our world—climate change—was taking place, and nowhere at a more rapid rate than in the Arctic. A decade later, the Arctic had been subjected to thousands of scientific probes—its waters, its ice, its soils, its continental shelves, its atmosphere, its geology, its biota and ecosystems—in essence, a scientific full-court press. By 2010, it was clear that the Arctic was warming up overall twice as fast as the rest of the world, and predictions of concerns such as when the Arctic Ocean would be altogether free of summer ice placed such events increasingly soon.

In 2010, the world was on notice that accelerating global climate change, caused largely by the effects of human activity (in particular the expanding accumulation in the atmosphere of carbon dioxide, nitrous oxide, and other greenhouse gases, along with soot), would quite probably bring about catastrophic planetary changes unless checked—and checked soon.

So a decade after *A Fabulous Kingdom* appeared, we have added a fourth part of the book to characterize some of the astonishing new knowledge we have garnered of the Arctic . . . and characterize the remaining ignorance, which is to say the new questions being asked of this now perhaps even more fabulous part of the world.

Charles Officer and Jake Page, 2010

A FABULOUS KINGDOM

INTRODUCTION

THE NATURE OF THE PLACE

In the Arctic your senses of location and time are likely to go haywire. In our familiar temperate and equatorial latitudes we speak of north, south, east, and west, the familiar cardinal directions. At the North Pole, all directions are south. The meaning of time, as the notion is used in our temperate latitudes, diminishes the farther north one goes, until it is virtually irrelevant: because the meridians (longitude circles) converge at the Pole, so do the time zones. What time of day is it at the Pole, where you could place your foot in all the world's time zones at the same instant? At the Pole the Sun rises once a year and sets once a year, with the Moon rising and setting once a month.

The long periods of darkness during winter and long periods of sunlight in summer in the polar regions—and to a lesser extent in the temperate regions—are caused by the fact that the equatorial plane on which the Earth rotates is at an angle to the plane on which the Earth revolves around the Sun, the plane of the ecliptic. The angle of tilt between the two planes is 23.5 degrees. The moment when the Sun is farthest south is on December 22, known as the winter solstice. On this day the entire region north of latitude 66° 30′ N is in total darkness. Conversely, on June 21 every year, which is the summer solstice, the same region has twenty-four hours of daylight. The North Pole itself has six months of daylight, from about March 21, the vernal equinox, to September 21, the autumnal equinox, and six months of darkness for the rest of the year. The Arctic Circle is defined as the latitude 66° 30′ N, a convenient division between the Arctic and the North Temperate Region south of it.

A different kind of map is needed in the Arctic. The conventional map we are most familiar with is called a Mercator (or modified Mercator) projection, after the sixteenth-century cartographer. The trouble with any map is that it has to represent a three-dimensional object, the planet, on a two-dimensional surface, and so it must distort part of the world. The simplest of Mercator projections arises, figuratively, from the exercise of placing a cylinder around

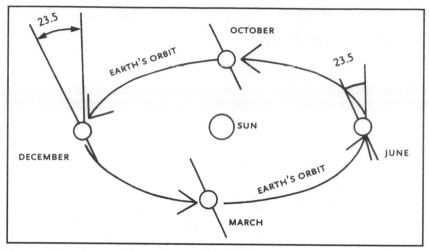

The annual revolution of the Earth around the Sun (from Maloney 1978)

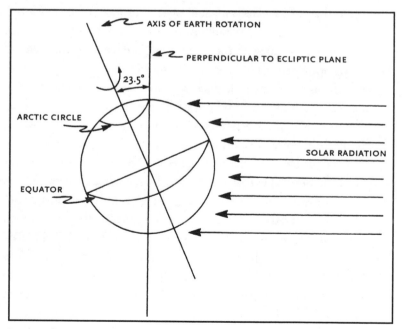

Earth and Sun orientations at the winter solstice

the world, touching it at the equator, with its axis in a north-south direction. If you project out from the center of the Earth through every point on the Earth's surface and onto the cylinder, then unwrap the cylinder, you have a Mercator projection. It gives a pretty good representation of things at tropical and temperate latitudes, but it is of little use at the higher latitudes. There everything is out of proportion, much too large, with Greenland, for example, being larger than all of North America, and in the extreme, the North Pole is off the map altogether—out at infinity.

For polar regions, most maps in use today are centered at the North Pole, and all the directions (called azimuths) and distances are true from the Pole. These maps are called azimuthal equidistant projections. The latitudes are circles around the Pole, and the longitudes radiate out from the Pole. Such maps are made arithmetically, unlike Mercator maps, which are geometric projections. But, of course, an azimuthal equidistant projection is perfectly accurate only at the Pole; elsewhere it produces its own distortions, which are larger the farther you get from the Pole. To get a true idea of the sizes of the

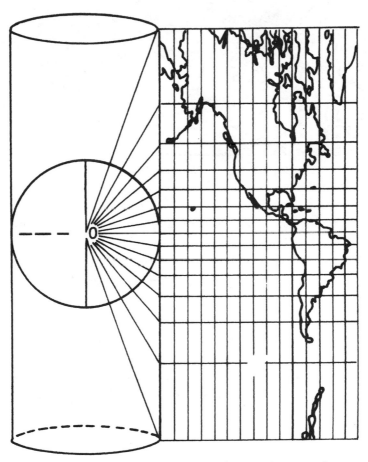

Mercator central projection upon a cylinder (from Maloney 1978)

Location map for the North Pole region (from Parkinson et al. 1987)

Earth's landforms and oceans, and a real sense of their directional relationship to each other, there is nothing like a globe.

The Arctic Ocean is roughly circular in form, with its center slightly offset from the North Pole. It is relatively isolated from the deep waters of the world and surrounded by a sequence of landmasses. Starting from the northern shores of Greenland and proceeding clockwise are Ellesmere Island, with Devon and Baffin Islands to the south; the Canadian Archipelago; the shores of northwestern Canada; Alaska; then around to the vast extent of Siberia, with the islands of Novosibirskye, Novaya Zemlya, Franz Josef Land, and Svalbard (formerly Spitzbergen) offshore; and ending with northern Europe (specifically Finland and Norway).

These Arctic lands—most of them, at least—are underlain by what is called permafrost. Except for a thin layer that melts in the summer, called the active layer, the extreme cold of the Arctic has permanently frozen the ground to depths of 800 to 1,500 feet, and even deeper in Siberia. To the south, in what is called the subarctic, the permafrost can be up to 400 feet deep, and farther south it underlies great layers of peat and boggy areas. Since continuous permafrost totally cuts off drainage underground, shallow lakes are common throughout the Arctic landmasses, and in warmer months standing water is home to legendary swarms of blackflies and mosquitoes. During the summer, waterlogged soil flows downhill over frozen ground, creating long, smooth slopes in areas where mountains do not rise from the land. Much of the exposed rock of the northern parts of the Arctic is broken up by frost into angular boulders.

To return to the ocean, the major bathymetric (deepwater) feature of the central Arctic is the Lomonosov Ridge, which divides the deepwater basin of the Arctic into two parts, the Eurasian Basin in the Eastern Hemisphere, and the Canadian Basin in the Western Hemisphere. Surrounding the Arctic

Bathymetry of the Arctic Ocean (from Parkinson et al. 1987)

Ocean are several seas, considered separate mainly because their ice cover is seasonal, unlike the permanent ice pack of the central Arctic.

The lands bordering the Arctic Ocean are sparsely populated by nomadic peoples. Until very recently, hunting was the only way to make a living in such a northerly climate. Plant life is nonexistent in areas of permanent ice, and the tundra and other exposed surfaces are not friendly to the kind of plants that normally sustain humans. Agriculture is, of course, virtually impossible. About a million people live in the Arctic, more than half of them in Siberia. The Inuit (formerly called Eskimos, a name given them by others) number about a hundred thousand, inhabiting a broad expanse from Greenland through northern Canada to Alaska. That nearly a million people do inhabit the Arctic year round is astonishing, what with the extreme harshness of the climate and the desertlike bleakness of the landscape. Indeed, the Arctic is a desert—a cold desert—because virtually all its fresh water is locked up as ice and annual precipitation measures only 6 to 9 inches, making it a place of practical aridity.

The polar climate is a result, in great part, of the heat imbalance of the spheroidal Earth. Given the angle at which the Sun's rays strike the Earth, more radiant energy is received near the equator than at the poles. Further-more, much of the radiant energy that does reach the polar regions is reflected back into the atmosphere and beyond by polar snow and ice. The global tendency is to redress the heat imbalance, to redistribute the heat dynamically by means of the general circulation of the atmosphere. Gener-ally, warmer and less dense air at the equator rises and moves toward the poles, while colder and denser air at the poles sinks and moves toward the equator. This would create two separate cells of circulating air—as if a wide sleeve were wrapped around the Earth north and south of the equator. But the Earth rotates, spinning on its axis, and this causes each pole-to-equator system to break up into three separate circulation cells: one is polar, the next is at midlatitude (called the Ferrel cell), and one is equatorial (called the Hadley cell).

The Earth's rotation creates what is called the Coriolis force, which dic-tates that air in the Northern Hemisphere, which moves north if it is warm and south if it is cold, is also deflected to the right of the north-south mo-tion. In the Southern Hemisphere, the effect is opposite; air is deflected to the left. So when cold, dense air at the North Pole sinks and moves south, it is deflected to the right, or in a westerly direction, creating winds that are called polar easterlies. (Winds are designated by the direction they flow *from* rather than *to*.)

In the Hadley cell in the Northern Hemisphere—the cell nearest the equator—warm, less-dense air rises and flows northward as it is replaced by colder air from the north, so here too the north-moving air is deflected to the west by the Coriolis force, creating the northeast trade winds.

What happens in the cell in the middle, the Ferrel cell? Air is rising at the southern boundary of the polar cell and descending at the northern boundary of the Hadley cell. At the Earth's surface here, the air is moving north and is deflected to the right (the east), creating what are called the prevailing westerlies. Much of the United States lies under the midlatitude Ferrel cell with its prevailing westerlies, which is why weather tends to come from the west. In the Southern Hemisphere the cold air comes from the south instead of the north, but the direction of the Coriolis force is flopped as well, the results being polar easterlies, prevailing westerlies, and southeast trade winds—much the same as in the north.

The value of these circular patterns for the Atlantic Ocean in the days of sailing vessels is obvious: ships sailed from Europe with the northeast trade winds blowing from astern, propelling the square-riggers across the water steadily. They could then head north on the Gulf Stream and back to Europe on the prevailing westerlies. But there were traps for the unwary. At the equator, as we have noted, warm air rises. Some flows north, some south, creating the two trade winds. In between, the air flows weakly and horizontally at the Earth's surface; this is called the intertropical convergence zone, or to sailors of wind-driven vessels, the doldrums. Similarly, the winds are also weak between the equatorial and midlatitude cells—a zone called the horse latitudes. As in the doldrums, ships were often becalmed there, and the crews jettisoned any expendable cargo (presumably including horses) to lighten the load they had to tow behind rowboats.

At the North Pole the winds are generally calm, increasing in magnitude away from it. Table I.1 shows the frequency distribution of wind speeds over the central Arctic Ocean. They are not high as a rule, averaging 9 to 11 miles per hour. They are highest in April and May, but never more than 33 miles per hour.

During the Arctic's sunless winters the skies are typically clear, and it is extremely cold; January temperatures over the pack ice average –22° to –33° F. In summer, when with the return of solar radiation come melting snow and ice and the resultant open water, temperatures are held near the freezing point for water (32° F), and it is likely to be damp and foggy. Annual precipitation, as noted, is about 6 to 9 inches, falling mostly in summer and early fall. Typically the landmasses lying around the Arctic Ocean are somewhat warmer than this in both summer and winter.

Table 1.1 Frequency Distribution of Wind Speed over the Central Arctic Ocean
Wind Speed (m/sec)

Month	0	1	2	3	4	5	6	7	8	9	10–14	15–19	20	Total of observations
Jan.	11	7	8	10	13	12	8	8	6	4	10	2	1	564
Feb.	10	6	11	15	17	15	9	5	5	1	6	0	0	548
Mar.	6	6	8	18	22	15	7	6	4	2	5	1	0	585
Apr.	6	5	15	15	17	15	8	7	5	4	3	0	0	479
May	7	5	11	16	16	15	11	7	6	3	3	0	0	744
June	5	5	9	15	13	15	11	9	6	4	7	1	0	669
July	4	3	9	12	13	16	10	9	9	6	8	1	0	609
Aug.	4	4	7	11	11	15	11	11	8	5	11	2	0	570
Sep.	8	4	9	13	15	15	8	10	5	4	7	2	0	545
Oct.	7	5	9	12	12	12	10	9	7	4	11	2	0	586
Nov.	9	7	10	13	16	15	7	6	6	4	6	1	0	607
Dec.	11	10	14	14	17	12	6	5	4	3	4	0	0	607

1m/s=22 mph

(From Vowinckel and Orvig 1970)

Just as Arctic winds rarely achieve high speeds, the ocean currents tend to be stately. The vertical structure of the ocean currents is determined, as one would expect, by the density of the masses of water, with denser water flowing in under less-dense water. Density is determined by the water's temperature and salinity, with the latter being more important. The colder and saltier the water, the denser it is. Much of the water flowing into the Arctic Ocean is a warm and saline undercurrent, flowing along the coast of Norway, referred to as the Norwegian Current. The major outflow is the surface transport of the East Greenland Current south through the Fram Strait.

Within the Arctic Ocean water circulation is governed, in part, by the Lomonosov Ridge; in the Western Hemisphere the clockwise gyre of water north of the Canadian Archipelago is called the Beaufort Gyre. In the eastern hemisphere, the Transpolar Drift System flows across from Siberia to the Fram Strait. Off Siberia, the flow averages about 1 to 1.5 miles a day, increasing to about 4 to 5.5 miles a day in the narrower causeway of the Fram Strait.

Schematic of the large-scale horizontal circulation patterns in the surface waters of the north polar region; the four major rivers providing inflows to the Arctic Ocean are also shown (from Parkinson et al. 1987)

The Arctic sea ice is always on the move. It follows the drift of the underlying ocean currents and the changes in direction and speed of the wind. For polar explorers and Pole seekers, the most important feature of the Arctic—the single feature that needed most to be understood—was the structure and drift of this shifting, ever-changing ice pack. The ice never completely covers the Arctic Ocean, because differential motion, fracturing, and melting all lead to open waters. Some of these are narrow, roughly linear leads, ranging in width from yards to a mile, and some are broader polynyas, which can be thousands of square miles in diameter. Frequent deformation of the pack ice breaks up the otherwise uniform expanse into irregular shapes called floes, which are separate platforms of ice. Other important features are pressure ridges, formed when ice is compressed with enough force to crumble it into

A lead, approximately 20 meters across, partially covered with thin ice in the Beaufort Sea ice pack, August 1975; dark blue-black coloring of the lead contrasts with the turquoise blue of the melt ponds; ponds that have melted through the ice appear darker; note also the snow cover (from Parkinson et al. 1987)

End of a small pressure ridge near the North Pole (Walter Tucker, Cold Regions Research and Engineering Laboratory, Hanover, N.H.)

rows of elevated ice several yards in height and also extending some distance down into the water below. Pressure ridges are ubiquitous, and on average there are four ridges some 30 yards in height to climb over or detour around for every mile one treks across. The pack ice, then, is extremely difficult terrain, and it extends all the way to the Pole. The native populations never had

Multiyear ice in the Beaufort Sea, showing weathered hummocks and pressure ridges (Walter Tucker, Cold Regions Research and Engineering Laboratory, Hanover, N.H.)

any interest in going into the polar region until paid by European explorers to do so.

At its southern boundaries, the ice has a seasonal growth-and-decay cycle, nearly doubling in extent from the summer to the winter. During the summer melt period water percolates through the ice, and when winter approaches, the ice is left with a rolling, hummocky surface that adds to the difficulty in crossing it. The only relatively smooth and undeformed ice one encounters in the Arctic is first-year ice, formed at the edges of the ice pack and about two yards thick. Multiyear ice tends to be about three yards thick and may be decades old. In September, when the ice is at its minimum extent, the ice pack is confined mostly to the Arctic Ocean, with only a small amount reaching into the Greenland, Kara, and Barents Seas and the Canadian Archipelago. At this time virtually no ice is to be seen in the Bering Sea, Hudson Bay, the Sea of Okhotsk, and Baffin Bay. On the other hand, in March, when the ice is at its maximum, it covers the Arctic Ocean, the waters around the Canadian Archipelago, and large portions of other peripheral seas and bays. Through the eons, this schedule has varied as the Northern Hemisphere experienced long periods of unusual warmth or unusual cold.

For polar explorers a century ago, the movement of the pack ice was as important to know as the location, height, and extent of pressure ridges. In simple terms, you can't know what direction you need to go to reach, say, the North Pole, if you don't know which way the ice you're going to cross is drifting.

Average summer ice extent (minimum) and average winter ice extent (maximum), both shown as heavy lines (from Central Intelligence Agency 1978)

Today, thanks to the placement of manned (though drifting) stations on the ice pack by Russians, Canadians, and Americans over the past sixty-odd years, we have a fairly good picture of these motions. The ice generally follows the direction of the Beaufort Gyre and the Transpolar Drift System, but it can be quite erratic, sometimes doubling back on itself. It travels about four miles a day, sometimes less, sometimes as much as two miles more per day.

Finally there is the matter of navigation and bearings out on the Arctic ice pack. The early explorers did not have the advantage of satellite navigation. They couldn't even avail themselves of then-conventional celestial navigation, in which one measures the angle from the horizon to a star at a given moment in time. From the intersection of two or more such lines from two or more

Tracks of manned drift stations, 1958–1975, for both the Soviet Union and the United States (from Central Intelligence Agency 1978)

star sightings, and with the aid of the *Nautical Almanac,* a catalogue of star positions, your location is given. To use this technique, both the horizon and the stars (or planets) have to be visible simultaneously, limiting celestial navigation to early evening and early morning. On the polar ice pack in summer, however, the horizon is visible but no stars are; in winter the stars twinkle but there is no horizon to be seen in the dark.

In this situation you have to rely on a less accurate system, determining the height of the Sun above the horizon at local apparent noon, which calls for a series of Sun sights until the maximum elevation has passed. Through appropriate tables, the Sun's elevation can be translated into your latitude, and the time of the local *apparent* noon (the Sun's maximum height in the sky) translates directly into one's longitude. (Until the invention of the chronometer at about the time of the Renaissance, there was no way to determine longitude, and explorers setting out in earlier times simply couldn't know where they were.)

These Sun sights are all very well in much of the world, but as you approach the Pole there is little change in the Sun's elevation, and the concept of local apparent noon loses its meaning. Magnetic compasses are of minimal value in the polar latitudes, since the magnetic pole undergoes large and somewhat unpredictable variations. It is currently in the vicinity of latitude 76° N and longitude 100° W; however, these locations not only are indefinite but change irregularly over a period of years. It is preferable to get an estimate of geographic *south* from the Sun's position at its maximum elevation.

With the unpredictable vagaries in the drift of the ice pack, it is essential to take daily readings at noon. Dead reckoning—deducing position from your direction and speed—without considering the drift of the ice can lead not only to huge but unrealized errors, and it often did in the long history of Arctic exploration.

Imagine, then, being an explorer four hundred or even a thousand years ago, not knowing any of this as you proceed northward past the waters and landforms of your known world in a small though seaworthy craft, into a world inhabited (but only sparsely) by strange creatures in the sea—seals, walruses, narwhals with their unicornlike single horns, the occasional seabird arrowing off through the mist, strange ice forms floating in the fog like cosmic rubble and rising steeply above you, distant black-and-white shores soon lost to sight in the gathering frozen night. . . .

The Arctic has been described as bleak, beautiful, terrifying, depressing. It has driven Europeans into madness; worse, it has claimed lives with a carelessness that denies, for some, the presence of a loving God. One of its most eloquent troubadours, Barry Lopez, has trekked its length and breadth and found a wisdom "that lies in the richness and sanctity of a wild landscape, what it can mean in the unfolding of a human life, the staying of a troubled human spirit." He speaks of the North and its exploration as a continuing movement through uncharted waters, "an expression of fear and accomplishment, the cusp on which human life finds its richest human expression."

A magical kingdom, one might say.

ULTIMA THULE

1 SEA LUNGS, GODLY COMMERCE, AND PROJECTIONS

Pytheas, one of the first men from the classical world of the Mediterranean to explore the ocean and lands of the far north, came upon a region where the Earth, the sea, and all the elements were held in some kind of suspension "which you can neither walk nor sail upon." He described this phenomenon as resembling the "sea lungs," which was a name for certain jellyfish. What he might have had in mind is anyone's guess; perhaps it was a sea fog so dense it made him claustrophobic, as if, Jonahlike, he were trapped inside a giant jellyfish. Far-fetched? Yes, but would an astronomer of the fourth century B.C. have looked at the rough pack ice in the Arctic and been reminded, say, of the air sacs (the alveoli) of the mammalian lung? Not likely.

Pytheas was a citizen of the Greek colonial city of Massilia, present-day Marseilles, and an accomplished scientist and astronomer. Among his accomplishments was to associate the phenomenon of the tides with the motion of the Moon, something no one had noticed until then. The ocean tides are practically nonexistent in the Mediterranean, with its narrow neck opening to the Atlantic at the Straits of Gibraltar, which was called in those days the Pillars of Hercules. So Pytheas must have ventured through those pillars. He was also the first, or at least among the first, to use celestial navigation to locate himself at sea. With these nautical accomplishments, it is not surprising that in about 325 B.C. the merchants of Massilia selected him to see if he could open a trade route by sea to such northerly places as Cornwall in England, the south coast of Brittany, and the Baltic Sea. Massilia's merchants were already plying an arduous river and overland trade route to those places, involving a long trek up the Rhône, among others. A sea route would be easier, they reasoned, just as it had been for the Phoenicians, who had sailed there for almost a thousand years, starting in about 2000 B.C., for the same reasons: alluvial deposits of tin from

Cornwall and Brittany, and amber that washed up from the ocean on the shores of Denmark and near Lithuania. And when the Phoenician city-states declined and were overrun by Assyrians around 1000 B.C., Carthage emerged as the major sea power of the time and took over the tin and amber routes.

The first actual mention in the literature that has come down to us of a northern sea voyage is that of a Carthaginian named Himlico, whose voyage evidently took place around 500 B.C. In it he described a projecting ridge, "a high mass of rocky ridge [that] turns mostly toward the warm south wind" called Oestrymnis; it is probably the chalk cliffs of Dover. The account also mentions islands that are likely those off Brittany, rich in tin and lead. It speaks as well of a place called Hierne (Ireland), not far from Albion (England again), and of people who didn't make keels; "strange to say, they make their ships of hides sewn together" and "plough in skillful fashion far and wide the foaming sea, and the currents of monster-bearing Ocean in these small boats."

Yet the account of Himlico's voyage comes to us secondhand. His own account, if such there ever was, does not exist. Instead, we are told of Himlico and his sightings by a Roman author, Rufus Festus Avienus, writing almost a thousand years later, in the fourth century A.D. Better, then, to trust in Pytheas as the first of the classical explorers of the northern seas. He set out, we are told, at the same time that Aristotle was holding classes and Alexander the Great and his army were marching on India.

In all, it seems, Pytheas and his crew were gone for some six years, spending a fair amount of time in present-day England and Scotland, noting that people there grew wheat and corn; mined tin; had tools of iron, domestic animals, and chariots of wood; and made a "wine" from fermented grain. He sailed on northward, finally reaching a place he called Thule, where evidently the "sea lungs" stopped him. Not much farther north, he reported, the summer sun didn't set and the winter sun was never seen. He evidently believed that Thule was six days' sail north of Britain and one day south of a "congealed" or frozen sea, meaning the pack ice. Upon his return he wrote a treatise, *On the Ocean,* which unfortunately, like Himlico's own account, was lost. We know of Pytheas's treatise and his trip north only from subsequent writers, chiefly two Roman geographers who thought he was a liar.

The better known of the two was the geographer Strabo, who wrote of Pytheas about three hundred years after the fact and apparently from secondhand sources. Strabo read about Pytheas in the works of a shadowy explorer named Polybius, who was motivated to downplay Pytheas's accomplishments lest they outshine his own. Strabo also referred to the works of the mathematician and poet Eratosthenes, who believed there was such a place as Thule but didn't know how much more of Pytheas's account was reliable. Strabo concluded that Pytheas was a fraud, an archfalsifier of information, saying that other people who had since gone to Britain and Ireland never mentioned Thule, and anyway, people couldn't live as far north as he said they did. Strabo, of course, was wrong, and Pytheas was right.

Another major classical writer to discuss Pytheas's version of events was Pliny the Elder, the author of *Natural History,* in the late years of the first century A.D. He evidently had heard of Pytheas through yet other writers, but unlike the virulent Strabo he simply reported what he had read without taking much of a stand one way or the other. For example, he wrote:

> The light nights in summer substantiate what theory compels us to believe, that, as on summer days the sun approached nearer to the top of the world, owing to a natural circuit of light the underlying parts of the earth have continuous days for six months at a time, and continuous nights when the sun has withdrawn in the opposite direction towards winter. Pytheas of Marseilles writes that this occurs in the island of Thule, six days' voyage north of Britain.

No educated person in classical times, it should be pointed out, questioned the notion of the midnight sun and the long nights of winter. They were well aware that the Earth was a globe and that the changing angle of the Sun would bring about such day lengths at the "top" of the globe. They just had no idea what lay toward the top (or the bottom) of the globe. Speculation was rife: Was there a frigid sea beyond which a halcyon land existed, inhabited by blessed people called the Hyperboreans? Or was it a frozen mountain, or an open sea, or some kind of unimaginable and precipitous end of the Earth?

Today most historians seem satisfied that Pytheas was probably the first classical explorer to venture into the near Arctic, but there remains a good deal of disagreement about where Pytheas was when he came upon Thule. The main candidates are the Shetland Islands (north of Scotland), Iceland, and Norway. But the Shetlands, given the length of the day there at midwinter, and the fact that they are far more than a day south of the pack ice and less than six from Scotland, have been largely ruled out. An Icelandic explorer of the twentieth century favors Iceland; a Norwegian explorer, not surprisingly, favors Norway. One problem with Norway is that it doesn't have much sea ice near its coast. On the other hand, most Icelandic historians say Thule wasn't Iceland. Thule thus has eluded us and probably always will; indeed, our phrase "Ultima Thule," derived from Pytheas's island, means the farthest place, in essence an ultimate, perhaps impossible-to-attain, goal.

In any event, Pytheas had refound the sea route to the tin mines of Britain. It is likely that Massilian and other merchants followed in his wake, and it is perfectly possible that others approached or even entered Arctic waters over the centuries that ensued; we just have no record of such anonymous and unheralded doings. We know far more, in fact, about the people who at that time had already lived throughout the Arctic for five millennia or more, because they left signs of their presence throughout the region, later to be scratched out of the ground by archaeologists.

By the time Pytheas reached Thule, wherever that was, people living on most of the landforms that surround the Arctic Ocean were hunting whales and other sea mammals such as seals with harpoons. They were also following the migrations of caribou, herding reindeer, and burying their dead with exquisitely carved representations of the local fauna. These various Arctic peoples all had evolved much the same anatomical adaptations to living in so cold a place, tending to have thick, short bodies; relatively short limbs; and small hands and feet, plus an increased flow of blood to body parts exposed to extreme cold. In addition, the Lapps, those renowned reindeer herders of the north, tend to shunt blood from one artery to a paired one, which warms venous blood returning from the extremities to the heart. This in turn means that their hands and feet can become relatively cold without affecting organs such as the brain.

These well-adapted people were essentially the sole inhabitants of the Arctic for some twelve thousand years. But even though they all remained utterly anonymous in the course of history until some two hundred years ago, it was well into the twentieth century before Europeans learned much of anything about the Arctic that these indigenous people didn't already know. And as we shall see, until the airplane was capable of long-distance flight, no European (or American) explorer got very far in the Arctic or lasted very long there without the help or the carefully observed example of the indigenous peoples, chiefly the various Inuit peoples that Europeans came to call Eskimos.

If the earliest ventures into the Arctic arose as a result of commercial interests such as lead and tin and amber, the next recorded penetration of the Arctic by Europeans came about as the quest for a different sort of commerce altogether: commerce with God. By A.D. 800 the European world had changed radically from Pliny the Elder's times. Among other things, Huns,

Vandals, Visigoths, and a host of other northerly groups had pressured the overextended Roman Empire, shoved it back, and finally defeated it. During the centuries that followed, much of classical culture and civilization was lost except in more easterly realms, where Arabs would preserve a great deal and expand on it. And in Europe, the refuge of culture—the place where learning, intellectual enterprise, and spiritual thought survived like a small ember— was the remote and windswept monasteries of Ireland. Under pressure from both Rome (to conform to its doctrinal pronouncements) and the roving Vikings, many Irish monks left in the 700s and 800s for the Faeroe Islands and even Iceland, establishing new monasteries on remote promontories overlooking the cold ocean. There are plenty of stories about how some of these monks, sailing the high seas in their carraughs (boats made of ox hides) reached as far west as North America, but there is, disappointingly for the romantic of spirit, absolutely no evidence that this ever happened. In the 1970s an adventurer named Tim Severin constructed a carraugh of the kind that the Celts used, made of hides over a wicker basketlike structure, and in it he sailed from Ireland to Iceland and from there to Newfoundland, proving that it could have been done by the monks of old (but not, of course, proving that they did any such thing).

Indeed, there are grand legends of the Celtic monks searching for the Land of the Blessed, the untroubled and graceful place where vines bore fruit twelve times a year and people lived in peace. These legends became unified in an eighth-century narrative called *Navigatio Brendani.* The man known as Brendan the Navigator did indeed exist, but he almost surely never went to Iceland. Saint Brendan was born on the west coast of Ireland in the fifth century, sailed to Scotland, where he founded a monastery, and later became abbot of a monastery in Wales, dying in the sixth century back home in Ireland. Before long he was a folk hero as well as a saint, with the great narrative being committed to paper several centuries after his death and going through more than a hundred versions in virtually all the languages of Europe. The narrative is a rousing seagoing epic of wondrous stories and amazing meetings, most of which surely didn't happen, particularly to the good abbot, including a landing on North American shores where the monks were greeted by a very old man who wore no clothes but was covered by his hair and beard, which were pure white.

Three hundred years after the real Brendan had been laid in his grave in western Ireland, the Vikings, those land-hungry, loot-hungry seafaring warriors from Scandinavia, were in full attack mode. Much of Europe would fall to these marauders, the terrifying prows of their ships suddenly appearing in coastal and river communities, of which few survived intact. Danish Vikings, for example, destroyed Paris twice in the mid-800s and sailed through the Pillars of Hercules to terrorize both Italy and Morocco. Their takeover of all of England was blocked only by a young Welsh lord named Alfred, who rallied the various English groups into a single force in 878 and held the Vikings to only partial control of the British Isles. Alfred, a man of many parts—soldier, administrator, scholar—became known as the first true king of England: Alfred the Great.

Earlier, Danish Norsemen had "discovered" Iceland, but they were mostly fishermen and farmers, colonizing the island and evidently driving out the remaining Celtic monks from their meditations. At about the same time, around A.D. 870, a Viking named Ottar ventured north into the polar sea, most likely to hunt for creatures such as walruses, thus becoming the first European known to have reached the Arctic, though others must have reached it before him. In his account, made to King Alfred (and he, the good scholar, took it down), Ottar sailed north along the coast of Scandinavia to North Cape, then east for five days through the Barents Sea to the Kola Peninsula, and then south into the White Sea. He evidently found the southern shores of the White Sea to be inhabited. Hearing of this, later Vikings would follow his route, bent on plunder.

It was probably a Norwegian, Gunnbjörn Ulfsson, who discovered Greenland in the next century, but it comes down through most histories as an exploit of Eirik Raude or Erik the Red, a Norwegian and apparently a major landowner in Iceland, where he had settled after being banished from Norway for murder. In 982 his serfs in Iceland set an avalanche tumbling down onto another man's home (or so it is written in Finn Gad's 1970 *History of Greenland*). The man's kinsmen exacted revenge by killing Erik's serfs, which led Erik to exact his revenge in turn, killing the slayers and a few others to boot. The penalty in Norse communities for unjustifiable homicide was loss of personal property and banishment from the community for three years, so Erik sailed off to the west, reaching the great landmass that Ulfsson most likely had already come upon. For three years he poked around the southern coastal areas and up into the fjords of this unwelcoming place, returning to Iceland in 985 with glowing accounts of what he dubbed, in an early example of boosterism, Greenland.

The sales job worked, and in 986 twenty-five ships set out for this new land. Fourteen of those ships, bearing some five hundred people, arrived safely, and the settlers created a colony on the (subarctic) south shore, building houses of stone and turf and raising some diminutive breeds of

Early northern voyages by the Vikings (from Central Intelligence Agency 1978)

livestock, hunting seals and walruses, and fishing. Soon another colony was established farther to the southwest; the Greenland communities would thrive for about three centuries, trading their raw goods for iron, grain, and manufactured implements.

About the time Erik led the colonists off to Greenland, a merchant named Bjarni Herjulfsson, whose normal route was between Norway and Iceland, decided to follow his father (one of the colonists) to Greenland. He missed the coast and came to a land "well wooded with low hills," then north to another that was "flat and wooded," and north yet again to a land that was "high and mountainous and topped by a glacier." He didn't land at any of these places but headed east, eventually heaving to at the second, western settlement of Greenland, where he remained. Evidently he had seen New-foundland, Labrador, and Baffin Island, in that order. And then, in the year 1001, Erik's son, Leif, bought Bjarni's ship and set out for the lands the merchant had sighted, evidently with a view to collecting some timber. Coming first to Baffin Island, Leif headed south to Labrador and then to Newfound-land, where he, or subsequent Norse explorers, established a temporary set-tlement on the shore at a place we call L'Anse aux Meadows. There in the 1960s Helge Ingstad, a former governor of East Greenland and Spitzbergen,

Newfoundland, Labrador, Baffin Island, Greenland, and the L'Anse aux Meadows site (from Magnusson and Pálsson 1965)

and his archaeologist wife, Anne Stinne Ingstad, uncovered the remains of the settlement: eight dwelling places, a forge, and artifacts, mainly slag and carpentry debris. It was evidently a base camp for further exploration, as there were few signs of garbage and no burials. The settlement apparently was abandoned in 1014, though other Norsemen probably plied the coastline for a few years thereafter, perhaps as far south as Maine. But eventually difficulties with the local Indians, a group we know as the Beothuks, were too much for the overextended Norsemen at Newfoundland, and they left.

It is well known now that Leif referred to the place he settled on as Vinland. But wild grapes are not indigenous to Newfoundland, and this has caused plenty of scholarly and unscholarly speculation. Until the discovery of the site at L'Anse aux Meadows and its careful dating, one could insist that Leif had to have meant Maine, where wild grapes do grow. But Leif was exploring during what is called the Medieval Warm Period—an era during which a warm and moist climate graced both Europe and North America. Maybe there were grapes then in Newfoundland. Or maybe he had learned a thing or two about boosterism from his father.

In any event, the Vikings came and went—unlike later Europeans, without even infecting any of the native population with smallpox or adding anything to Indian culture or oral history. Meanwhile, the Medieval Warm Period ended and was soon replaced in about 1300 by the Little Ice Age, when the climate turned colder by some 2° F. This interval lasted for about half a millennium; in the sixteenth century Pieter Breughel could paint his countrymen skating on frozen canals, the Thames froze over, and the dwellers in the small southern town that would become the capital of the United States could skate across the Potomac. Alpine glaciers ground over Swiss towns, and early on, along the southern coasts of Greenland, sea ice began to encroach, cutting off communication from Iceland and Scandinavia for much of the year. By

Estimated variation in yearly temperature for central England during the Medieval Warm Period and the Little Ice Age (from Lamb 1982)

1350 the western settlements on Greenland were abandoned; a few stragglers hung on along the eastern coast until about 1500, when the last ones left, some of the others having married into the native Inuit population.

All these Norse settlements in Iceland and Greenland were, of course, south of the actual Arctic Circle. The Hyperborean region continued to elude European aggrandizement. The native polar peoples—Inuit, Lapps, and others—had another five hundred years to live in relative peace in their grand, lonely world among the fish and the great mammals of the sea and ice. For them it was home, the center of their universe. For the European mind, the North continued to be, mythologically, the place from where dangerous people and noisy gods swept south and, at the same time and equally mythologically, a kind of promised land, a place where fortunes were to be made and national destinies resolved. In the sixteenth century, an explorer could present to the Virgin Queen of England the horn of a narwhal, and Elizabeth and all in the royal court would be happy in the belief that it had come from a unicorn.

One can imagine the eagerness with which geographically minded scholars half a millennium later welcomed new accounts of far-off places, or of places poorly delineated before. During this era the art and industry of mapmaking began again after a long hiatus. It was during the classical age of Greece, Rome, and Alexandria that scholars had begun to map the known world and the regions that might lie beyond, bringing mathematical tools to the task as well as skill and imagination. For a long time, major feats of knowledge, scholarship, and archive keeping had taken place in Alexandria's library, but the library was sacked by a Christian mob in about A.D. 300, and the period of knowledge came to an end. In the ensuing centuries after the fall of Rome, such enterprises as cartography took a backseat to matters of faith and Church politics. For a time, the Church insisted for doctrinal reasons that maps show the world as flat. But this began to change, as did so much else, in the period we call the Renaissance—which was also the beginning of the Europeans' Age of Exploration.

The year 1492 was not just Columbus's; it saw the first attempt at rendering the Earth on a spherical map, a globe. This was a time also when there was a good deal of dead reckoning in spite of the fact that the magnetic compass existed as early as the twelfth century (in China) and Europeans had begun to make rudimentary sea charts of nearby waters. Even so, for a long time, reckoned in centuries, a navigator would plot a course on such a chart (called a portolano) from his harbor to another point across an expanse of water, set forth, and often miss his target, just as had poor Bjarni Herjulfsson, who, though lost, may have been the first European to lay eyes on the New World. Even in Columbus's era, longitude and latitude were still only minimally understood—particularly longitude, which meant that a sailor was essentially lost whenever he sailed east or west any major distance beyond sight of familiar land. What actually lay beyond well-known waters was still a mystery, colored by guesswork, wrapped in fantasy and myth. Nor was this inconvenient lack of detail much diminished when the first Mercator projection appeared on a map.

Gerardus Mercator was the Latinate name taken by Gerhard Kremer, a German born in 1512 and raised in Flanders. In his studies to become a priest, Gerhard took seriously the problem of the contradiction between the teachings of Aristotle and those of the Bible. He eventually decided in favor of mathematics and astronomy and became the pupil of Gemma Frisius, a doctor, mathematician, and geographer from whom he learned, among other things, the making of scientific instruments of the era, including the astrolabe, a device for reckoning latitude. Before long Mercator began producing maps and introduced not only the word *atlas* for a collection of maps but also a flowing, calligraphic style of labeling that became the standard. And, of course, he introduced the Mercator projection for maps, chiefly to simplify the lives of mariners, allowing them to steer courses over long distances merely by plotting straight lines. By the time he was about fifty years old, he was the century's leading cartographer and geographer, and in 1569 he published an atlas of the world that would profoundly affect Arctic exploration for another three hundred years.

To produce such an atlas was no small undertaking, particularly because so much of the world remained unknown to Europeans, or known only through reports from a handful of explorers and maps based on such incomplete reports, some of which we now know to have been made almost entirely from whole cloth. By this time European cod fishermen and whalers had long been plying the eastern coast of North America and, arriving from the south into Florida, the Spanish had been a major presence in the southeastern part. But this was an era of mostly private, for-profit ventures in the New World, and the adventurers (such as Hernando de Soto, who plowed through the American Southeast all the way to the Mississippi River and beyond in the 1540s but kept his route to himself) were not about to share their hard-won geographical knowledge with others even of their own nationality, much less other European competitors. So mapmakers of the time were forced to employ a great deal of what we would today call hearsay, and this pertained in the extreme to Mercator's rendering of the Arctic.

To begin with, Mercator was aware of the problem we still face when looking at a Mercator projection of the world: Greenland, for example, appears to be larger than North America, when in fact it is one-tenth the size. He knew that were he to extend his projection to the North Pole, the top of the map would need to stretch away into infinity, so he provided an additional map, showing the pole as if seen from above it. Writing of the basis for his rendering, he explained that much of it came from *The Travels of Jacobus Cnoyen of Bois le Duc,* an account whose best information in turn came from a priest who had served the king of Norway in 1364. This priest had explained that in 1360

> an English minor friar of Oxford [Nicholas of Lynn], who was a mathematician, reached those isles [the Hebrides and Iceland] and then, having departed therefrom and pushed on further by the magical arts, he had described all and measured all by means of an astrolabe. . . . He averred that the waters of these 4 arms of the sea were drawn toward the abyss with such violence that no wind is strong enough to bring vessels back again once they have entered.

We know something of Nicholas of Lynn, a Carmelite theologian at Oxford in the fourteenth century who Geoffrey Chaucer says (in a scientific treatise he wrote as well as *The Canterbury Tales*) determined Oxford's latitude with an astrolabe. He also carried out such measurements for the king of Norway, but there is no evidence that he proceeded any farther toward the North Pole.

In 1360 a manuscript entitled *De Inventio Fortunata* appeared, attributed by many—though not all—to Nicholas. No copy now exists, but it was passed on to Mercator by the Jacobus Cnoyen he cited, a Flemish adventurer. Mercator took the manuscript's description of what existed at the Pole as true and incorporated it into his map.

Yet another source Mercator used was the existing maps and description of the exploration of Nicolò and Antonio Zeno, brothers from a prominent Venetian family who in 1380 sailed northward and came across an island they called Frisland, which was "much larger than Ireland" and lay somewhere between Iceland and Greenland. Frislanders, they reported, carried on a lucrative trade with "Flanders, Brittany, England, Scotland, Norway and Denmark." The brothers Zeno had met the prince of a nearby island whose name was Zichmini and who had just defeated the king of Norway. The narrative continues with the discovery of Estotiland, which on the Zenos' map appears to be the Labrador coast of North America. The map also shows a large land mass extending north from Greenland into the Arctic Ocean.

It appears that the Zeno brothers' report and map were lost among the family letters, and it was not until 1558 that one of their descendants, also named Nicolò, published their account. Of course, there was no such place as Frisland, no Frislanders, no trade with Europe, no Zichmini, and no such defeat of Norway's ruler. It was in fact a total fraud, but one intended to make it appear that Venetians had discovered North America a century before Columbus, who hailed from the competitor city-state of Genoa.

This information was incorporated into Mercator's and subsequent maps, along with the existence of Lodestone Mountain, a vast landform with a magnetic field so strong that it was said to draw the nails out of any approaching ship and cause erratic behavior in magnetic compasses thousands of miles to the south. Mercator was using logic and the best sorting of available accounts that he could accomplish. And some of what he incorporated was not only plausible, but partly true. In fact, the magnetic pole is offset from the geographic North Pole, as was Lodestone Mountain, although the magnetic pole is not a magnetite mountain but instead the surface expression of a magnetic field generated in the liquid core of the Earth by magnetohydrodynamic currents. Mercator also noted a phenomenon occurring north of the Hebrides: "a monstrous gulf in the sea towards which from all sides the billows of the sea coming from remote parts converge and run together as though brought there by a conduit, pouring into these mysterious abysses of nature, they are as though devoured thereby and, should it happen that a vessel pass there, it is seized and drawn away with such powerful violence of the waves that this hungry force immediately swallows it up never to appear again." This was the Maelstrom, and there is such a place, an oceanic whirlpool off the northwest coast of Norway, near the Lofoten Islands. When it is active, it does capture small ships in its vortex, but it is not, as Mercator had it, at the North Pole.

Subsequent maps by others would vary in details, some keeping Mercator's four landmasses ranged around the Pole, others retaining the four rivers but having them flow outward from the Pole. But a major feature remained in almost all subsequent maps, and it was this that would profoundly affect the future of Arctic exploration: the open polar ocean. For this meant that there should be an easy trade route through the Arctic Ocean to the riches of India and China, northeast around the Asian continent, northwest past North America, or both. If such a passage were found, English and Russian ships would not have to make the long and arduous passages around the southern tip of Africa or South America, routes that were already in the hands of jealous and protective Spaniards and Portuguese. Spaniards, ensconced for a half-century already in Florida, had probed the eastern coast at least as far north as Chesapeake Bay, hoping to find sea passage through the continent to Cathay, a passage they believed had to be there. The French, ensconced along the Saint Lawrence River, were marrying into Algonquin Indian families and plying the waterways in canoes. To be sure, they were collecting beaver pelts, just as the Spanish further to the south were collecting souls, but the French also hoped to find the network of rivers and tributaries that led across the continent to the riches of the Orient.

Indeed, the search for both the Northeast and the Northwest Passages was well under way before Mercator's enticing map appeared. In 1497, five years after Columbus's first voyage, another Genoese mariner set out from Bristol, England. John Cabot, born Giovanni Caboto, had taken up Venetian citizenship

Map of the polar regions (Mercator 1569)

and failed to persuade Spanish or other backers to send him west to China, so he came to England, where he persuaded King Henry VII and some Bristol merchants to finance him. He sailed in May 1497, fetched up on what he called New Found Land (quite surely Newfoundland), saw no inhabitants but picked up a few traps and other artifacts, and was convinced that he had made a successful crossing to a remote and fairly primitive shore of Cathay. He returned to England, arriving in August, whereupon the king awarded him ten pounds for his effort.

Cabot left again the following year, this time with more significant backing and five ships laden with trade goods. His plan apparently was to find his way back to his New Found Land and sail southwest along its coast until he came to the wealthy lands so aptly and tantalizingly described earlier by Marco Polo. But nothing was ever heard from him or his five ships again. Though he was almost certainly the European discoverer of North America, he left no account of his earlier voyage and, in one of the more bizarre oedipal confusions in history, had a son who ran off with his prize.

Sebastian Cabot is reckoned to have been thirteen years old when his father made his successful journey to Newfoundland, and there is every reason to believe that he was not a member of the expedition. But he later managed to persuade people that he had been on board, explaining at least once that his father had died a few years before the actual voyage, and for nearly four centuries he got credit from most historians for John's voyage of discovery. (As

Northeast Passage and adjacent geography (from Central Intelligence Agency 1978)

Northwest Passage and adjacent geography (from Central Intelligence Agency 1978)

late as 1897, the government of the province of Newfoundland issued a com-
memorative stamp honoring John Cabot and bearing a portrait of him. But no
portrait of John survived, if one was ever made. Instead the stamp showed a
rendering of the one portrait that survived of Sebastian, as an old man, which
of course his father never got to be.)

Sebastian Cabot was evidently a man of many other talents as well as
self-promotion. Later he recounted to a friend that he had outfitted two ships
at his own expense in Britain in 1508 and led a crew of three hundred men
due north until, in July, they encountered continuous daylight and so much
ice in the sea that he was obliged to turn west and south, penetrating as far
west as the entry to what was surely the passage to Cathay (likely the island of
Cuba), or—according to another report to a different friend—sailing into a
great opening to the west from the Arctic Ocean (what could have been
Hudson Bay), surely the entrance of the Northwest Passage. This voyage was,
it turned out, a complete fabrication.

Subsequently Sebastian went to work for Charles V of Spain, serving as
pilot-major for the crown, a job that entailed training and testing all pilots as
well as performing other nautical duties. He became adept at making nautical
instruments and produced a map of the world based on "his" explorations,
among others. He did make a transatlantic voyage for the Spanish king, this to
South America, seeking a better passage than that of the successful Magellan.

But his experience turned out to be such a disaster that, rather than face banishment to Africa, Sebastian returned to England and soon enough became the head of a company established to fund an attempt to find the Northeast Passage. By now he was seventy or more years old, but as this brave expedition sat at anchor in harbor, about to set forth, the old man tottered on board and performed a bit of a jig. And as the three ships set sail, the true era of seeking a northerly passage began. It would become a long-term goal of several northern European nations, a bright and compelling dream—what might indeed be called one of European civilization's Ultima Thules.

2 FRIZADORES FOR CATHAY, AND POLAR BEARS

May 10, 1553, was a grand day for the Merchant Adventurers and for the ailing King Edward VI of England. Three ships, having been carefully prepared for their journey by shipwrights and victualers, and laden with cargo for trade, proceeded under tow down the Thames from the town of Radcliffe. Along the riverbanks people cheered, and when the little fleet reached Greenwich, where the king was waiting, cannons saluted the monarch and the people roared their approval. The Merchant Adventurers, a company formed "for the discoverie of Regions, Dominions, Islands and places unknowen," was led by Sebastian Cabot.

Thirty years earlier, returning to England from a few years in Spain after his alleged 1508 voyage, Sebastian had tried to seek financial backing for another voyage but ran into an obstacle erected by the British merchants. They wrote to King Henry VIII that it would be unwise to finance a trip to the New World "upon the singuler trust of one man, callyed as we understand, Sebastyn, whiche Sebastyn, as we here say, was never in that land hym self, all if he makes reporte of many thinges as he hath hard his Father and other men speke in tymes past."

It must be taken as a credit to Sebastian Cabot's persuasiveness that he had talked his way back into the graces of the London merchant circles, but he did by now know a thing or two about sea voyaging, however limited his own actual experience. It might have been his idea to sheath the three ships with lead against the burrowing worms that were said to infest the waters off Cathay. In any event, geographers (and no doubt Sebastian) had persuaded the merchants that the passage to Cathay could most easily be accomplished by sailing east through the wide swath of open sea along the Arctic coasts of Scandinavia, Russia, and beyond.

To lead the expedition, the Merchant Adventurers had selected a non-sailor as captain-general. This was Sir Hugh Willoughby, a "valiant" soldier who had seen duty in the Scottish border wars and was "well-borne," and tall of stature to boot. The three ships under his command were the *Bona Esperanza* (120 tons and the flagship), the *Bona Confidentia* (90 tons), and the *Edward Bonaventure* (160 tons). Progress north to the Norwegian coast was hampered by uncooperative winds, and when the little fleet reached the northern end of the Lofoten Islands at the end of July, they encountered a violent storm that separated Willoughby's *Esperanza* and the *Confidentia* from the largest ship, the *Edward*, which was under the command of a seasoned mariner, Richard Chancellor. Chancellor took himself to an island off the Danish coast, now called Vardo, which had been chosen as a rendezvous point against just such a contingency.

The other two ships, however, sailed aimlessly to the northeast and then the southeast; finally, on September 18, finding themselves utterly lost, they anchored in a harbor in the mouth of a river on what they took to be the mainland but was in fact Lapland. Around them, Sir Hugh noted in his journal, were riches of "seale fish & other great fishes . . . beares, greate deer, foxes . . . and such other which were to us unknowen and also wonderful." Sir Hugh, a landlubber, nevertheless made a wise nautical decision: given the richness of the wildlife, the fact that his ships had been provisioned for six months, and the additional fact that the weather was turning "evile," he decided that the two ships and their crew of sixty-three, including himself, would overwinter in the river harbor. Sir Hugh ceased writing in his journal once a few parties had gone forth and found no inhabitants in the area; they evidently settled down to the nerve-racking and probably boring job of waiting out the winter.

By January the Arctic winter may have been getting to Sir Hugh, for he wrote a will in that month. The will was found by Russian fishermen the following summer, when they came upon the two ships and the corpses of all sixty-three men.

Meanwhile, Richard Chancellor, on the *Edward*, had waited at the rendezvous for seven days and then pressed on to the White Sea and Arkhangel'sk, trekking from there overland to Moscow and a cordial reception from Tsar Ivan IV (also known as Ivan the Terrible), who granted the Merchant Adventurers a license to trade with Russia via this northern route. A more conventional route at the time was through the Baltic Sea, which was firmly under the control of the Hanseatic League, a confederation of merchants from various German cities—what might perhaps be thought of loosely as the first multinational corporation. The league acted as intermediary between east and west and controlled such enterprises as the Russian fur trade. The opening in this closed system made by Chancellor in Moscow broke the Hanseatic League's hold, and the Merchant Adventurers were soon replaced by the Muscovy Company, with the aged but still hustling Sebastian Cabot in a leadership position until he died a few years later.

Meanwhile, it became apparent that Willoughby and his crew had not died of starvation. The rescuers found plenty of food stores on board, and although most of the wildlife would have migrated south for the winter soon after the ships set anchor in the river harbor, foxes would have remained as a plentiful supply of live meat. It was long assumed that they had died either of the cold or from scurvy, a disease that was ubiquitous on sailing ships during extended trips where the food stores consisted conventionally of "fleshe, fishe, bisket, meat or bread . . . beere, wine, oyl or vineger." But a letter, uncovered long afterward, has shed a different light on these events. On November 4, 1555, Giovanni Michiel, the Venetian ambassador to London, wrote the doge of Venice:

> The vessels which departed some months ago, bound for Cathayo, either from inability or lack of daring, not having got beyond Muscovy and Russia, whither the others went in like manner last year, have returned safe, bringing with them the two vessels of the first voyage, having found them on the Muscovite coast, with the men on board all frozen, and the mariners now returned from the second voyage narrate strange things about the mode in which they were frozen, having found some of them seated in the act of writing, pen still in hand, and the paper before them; others at table, platters in hand and spoon in mouth; others opening a locker, and others in various postures, like statues, as if they had been adjusted and placed in these attitudes. They say that some of the dogs on board the ships displayed the same phenomena. They found the effects and merchandise all intact in the hands of the natives, and brought them back thither with the vessels.

Looking at this account four hundred years later, a British medical historian, Eleanora C. Gordon, realized what had probably happened to Willoughby and his crew. The crew might well have run out of firewood, which would have been sparse at best on these shores. So they would have turned to burning sea coal and probably, in all innocence, sealed up the chimneys and portholes against the cold. Carbon monoxide, the silent, odorless, and tasteless gas that is produced by burning coal, would have killed them all virtually simultaneously, accounting for the bizarre sight that confronted the Russian fishermen who found them.

In 1556 the Muscovy Company sent another trading expedition off to the White Sea: two ships, the *Edward Bonaventure* and the *Philip and Mary* (named for England's king and queen), under the command of John Buckland. Among other tasks, they picked up Richard Chancellor at Arkhangel'sk and recovered the two ships in which Willoughby and his company of merchants and seamen had perished. But the return voyage turned into a catastrophe. The *Confidentia* was wrecked off the coast of Norway, the *Esperanza* was lost at sea, and the *Edward Bonaventure* was wrecked off the coast of Scotland in November, Richard Chancellor dying in the wreck. The *Philip and Mary* alone made it to London (though not until the following spring), bringing with it Russia's first ambassador to the English court. In spite of the loss of the three other ships, the Muscovy Company sent trading vessels to the White Sea almost annually for several years, bringing about an attractive trade with Moscow and the Russians. One of the traders, a man named Jenkinson, retained an interest in the sea route to Cathay, stimulated by discussions with people from Siberia about tides and currents, and a story about a strange skull found on Novaya Zemlya that had only one horn. Unicorns were known to live in Cathay, so this one must have been brought to the archipelago north of European Russia by the currents of the sea.

The Northeast Passage still beckoned. Privateers (which is to say buccaneers licensed by the crown, now Elizabeth I) such as Francis Drake and Martin Frobisher were bringing back plentiful booty taken from the Spaniards and to a lesser extent from the Portuguese, who were deriving fabulous wealth from their control of the southern sea routes. So the merchants of the Muscovy Company launched another attempt in 1580. They were egged on, we can be fairly sure, by Gerardus Mercator, who had stated that "the voyage to Cathayo by the east is doubtless very easie and short, and I have oftentimes marveiled, that being so happily begun, it hath bene left of." It is not clear what happy beginnings Mercator referred to, but it certainly wasn't the first two expeditions of the Muscovy Company, which perhaps should have maintained its original and limited goal of Russian trade via the White Sea. But the company granted commissions to two experienced sea captains, Arthur Pet and Charles Jackman, both of Middlesex, "for a voyage to be made by them for the discoverie of Cathaye."

That the merchants had become cautious over the years is suggested by the fact that the two "good barkes," the *George* (40 tons) and the *William* (20 tons), had crews of ten and six, respectively. Pet, in command of the *George*, was also named admiral of this modest fleet, with Jackman as vice admiral. They set out in May 1580, each ship carrying a two-year supply of food and trade goods of such variety that it took two pages to list them. The cargo included frizadores (plush silk), motleys (cloths of many colors), "Jerzie yarne," hinges, "hullocke" (sailcloth), parchment, glue, soap, saffron, antimony, and the biggest map of England they could find. The admiral and vice admiral were enjoined also to push the sale of aqua vitae, which the English had found they could make very cheaply.

Taking advantage of favorable winds, the two ships set off on May 5, 1580, and soon lost sight of each other, coming back together at Willoughby's rendezvous point, the island of Vardo, in late June, with the *William* suffering from leaks and damaged steering. Unfavorable winds held them there until July. Thereafter they encountered ice, "a great fogge," and further miserable weather, while the *William* had to contend with a broken stern post, leaving the rudder hanging loose. In late August, sailing along the shoreline to avoid the ice, they ran aground on a hidden shoal, finally got off, and lost sight of each other, the people on the *George* never again laying eyes on the *William*. Admiral Pet labored on for a few more days, fighting ice and weather, but the ship was damaged and leaking and there was nothing to do but return to England, which he did through continuing foul and perilous weather. Pet learned later that the *William* had overwintered in Norway but was lost at sea the following year, trying to get home in the company of a Danish ship. The only notable accomplishment of the expedition was that they managed to pass south of Novaya Zemlya and become the first such voyagers to enter the Kara Sea. Given such a disappointing result, the merchants did nothing further about the Northeast Passage for almost another twenty years.

Meanwhile, however, Dutch merchants had the same hunger for trade with Russia via the White Sea: an overland route, as well as a sea route to Cathay. In this regard, a group of Antwerp merchants came together to finance an experienced Dutch navigator, Willem Barents, then in his forties, to find the Northeast Passage. Barents made three journeys altogether, the first in 1594 with three ships, two of which went south around the Novaya Zemlya archipelago and into the Kara Sea while Barents himself went north around it. All three ships were forced to turn back by the ice in the Kara Sea. A year later, with seven ships, Barents again found the strait between Novaya Zemlya and the mainland full of ice, forcing his return. The voyages were not total failures, however, in that Barents was an indefatigable record keeper, and his charts and meteorological observations—helpful for long afterward—can be thought of as the beginnings of modern science in the Arctic.

Undaunted, and bankrolled yet again, Barents left Holland once more in May 1596 with two ships and headed straight north, eventually coming within sight of Spitzbergen (now called Svalbard). He left one ship in those waters to explore this new archipelago and was evidently forced east by what he could not have known at the time was the Arctic ice cap. At one point, on September 6, the crew encountered one of the unspeakable horrors that must have haunted the thoughts and dreams of most men arriving in the Arctic. Some of Barents's men were ashore when a "great leane white bear" stole out and grabbed one of the men by the neck. As another sailor nearby fled, the bear fell upon the hapless crew member and

> bit his head in sunder, and suckt out his blood, wherewith the rest of the men that were on land, being about 20 in number, ran presently thither, either to saue the man, or else to driue the beare from the dead body; and hauing charged their peeces and bent their pikes, set vpon her, that still was deuouring the man, but perceiuing them to come towards her, fiecely and cruelly ran at them, and get another of them out from the companie, which she tare in peeces, wherewith all the rest ran away.

Polar bears, also called ice bears and sea bears, spend as much time in the water as on land and are quite rightly known to scientists as *Ursus maritimus*. Weighing in at up to 2,000 pounds (which is larger than most horses) and rearing up to *12* feet on their hind legs, they are not the largest of bears; that honor falls to the Kodiak bear, which is half again as large, and to various extinct cave bears. But polar bears are probably the most dangerous to any hapless human. Though they are capable of deftly plucking a shellfish loose from its bed with a claw, they can also, it is said, knock a small whale unconscious with a single swipe of a front paw. They have largely white coats, as do so many other Arctic mammals, such as the Arctic fox, hare, and others, and white fur on the bottom of their feet, which helps their feet to function variously as snowshoes or paddles. They can swim immense distances, their woollike undercoat keeping them from getting wet to the skin, which in turn is underlain by a layer of blubber that is their main insulation against the cold. They surface almost silently. On land— or, more to the point, on ice floes, which they inhabit all summer, rarely coming to actual land—they can run in spurts at 25 miles an hour, plenty fast enough to intercept seals, which are the major portion of their diet. The bears are considered great wanderers, but recent research has shown that there are several more or less distinct populations, each with its preferred regions.

Females den in winter, usually well to the south of the ice floes, arranging the snow and ice cover with the same care, and along the same lines, as the Inuits arrange their iglus—to maximize the flow of fresh air while maintaining a constant temperature of about 32°F freezing. The cubs, usually two or three, are born deaf, blind, and helpless and rely on the mother's bodily warmth and her milk, which is as thick as cream, to survive their early weeks. Equally rich is the milk produced by many of the seal species that frequent the Arctic seas; they include walruses and narwhals, those "sea unicorns" whose single horn is in fact a protruding tooth unique to the males. Hooded seals, though, may have the record for richness of mother's milk—and the shortest lactation period of any mammal. Hooded seals give birth to pups on the Arctic ice just as it is about to break up with the onset of spring—the time when the pack ice is at its weakest, meaning that predation from polar bears is least likely and the vulnerable pups have the greatest chance of survival. The pups weigh about 45 pounds at birth, and four days later they are weaned—now weighing 90 pounds. This astounding rate of growth is possible because the hooded seal's milk is 60 percent fat (whipping cream is 40 percent fat), and the mother produces some 60,000 calories daily, enough to feed twenty-five humans.

None of this, of course, was known to the early European explorers, to whom the polar bear became a terrifying threat when out on the ice—and a possible source of food if one was lucky enough to get in a good shot or two before a nearby bear either attacked or vanished into the seemingly endless expanse of white.

Barents continued east past the northern tip of Novaya Zemlya until his ship was captured in the ice of the Kara Sea. Rather than hole up on the ship itself, the crew had the good sense to build shelters on the shore from driftwood and ship timbers, and there they waited. On November 4, almost three months after Barents's crew became trapped, the Sun disappeared from the sky and did not reappear until January 24; it was two and a half months in the dark. One of the ship's officers, Gerrit De Veer, kept a diary of this long, cold wait, and his entry for December 7 is a telling reminder of an earlier expedition:

> The 7 of December it was still foule weather, and we had a great storme with a northeast wind, which brought an extreame cold with it; at which time we knew not what to do, and while we sate consulting together what were beste for vs to do, one of our companions gave vs counseill to burne some of the sea-coles [soft coal] that we

had brought out of the ship, which wuld cast a great heat and continue long; and so at evening we made a great fire thereof, which cast a great heat. At which time we were very careful to keepe it in, for that heat being so great a comfort vnto vs, we tooke care how to make it continue long; wherevpon wee agreed to stop vp all the doores and the chimney, thereby to keep in the heate, and so went into our cabans [cots] to sleepe well commforted with the heat, and so lay a great while talking together; but at last we were taken with a great swounding and daseling in our heads, yet some more than other some, which we first perceived by a sick man and therefore the least able to beare it, and found ourseules to be very ill at ease, so that some of vs that were strongest start out of their cabans, and first opened the chimney and then the doores, but he that opened the doore fell down in a swound (with much groaning) vpon the snow; which I hearing, as lying in my caban next to the doore, start vp (and there saw him lying in a swoon), and casting vinegar in his face recoured him againe, and so he rose vp. And when the doores were open, we all recovered our healthes againe by reason of the cold aire; and so the cold which before had beene so great an enemy vnto vs, was then the only reliefe that we had, otherwise without doubt we had [all] died in a sodaine swound. After yt, the master, when we were come to our selues again, gave euery one of vs a little wine to comfort our hearts.

Thus they escaped being suffocated by carbon monoxide—the fate that almost surely met Willoughby and his crew.

Once the ice broke up in June, Barents's ship was far too damaged to be of use, so on June 13 the survivors embarked in two open boats, making a heroic passage home. But Barents himself was not long among them, dying about a week after they set out for home. The rest sailed north around the tip of Novaya Zemlya, down its northwest coast, and west along the Russian shore to Scandinavia, where on August 30 they were rescued by the second ship of the expedition, on its way home from Spitzbergen, where it had overwintered. Of the original seventeen crew members of the expedition, twelve made it back to Holland—the first time Europeans had overwintered in the Arctic. But there was nothing straightforward about the return trip. The men, without their trusted master navigator, encountered foul weather, dangerous ice, and terrible mists and fogs, and De Veer's journal provides a mournful insight into how difficult the effort was. At one point, laboring from morning into the afternoon to bring their frail

The shelter constructed by Willem Barents and crew in which they spent the winter of 1596–97 (from De Veer 1609)

craft out of harm's way, he wrote, "In al that time we rested not, which made vs extreame weary and wholly out of comfort, for that it troubled vs sore, and was much more fearfull vunto vs then at that time when Willem Barents dyed."

A few more attempts by Dutch and British would be made to find the Northeast Passage. Finally the British hired Henry Hudson to have a look on their behalf. He made two trips, in 1607 and 1608. In the first expedition he sought a passage via the North Pole and succeeded in mapping much of east Greenland as well as reaching a farthest north for that time of 80° 23' N. But, of course, he found no Northeast Passage. The second voyage took him to Novaya Zemlya, where ice prevented him from entering the Kara Sea. And thus would end any remaining enthusiasm among northern Europeans for slipping through a convenient waterway east to Cathay.

Both Barents and, later, Hudson were tempted to sail straight north to the North Pole and thence to Cathay. If ever a siren dwelled in the Arctic Ocean, beckoning to intelligent and well-traveled navigators and intrepid explorers, it was the notion of an open Arctic sea. Mercator's map of the world, and most other such maps, clearly showed such a sea. But the thought was present in the European mind long before the maps.

As early as 1527 Richard Thorne, an English merchant living in Seville, took note of the great advantages accruing to the Portuguese, who were opening up an eastward route to the Spice Islands; and to the Spanish, who were opening a westward one in the wake of Magellan's circumglobal effort. Thorne set forth a proposal that the English explore a third route that would be much shorter and relatively safe. Of course, nothing was known in Europe about what lay north of the Arctic Circle, but Thorne probably had in mind some memory of the Greek notion of an ocean that encircled the world, leading him to assume that a polar sea connected the Atlantic with the ocean that Magellan had so recently crossed. Also, he may have been influenced by Spanish chartmakers of the time, who had the astonishing habit of not putting on their maps anything that they had not actually visited. Hence, Spanish maps of the Arctic were free of landforms.

Thorne was evidently well aware that, for all the ignorance that existed about the Arctic, it was generally considered an extremely dangerous place, and so he affirmed in his proposal that the polar seas were safe, because they had "in them a perpetuall cleerenessse of the day without any darknesse of the night: which thing is a great commoditie for the navigants to see at all times rounde them, as well the safegardes as daungers." Of course, in proposing this third route across the North Pole, Thorne was guilty of wishful thinking, arising from a nationalistic sense of commercial competitiveness, but he would not be the only one guilty of that. As late as the end of the nineteenth century, respected explorers, oceanographers, and other scientists would adduce a great variety of theories and guessed-at phenomena to assure themselves of the existence of the open polar sea—now more for glory than for commerce. Even the putative habits of whales and the instincts of migratory birds would be summoned up in its favor. And not even the discouraging results of Barents's and Hudson's early attempts—and the failures of others who came later—would diminish the siren call in the following centuries, when it would inspire many seeking the Northwest Passage, and those who would seek the plum of being first to stand on the North Pole.

Indeed, the search for the Northwest Passage had been under way for more than twenty years before Barents's last voyage. A British expedition led to the first English attempt to start a colony in the New World—nine years before English colonists tried and failed to colonize North America at Roanoke,

Virginia, twenty years before conquistadors established a permanent Spanish presence in New Mexico, and twenty-nine years before John Smith and company arrived at Jamestown. The result of a buccaneer's dream, it constituted the first gold rush in North America and wound up creating an embarrassing scandal in the commercial circles of Elizabeth's England.

3 FOOL'S GOLD, HOOCH, AND MUTINY

Martin Frobisher, a contemporary of Sir Francis Drake, was a stolid and occasionally short-tempered Welshman of great size and formidable strength. Evidently he was a man of few words, perhaps even a bit awkward in social situations. But Frobisher was the first Englishman to seek the Northwest Passage. During a career in England's African trade (he was sent away from the Yorkshire home where he grew up, a problem child) and as a successful patriot sailor, or buccaneer à la Drake, he harbored a dream that he would find the northern route to Cathay, thinking it had to lie somewhere past Greenland. Finally, after fifteen years of effort, he persuaded one London merchant, Michael Lok, that such a voyage was "not onely possible by the north-west, but also, as he could prove, easie to be performed." (We are fortunate that for much of this period in his life Frobisher, who wrote little, was followed about by his own Boswell, a friend and shipmate, George Best, who chronicled Frobisher's thoughts and deeds.)

Lok managed to raise 875 pounds, enough for Frobisher to set sail on June 15, 1576, with two barks, the *Gabriel* and the *Michael* (25 and 20 tons, respectively), along with a pinnace (a smaller, unarmed ship of a mere 10 tons) and a total complement of thirty-two men. (By comparison, Columbus's *Santa Maria* was a ship of 100 tons, and the *Mayflower,* which would sail forty-five years later, was 180 tons. A bark is a ship with two main masts and a shorter foremast. A pinnace is a much smaller two- or three-masted light sailing craft.) As he sailed by the royal party standing onshore to see them off, Frobisher received a frail wave from Queen Elizabeth.

Off the coast of Greenland, which Frobisher assumed was the Zeno brothers' Frisland, a ferocious storm sank the pinnace and persuaded the officer of the *Michael* to turn tail and return to England. The *Gabriel* sailed on, arriving on July 28 in sight of a body of water that led northwest, between 62° and 63° N latitudes. Frobisher sailed into this presumed "strait," which he also

Martin Frobisher (Bodleian Library, Oxford)

assumed was the Northwest Passage, believing that he had North America to port and Asia to starboard. Emerging from the fog, he saw that the shoreline of the strait was barren and ice-bordered, an unpromising rocky land in a gray world. For days they explored what they called Frobisher's Strait, looking for signs of life, and on August 19 some of his men, poking about in a skiff, were approached by five Inuit in kayaks. This meeting led to another the following day, which saw the exchange of such things as bells and looking glasses for sealskins. On August 21 five crew members rowed ashore for yet more trading and were never seen again. They had taken the only skiff, and the snow was beginning to fall. A search was impossible.

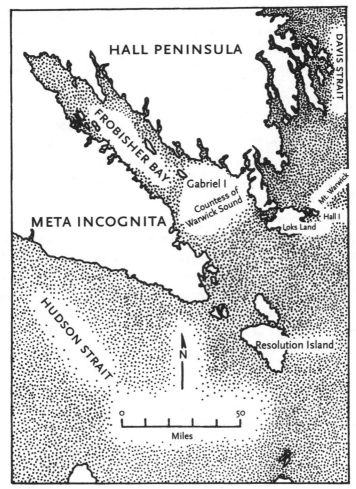

Frobisher Bay (based on a map in Tokens of Possession, Kenyon, 1975,
Royal Ontario Museum)

Frobisher, a decisive leader, prepared to leave, but then some kayaks
approached through the falling snow. Dangling a trinket over the side,
Frobisher tempted one Inuit to come close enough to snatch him (and his
boat) out of the water by sheer strength and plop the no-doubt-terrified man
on the deck. With that, they headed back to England, arriving with little to
show but the Inuit (who died shortly afterward of a bad cold), some wild-
flowers, and a piece of black rock someone had thought to bring along.

According to George Best, the wife of one of the adventurers received a
piece of the rock, "which by chance she threw and burned in the fires, so
long, that at the length being taken forth and quenched in a little vinegre, it

glistened with a bright Marquesset of golde." Whether that actually occurred, the merchant Lok was inspired to have the rock assayed. Three assayers said it showed no sign of "golde," but a fourth, an Italian alchemist and assayer named Agnello, pronounced it to be gold-bearing, and that was enough for everyone concerned to forget about the Northwest Passage. Frobisher was quickly sent back for more gold, this time with actual financial participation by the queen. So delighted was Elizabeth, in fact, that she permitted him to kiss her hand before he left on May 15 of the following year (1577) with three ships, including a much larger one called the *Ayde,* 200 tons, to go along with the *Gabriel* and the *Michael* again, with sufficient stores for 143 men for six months. Their chief task was to bring back 200 tons of ore; only if time permitted could they go exploring for the route to Cathay.

By this time, late in the sixteenth century, England was excluded both from the southern routes to spices and other riches in the Far East and from any mineral wealth in the New World. But according to the maps of the period, it appeared to English navigators that North America tapered to the north, just as South America tapered to the south, making a northern trade route possible; and of course if gold and silver were to be found in the southern Americas, why not in the north as well? Southern gold and silver, mined by enslaved Indians, had already begun to create an economic monster out of Spain—adding military strength to the Spaniards, which in turn added more control over the wealth of the New World, and so on in a threatening gyre. So Frobisher's (or at least Lok's) gold-rich ore became an understandably instant priority.

Even though Frobisher was a poor navigator and failed to "fix" his courses (with the result that it would take another couple of centuries for Englishmen to find their way back to Frobisher's Strait once he was finished there), he returned, reaching his destination in mid-July. Immediately a fracas blew up with some Inuits onshore, and Frobisher took an arrow in the buttock, fleeing, according to the chronicler Best, "rather speedily." Ten days later they found a small island, where they spent several weeks mining and loading ore, leaving the strait in late August with some 200 tons of ore and sailing into Bristol to a hero's welcome. They brought with them three Inuit hostages, a man, woman, and child, all of whom thrilled the English, the man performing feats in a kayak and with his hunting darts, but all three perished within two months of their arrival, the only sorry note amid a triumphant return. The investors immediately put up enough money for a third trip, consisting of fifteen ships and four hundred men, to leave the following May, charged with returning with 2,000 tons of ore, as well as leaving behind a hundred men in a permanent mining colony. So much, the English were telling themselves, for the vaunted hegemony of Spain.

And so, before the second expedition's ore had been any more than inconclusively assayed for its gold content, Frobisher set off again, this time with a gold chain placed around his neck by the queen and a grand flotilla under his command—in fact, the largest fleet to enter the Arctic until the Second World War, almost four hundred years later. The voyage soon proved treacherous, with Frobisher writing of "the yce comming on us so fast, we were in great danger, looking every houre for death." Soon thereafter they sailed into a dreadful mist, later "an horribile snowe." One ship collided with a whale, and they encountered a tempest and huge walls of ice, one of which sank the ship carrying a prefabricated house for the mining colony. The worst storm they had ever encountered left the fleet lost in Hudson Strait. Eventually they found their island, but it seemed too late to establish a colony without the prefab house, and the pilot of one ship instigated a mutiny on board and took his ship home. The remainder of the fleet left on September 1 with about 1,100 tons of black rock, lost some forty Cornish miners overboard in a terrible storm, and discovered that no one really cared about their return except for a few disgruntled investors, for by this time the company of venturers had learned that the black rock contained little or no gold. It was iron pyrite, or fool's gold. The company went bankrupt, and Michael Lok was left liable for the losses. He blamed Frobisher, who called his erstwhile backer a knave, and Lok went to jail personally bankrupt, leaving a wife and children languishing in poverty. Frobisher was reprimanded, went off to help put down a revolt in Ireland, and then ably defended England against the Spanish Armada in 1588, for which he was knighted for his bravery. He died in 1594 battling the Spaniards on their own ground, laying siege to a fort.

What British explorers would find some three hundred years later was the remains of Frobisher's mining efforts on the small island, which lies within one of the large bays of southern Baffin Island, not a strait, and not the entrance of a northwest passage. It is now called Frobisher's Bay. He had not come anywhere near finding the passage, but he had helped keep the notion of it alive.

One breast in which the dream of the passage stayed alive was that of John Davis, a highly respected seaman and navigator who had been a childhood friend of Sir Walter Raleigh and would later count among his acquaintances leading mathematicians and cartographers. Almost the opposite of Martin Frobisher, he was for the most part given to peaceful pursuits and nautical scholarship, producing a volume that would become the navigator's handbook

Canada's first mine; the great trench excavated for ore by Frobisher and his men

for generations, inventing a standard device for measuring latitude, and writing a masterly summary of geographical knowledge of the world in 1595. From 1598 on, he was in the service of the East India Company, discovering the Falkland Islands in the South Atlantic, charting the coast of Sumatra, and regrettably falling prey to Japanese pirates off Malaysia, dying at their hands two days after Christmas in 1605.

Before most of these deeds, however, Davis made the second notable English attempt to find the Northwest Passage, sailing first in a voyage financed by a consortium of merchants in 1585, six years after Frobisher's unpropitious final return from northern seas. In the poetically named *Sunneshine* (50 tons) and *Mooneshine* (35 tons, and which Davis oddly enough insisted on calling the *Moonelight* and which he outfitted with a four-piece orchestra), he reached Greenland and then the eastern coast of Baffin Island at 66° 40′ N before returning, convinced that the passage lay either west, up what is now called Cumberland Sound, or farther north. But before leaving, Davis's ships were spotted by a group of Inuits, who, the English thought, howled like wolves. Davis had the orchestra strike up a tune and ordered his officers and seamen ashore to dance. The Inuits watched in fascination and offered the Englishmen pieces of their clothing. The next morning the Inuits were back, dancing to a drum.

The following year he returned with two additional ships and a pinnace, making a total of five. One ship and the pinnace were sent looking for the northward passage, but a massive buildup of sea ice sent them home. Another of the ships was lost in a storm, and yet another had to be sent home, as it was unwieldy in ice. All that was left was Davis's *Moonelight,* and she was halted by ice at 67° N and returned to England in October.

The following spring Davis set sail once again, with two ships and a pinnace. Encountering excellent conditions, he set the two ships to cod fishing to defray some of the expedition's costs and proceeded in the little pinnace along the west coast of Greenland to a farthest north of 72° 12′ N before being turned back by the wind. Coming south down the Baffin Island coast, he charted numerous gulfs, inlets, and straits, including the entrance of the Hudson Strait (which he called the Furious Overfall, because of its fierce currents), and the shoreline of Labrador to boot. In all, it was a remarkable feat, sailing such a great distance through Arctic waters in what amounted to a sailboat, making the first effort at documenting ice conditions, weather, and terrain, and making sympathetic observations of the lives of the Inuit. In short, his was a scientific expedition as well as a voyage of exploration.

Ultimately unsuccessful in his quest, he remained convinced of the existence of the Northwest Passage, but his attentions, and those of England itself, were diverted from any further voyages seeking it by new troubles with Spain. Ten years after his last Arctic voyage, Davis wrote favorably of the nature of these northern lands and waters, saying they were not at all uninhabitable: "I found the ayre very temperate, yea and many times calme wether marveilous hot; I have felt the Sunne beames of as forcible action in the frozen zone in calme neere unto the shore, as I have any time found within the burning zone."

He went on to praise the inhabitants as "people of good stature, shape and tractable conditions, with whom I have converced and not found them rudly barbarous, as I found the Caniballs which are in the straights of Magilane and Southerne parts of America."

Though Davis's three voyages resulted in very little new country seen or new waters probed, it has been said that his efforts, particularly his assiduous charting, were what made it possible for the next two major seekers of the Northwest Passage to go as far as they did.

Henry Hudson, as we noted briefly before, made two voyages on behalf of English merchants seeking the Northeast Passage, both of which failed—and these failures discouraged England from any further attempts to reach Cathay via the east. Hudson was a greatly respected navigator, and the English merchants concluded that if he couldn't accomplish such a voyage, probably no one could. Hudson came from a wealthy family (his grandfather was one of the founders of the Muscovy Company). He may have served in the battle with the Spanish Armada, and he may have sailed with John Davis on one of his voyages. In any event, by 1607 he was a captain, and in 1609 he was at sea again, this time for the Dutch East India Company, whose directors thought it worthwhile to make one more attempt at the Northeast Passage, especially since their rivals, the French, had begun talking to Hudson about mounting such an expedition on their behalf. The Dutch provided Hudson with a ship, *Halve Maen* (or *Half Moon*), an ungainly craft of some 80 tons that Hudson sought, unsuccessfully, to replace with one that was more seaworthy. Eventually, he sailed on the *Half Moon* with a crew of twenty men, half English and half Dutch, most of whom did not speak or understand the other language. Setting out in early April, they encountered headwinds, fog, and ice and were unable even to reach the coast of Novaya Zemlya.

At this point there was a mutiny. It might have been led by a man named Robert Juet, a troublemaker whom Hudson had sailed with on an earlier expedition. (Hudson had a tragic and, it would turn out, fatal weakness. He was a very poor judge of character and was unable to control his men when an expedition was under stress—stress often caused by the men he misjudged.) Or the mutiny could have been caused by the Dutch sailors, who were unaccustomed to sailing in the cold. Hudson hauled out some maps of the New World that he had been sent by Captain John Smith of the Jamestown colony in Virginia and persuaded the crew that they should sail west to North America and a warmer climate.

By early July the *Half Moon* was off the coast of Newfoundland, having survived several violent storms, one of which swept the foremast into the sea. Hudson sailed as far south as Chesapeake Bay but did not visit John Smith. Instead he went north, looked in on Delaware Bay, and sailed into New York Harbor, claiming the area for Holland.

In the following days the *Half Moon* encountered some local Indians, who traded with the crew, but soon a few fracases broke out, in one of which a crew member was killed with an arrow through his throat. In response, the crew captured two Indians as hostages; one of them was later released, and the other escaped. Sailing up the river that would eventually be named for Hudson, they encountered other Indians, these being friendly, and the crew got a couple of them drunk on wine and aqua vitae, which they took to calling "hooch," a term that apparently derived from the local Indians' word for hard liquor, *hoochenoo*. After sailing 150 miles upriver, reaching present-day Albany and shallow water, they headed south and were later attacked by about a hundred Indians in canoes. Hudson ordered that the guns be fired, and several Indians were killed. Once out of the river, Hudson left for England, arriving there in November.

After being forbidden by the English government to work again for a foreign government and being put under modified house arrest, Hudson convinced several English merchants and the Prince of Wales to back yet another voyage, this one specifically to seek the Northwest Passage. Once again, and for unknown reasons, Hudson included Robert Juet in the crew, and this time he unwisely added a man named Henry Greene to the ship's complement. Greene had been a guest in Hudson's house and had a reputation as a gambler and troublemaker. When the *Discovery* was off Iceland, Greene got into a fistfight with the surgeon, Edward Wilson; Hudson intervened, defending Greene, while the crew supported the surgeon. Juet then got into the act, saying that Greene had been hired to act as a spy on the crew. Hudson heard about this and decided to put Juet ashore, but he was talked out of it and did nothing further about Juet's insubordination.

By August, after narrowly avoiding a mutiny, Hudson entered the Furious Overfall, with its ferocious currents, and before long came to Hudson Bay, where he and Juet had yet another falling out, with Hudson ordering his trial for mutiny. By way of punishment, Juet was demoted, and the *Discovery* sailed on. Warned of dangerous rocks near a shore, Hudson nevertheless ran the ship aground, losing face with the crew, and later, in the bleak subarctic waters of James Bay, they became iced in.

Tempers flared, and the crew began to suffer from scurvy. In mid-June the *Discovery* weighed anchor, and Hudson doled out the remaining stores of bread and cheese, only to be accused by the crew of hoarding. The ship got caught again in the ice, and somewhere in the middle of James Bay the men mutinied, led by Greene and Juet. Hudson was put on the ship's shallop (a small skifflike boat) along with several other men and his young son John. They were never seen again. Quite likely they died of exposure and starvation, but there is a tantalizing legend, among the Inuit of the area, that they once came across a small boat filled with dead white men and one live boy. Not knowing what to do with the boy, they chained him inside a house, where, presumably, he perished.

The mutineers hardly fared much better. Greene and several others were attacked and killed by what they thought were friendly Inuit; Juet later died of hunger after the crew had been reduced to eating bird bones fried in candle grease. Half dead, the remaining mutineers made it back to London in September, nearly a year and five months after they had set out. By the time they were tried, in 1618, several had already died, and the rest were let off mainly because the mutiny's instigators had all died on the way home. And, of course, they were helped by claiming to have found the Northwest Passage, making available Hudson's own chart that showed the east coast of Hudson's Bay. The London merchants were convinced and soon enough financed several more expeditions, one in 1612, by James Hall, who was killed by Greenland Inuit; another in 1613, by Thomas Button, who entered Hudson Bay, called it Button's Bay, and overwintered near Churchill; and a third in 1614, by William Gibbons, who spent the winter on the coast of Labrador. The latter two expeditions used Hudson's ship, the *Discovery,* and it was called into service yet again in 1615.

In a curious twist of irony, the 1615 expedition was captained by Robert Bylot, one of Hudson's mutineers, who had managed to pilot the *Discovery* back to England. His pilot for this voyage was William Baffin, one of England's most proficient navigators, self-taught in astronomy and mathematics, and already an accomplished Arctic hand. The expedition returned to Hudson Bay and circumnavigated it, and Baffin concluded that no passage existed out of the bay to the west. The following year Baffin sailed yet again on the *Discovery,* with Bylot in command, and explored 300 miles farther north than John Davis had, reaching 77° 45' N. No European would go farther north for another 236 years.

In his journal, Baffin wrote of the Arctic summer: "It would be superfluous to write of the weather because it was so variable; there were few days without snow and was often freezing, insomuch that on Midsummer Day our shrouds, ropes and sails were so frozen that we could scarce handle them; yet the cold is not so extreme that it cannot be endured." Baffin clearly found the Arctic summer different from what John Davis experienced.

Baffin also charted the coast of Labrador and the shoreline of the bay that bears his name, including the entrance to Lancaster Sound, which Baffin did not realize was, in fact, the entrance to the Northwest Passage. Upon their return, Baffin's charts and his account were heavily censored, apparently because the merchant company sponsoring the voyage did not want any competitors to benefit from them. And it was a cruel fate that this last, highly successful exploratory trip by Baffin came to be thought of as too good to be true—in other words, a hoax—and Baffin Bay was removed from the maps of the time. It would not be found again until two centuries had passed and the European quest for the Northwest Passage resumed.

The attention of the English was beginning to turn to mining the unexpected riches of the Arctic. Henry Hudson had returned from his 1607 voyage with accounts of whales in the vicinity of Spitzbergen, and a major whaling industry sprang up almost immediately, in competition with the Dutch. Whales both live year round in Arctic waters and come there as summer visitors, feeding on upwelling blooms of plankton, with killer whales feasting on dolphins. Finback, humpback, blue, and sperm whales would form the basis of the Arctic whale fisheries of Europe and America.

Before too long the English were visiting Hudson Bay and inland in a grand geopolitical quest for riches of another sort: pelts. The Hudson Bay Company was founded some fifty years after Baffin's last Arctic voyage, and for the next century it would play a major role in the competition among England, Holland, France, and Spain for hegemony in North America. The search for the Northwest Passage was largely abandoned.

By 1648, however, England was preoccupied by a different and far less happy circumstance than the fur trade. It was embroiled in the civil war that would, in due course, send the royal family out of the country and turn the nation over to the Cromwellian years of repressive Puritanism that would last till 1660.

Elsewhere in the year 1648, ninety Russian men set out in seven vessels from the Kolyma River with the intention of sailing east to find new territories, and in particular to explore the country near the Anadyr' River, which was, Kolyma locals said, rich in furs. Most of the men on the voyage were hunters and traders, but a small group of representatives of the state went along, most notably a onetime Cossack named Semyon Ivanov Dezhnev. In the 1640s Dezhnev had served in Siberia and traveled widely in the north country.

Four of the seven vessels were wrecked along the Arctic coast, the crews either drowned or killed by natives. The other three passed around the eastern end of the Chukotka Peninsula, through the Bering Strait, and around the northeastern tip of Asia, reaching the Anadyr' River. By late September, the three remaining ships were fighting the native people of the region, and in October a storm carried off two more vessels, which were never seen again, leaving only the ship with Dezhnev aboard. And that ship was wrecked south of the Anadyr', after which Dezhnev led the twenty-five survivors overland to the lower Anadyr', where they built the first Russian outpost on the river. Dezhnev apparently stayed in the area for another twelve years, eventually returning to Moscow, where he died. There were few records of the voyage. Dezhnev's own account languished unread in archives at Yakutsk until 1736, when it was uncovered by a German historian. But by then Vitus Bering had sailed through the strait that bears his name (it is the western terminus of the Northwest Passage), not that of Dezhnev, who is its real, though forgotten, discoverer.

Bering was a Danish navigator who, after a voyage to the East Indies, was asked by Tsar Peter of Russia to join his naval service. Twenty years later, in 1725, in the waning years of his life, the tsar wrote to his admiral of the fleet:

> Bad health has obliged me to remain home. Recently I have been thinking over a matter which has been on my mind for many years but other affairs have prevented me from carrying it out. I have reference to the finding of a passage to China and India through the Arctic Sea. On the map before me is indicated such a passage bearing the name of Anian. There must be some reason for that. In my last travels I discussed the subject with learned men and they were of the opinion that such a passage could be found. Now that the country is in no danger from enemies we should strive to win for her glory along the lines of Arts and Sciences. In seeking such a passage who knows but perhaps we may be more successful than the Dutch and English.

This enlightened man, known to us as Peter the Great, would die before the expedition could get under way, but he had thought to select the leaders—Vitus Bering, along with Morten Spanberg and Alexey Chirikov as Bering's lieutenants. They were commissioned to find out if Asia and America were joined or separate and to map the northern shores of Siberia, as well as to look for the elusive Northeast Passage to China. It was an enormous effort, requiring five years in all, chiefly because they had to transport all of their supplies overland from St. Petersburg to Okhotsk, overwintering on the Yenisey River and at Yakutsk. It could be thought of as the Russian equivalent of the Lewis and Clark expedition through the Louisiana Purchase to the Pacific and back. The cold was, not surprisingly, vicious, and several men deserted, while two died along the way. When they finally reached Okhotsk in October 1727, local carpenters who had been previously commissioned there finished building a vessel, the *Fortuna*, which took them in two trips across the Okhotsk Sea. From there they passed the Kamchatka Peninsula.

The following August they came upon and named St. Lawrence Island and soon passed 65° 30′ N, thus traversing the strait that would be named for Bering. But thanks to the continuous fog, they did not actually see the American shore and therefore lacked proof that Asia and America were separated. They spent the following winter on the Kamchatka Peninsula and returned to St. Petersburg overland from Okhotsk, arriving in March 1730. Bering was convinced he had passed through the strait, but others were not, and the matter required another trip. The next one would be more ambitious than the first, far more wide-ranging, with several parties and many more scientific activities to be undertaken. Collectively they were called the Russian Great Northern Expeditions (Table 3.1).

In all, five parties were sent out simultaneously in 1733 to various parts of the Arctic, plus two others to regions of the Pacific. They were to map the Arctic and Pacific shores and gather information on the flora, fauna, and geology of the region. Bering was in nominal command of all the parties, but practically speaking he was in command of the Pacific section, in which Spanberg was to survey the Kuril Islands south to Japan; Chirikov, with a French astronomer, Louis Delisle de la Croyère, was to head for the American mainland, and Bering, with a German naturalist, Georg Stellar, was to sail into the Bering Sea. All three succeeded, with Bering sailing along the Aleutian Islands chain as well and Stellar discovering the now extinct (and misspelled) Steller's Seacow, a seallike creature that would soon be hunted out. The groundwork had been laid for a Russian presence on the northwest coast of North America, a presence that would eventually stretch as far south as Oregon.

Table 3.1 Russian Great Northern Expeditions, 1733 to 1743

Region	Investigators	Dates
Arkhangel'sk to Ob River	Stepan Murav'yev and Mikhail Pavlov	1734–1736
Arkhangel'sk to Ob River	Stepan Murav'yev and Aleksey Skuratov	1736–1739
Ob River to Yenisey River	Dmitriy Ovtsyn	1734–1739
Yenisey River to Taymyr Peninsula	Fedor Minin and Dmitriy Sterlegov	1738–1741
Peninsula to Lena River	Vasiliy Pronchishchev and Semen Chelyuskin	1735–1737
Taymyr Peninsula to Lena River	Kbariton Laptev	1739–1742
Lena River to Anadyr' River	Petr Lasinius and Vasiliy Rtishohev	1735–1736
Lena River to Anadyr' River	Dmitriy Laptev	1736–1743
Pacific Coast	Vitus Bering	1733–1743

(From Holland 1994)

But fate was not to be kind to the leaders of the Pacific section of the Russian Great Northern Expeditions. Bering, who with his crew was getting scurvy, was wrecked on an island off the coast of Kamchatka, and on December 8, 1741, he died there. In all, thirty members of his party died, the survivors building a boat and making their way back to Mother Russia.

The French astronomer, de la Croyère, died on board ship in 1741. Stellar was improperly arrested in Siberia on his way back to Moscow and died in prison. Chirikov contracted consumption in Siberia and died three years after returning to St. Petersburg. The exploratory phase of the expeditions was essentially over, but the scientific missions continued for several more years. Spanberg was ordered to stay on in Siberia to help these affairs, but he disobeyed and left in 1745. For this he was sentenced to death but was later pardoned.

II THE MYTH OF THE OPEN POLAR SEA

4 CONNUBIAL FIDELITY AND *THE VICAR OF WAKEFIELD*

Early in the nineteenth century the British navy did in truth rule the waves. In 1805 Nelson defeated the combined navies of France and Spain at Trafalgar. And once the British had laid siege to Baltimore and set fire to Washington in the War of 1812, there was little else for the navy to do. Most of the seamen were discharged, their numbers reduced from 140,000 to 19,000. Most officers were kept on, but nine out of ten had little or nothing to do and existed on half pay. At the time, the second secretary of the Admiralty, responsible for the navy's internal operations, was a man named John Barrow, who was also a founder of the Royal Geographic Society. Barrow was not a seaman; nor was he an explorer, but he had developed a geographer's zeal for the still-mysterious Arctic and believed strongly that England should resume the Arctic explorations that had ended two centuries earlier with William Baffin's second voyage. The Northwest Passage remained to be discovered; the North Pole had never felt a human foot. And who better to undertake this work and achieve these goals than the world's greatest navy? New geographic and scientific knowledge, not to mention national prestige, would result.

Barrow was convinced, as many were, of the existence of an Open Polar Sea lying just beyond the pestiferous ice blockage at the Arctic Circle. He, like most others, also had a misconception about the northernmost part of North America. Essentially, it was thought that once you sailed past the first bend on the landform (which would soon be named Baffin Island), it would be clear sailing through to the Pacific. And so, with wondrous assurance, in April 1818 the British navy launched two expeditions, each with two ships. One expedition was under the command of David Buchan, with John Franklin as his second. Buchan's orders said:

From the best information we have been able to obtain, it would appear that the sea northward of Spitzbergen [Svalbard], as far as 82-1/2, or 84, had been found generally free from ice, and not shut up by land. Should these accounts, in which several masters of whaling-vessels concur, turn out to be correct, there is reason to expect that the sea may continue open still more to the northward, and in this event you will steer north, and use your best endeavours to reach the North Pole.

Just what reports from whalers were being referred to in these orders is not known. In fact, the navy really did not have much interest in the reports of whalers and fishermen who almost certainly preceded the actual explorers to many parts of the Arctic, albeit anonymously. (Similarly, uncounted Vikings had no doubt preceded other Europeans into the far northern reaches as early as A.D. 1300, during a period called the Medieval Warm Period, an interval of warmth that was followed by what is known to us as the Little Ice Age, which in turn lasted into the nineteenth century.) One of the most widely traveled whalers—and one who was well known in his own time—was William Scoresby, who was publicly skeptical about the existence of an Open Polar Sea and had already made known his opinion that ice conditions in the Arctic varied so much from year to year that the Northwest Passage, if it existed, could have no real commercial value.

The other expedition was to be led by a seasoned captain, John Ross, with a bright young lieutenant, William Edward Parry, as second in command. These two ships were to sail across North America via the Northwest Passage. And in the Bering Strait, the two expeditions were to meet up with each other for a triumphant sail home, the Buchan and Franklin ships having crossed the top of the world. There were exceptionally precise orders to Buchan about fixing a rendezvous point in the Pacific with Ross, about the ordering of the chain of command once the ships met, and about various contingencies for ensuring that the "journals and despatches" of the expeditions be copied and returned safely to the Admiralty. For all the detailed managing, however, the navy largely ignored the early experiences in the record of such men as Davis, Hudson, and Baffin, and even though the four ships were far superior to anything those men had sailed, the same cultural snobbery that made whalers and fishermen too low to consult made the Inuit too low and barbaric to emulate. So, for example, the Royal Navy went forth in the wrong kind of clothes for the climate, evidently in the belief that they could bring their own climate with them. Inuit apparel, made exclusively from the skins and fur of local animals such as seal and polar bear, was worn fur side out in warmer climes and fur side in where it was colder. Such clothing worked for the Inuit in much the same way it did for the fur-bearers themselves, not only providing insulation from the extreme cold and the winds, but also tending to repel water and to dry out quickly when wet. The woolens of the English navy were less resistant to cold and wind, and once wet by a spill through the ice, they took far longer to dry out.

Buchan and company sailed north to Spitzbergen, where they ran into gales and pack ice. Putting into Fair Haven, an erstwhile whaling port, for refuge and to make repairs, they then sailed home, arriving in England on October 22, almost exactly six months after they left. Theirs was the first— and last—attempt by the Royal Navy to sail a vessel across the North Pole.

Ross and Parry sailed up through the Davis Strait, accompanied by some forty whaling ships, and got as far north as Smith Sound. Cruising along the west coast of Greenland, they "rediscovered" Baffin Bay and along the way encountered a group of Inuit. The meeting, captured in a drawing by John Sacheuse, was remarkable for the incongruity of the two cultures. Sacheuse was a Greenland native who had been educated in England and had come along as interpreter. In his drawing, the two English officers are shown in full dress attire, the naval equivalent of top hat and tails. A seaman, on the ship, is freezing in standard navy clothing, while the Inuit are dressed in furs of various kinds. At one point the Inuit turned to look at Ross's ship and said, "Who are you? What are you? Where do you come from? Is it from the sun or the moon?"

Meeting of John Ross and William Edward Parry with Greenland Eskimos (Toronto Reference Library, Toronto)

Ross and Parry proceeded to Lancaster Sound, between Devon and Baffin Islands, and sailed into it for 50 miles. Seeing what appeared to be a range of mountains stretching across the water, Ross assumed that the sound was in fact a bay with no way through it, so he had the expedition turn back to England even though it had been provisioned to stay in the Arctic for two years. They arrived in England in November, about three weeks after Buchan and Franklin's return. The young lieutenant, Parry, had not seen the mountains Ross saw, nor had anyone else aboard, and Parry was convinced they did not exist but had been a mirage of some sort visible only to Ross. The refractive properties of the northern seas, explorers would eventually learn, often created wonderful optical illusions: mountains would appear and disappear, the Sun and its surrounding corona would suddenly become two suns and two coronas, and a greatly enlarged moon might become some other shape altogether.

Parry firmly believed that Lancaster Sound was the place to search for the Northwest Passage. He let this be known at the Admiralty, and the cautious Ross was soon retired at half pay, never receiving another naval command.

Geography of region investigated by John Ross and by William Edward Parry (from Berton 1988)

The bold and intrepid Parry was promoted to be the leader of the next three of the navy's Arctic expeditions.

Boldness is often an advantage for an explorer, but there is also no substitute for good luck. When Parry set out in 1819, the Arctic was enjoying a particularly mild winter and the channels were clearer of ice than they had been for a decade. He made Lancaster Sound easily, arriving a month earlier than the previous year, and found it free of ice . . . until he reached its western end. He detoured into Prince Regent Inlet and eventually made his way to the southern shore of Melville Island, where he overwintered as prescribed, in the gathering pack ice.

Franklin's last expedition, 1845–1847 (from Berton 1988)

In addition to intrepidity and good luck, planning is also critical. Parry set out with two ships, the *Hecla,* 375 tons, and the *Griper,* 180 tons. In all, the two ships carried ninety-four men. This was to be the first deliberate overwintering on board ship in the Arctic. In addition to scurvy (less of a threat now, since they knew to dole out daily rations of lemon juice), starvation, and exposure, a major danger for an overwintering crew was utter, mind-numbing boredom. It is not easy to imagine a group of men, presumably most of them not particularly well educated, having to spend some ten months stuck in the ice and cold and, for the most part, in the dark, where the passage of hours had virtually no meaning and there was nothing about but a vast, empty land—a bleak landscape of rock and ice, black, white, and gray, silent except for when the wind howled or, in the spring, when thousands of maniacally screaming seabirds would nest in the rocks that reached precipitously upward some five hundred feet. Tempers would flare, squabbles and fights would break out, and men would simply drink themselves into total oblivion, or go mad.

To head off boredom and its attendant woes, Parry had the deck of the *Hecla* covered with a huge tentlike arrangement, providing a space out of the wind in which the men could exercise daily, which Parry made a requirement. He often entertained the men at night by playing his violin, and he arranged for theatrical performances once a week on the quarterdeck. *Miss in Her Teens, or The Medley of Lovers,* a farce, was the most popular of these. The crew could also anticipate the publication once a week for twenty-two straight weeks of a newspaper, *The North Georgia Gazette and Winter Chronicle,* which contained essays, poems, articles, and whatever might have passed for news. Providing this sort of entertainment worked, and the approach was emulated by later British expeditions, which would be relatively free of mutinous behavior or strife.

The polar gloom was implacable, however, and men would take walks in the silence, "the deathlike stillness," Parry later wrote, "of the most dreary isolation, and the total absence of animated existence." Only wolves and foxes made an occasional ghostly appearance in the murky landscape.

While the ships were trapped in the ice, Parry decided to trek across the Melville Peninsula and map its geography and topography. He took a party of twelve men, pulling a cart with some 800 pounds of equipment, even though he was well aware of the Inuit practice of using dogs to pull sledges. The cart was another Parry innovation, but also an example of English patrician disdain rather than good planning.

As a nineteenth-century chronicler wrote about Parry's expedition:

> The strong, flat-bottomed boats . . . had thus to be laden and unladen, in order to be raised over the hammocks. . . . Frequently the crew had to go on hands and knees to secure a footing. Heavy showers of rain often rendered the surface of the ice a mass of slush, and in some places the ice took the form of sharp-pointed crystals which cut the boots like penknives. But in spite of all these obstacles, they toiled cheerfully on, until at length, after thirty-five days of incessant drudgery, the discovery was made that, while they were apparently advancing toward the pole, the ice-field on which they were travelling was drifting to the south, and thus rendering all their exertions fruitless.

Once out of the ice—which took until August—Parry attempted to sail westward again through Lancaster Sound but got no farther than the previous year, so he returned home. On this one voyage he had passed the meridian of 110° W and discovered (and named) more new Arctic features than anyone before him—and more than anyone else would in a single voyage for another eighty years. The expedition, in particular the ships' surgeons, had gathered a good deal of information about the local fauna, dissecting and describing such exotic creatures as polar bears and walruses, and making some fairly good guesses about the migratory patterns of caribou and many bird species. Parry returned to London a hero, and the king gave him a reward of £5,000 for partial discovery of a northwest passage, as did Parliament. In addition, he received a lucrative contract for the publication of his journal, setting a trend that would continue in the world of adventuring and exploring to this very day.

Parry's book, *Journal of a Voyage for the Discovery of the North-West Passage from the Atlantic to the Pacific,* appeared in 1821, and April of that same year saw him back on the way north on the *Fury* and the *Hecla,* with George Lyon the captain of the second ship and the object of the three-year voyage being to penetrate the southern end of Prince Regent Inlet, thought at the time to be the gateway to the Northwest Passage. They found the outlet and named it the Fury and Hecla Strait, but they were unable to pass through it in either 1822 or 1823. In 1822 Parry purchased from the local Inuits a dog sled and some dogs as well as Inuit clothing for a short overland excursion. This was the first known instance of Europeans making use of native survival technology in the Arctic, though it would not catch on and be used as a matter of course until much later.

A symbiotic relationship with the dog was one of the Inuits' most important adaptations to the cold world they inhabited, along with a physiology and metabolism that permitted more suitable circulation of blood; and the kayak, a fragile but seaworthy craft they made from driftwood and bone covered with skins. They used dogs, of course, to pull the sleds they built, also from driftwood and bone, and in this winter chore the dogs were usually assisted by both men and women. Not every Inuit had sufficient dogs to pull a sled; it took a minimum of five or six. But dogs could carry packs made of caribou skin and loaded with 25 to 30 pounds, and they were frequently used this way as well. A hunter in pursuit of polar bear or caribou would typically be assisted by one or more dogs; together they needed to be efficient, for besides feeding his family a hunter needed to feed his dogs as well, and an adult dog would eat more than 850 pounds of meat and blubber annually. A good hunter looked after his dogs with great care—even to the point of making boots for them to protect their paws from sharp ice crystals. But the Inuit dogs were not all that different from the wolves they were descended from. A family typically kept its dogs tied up, one reason being to keep their small children safe from attack. And their ultimate value lay in those all-too-frequent moments when starvation was stalking; one's dogs were the penultimate defense against that particular form of death and were eaten without much in the way of sentimental turmoil on the part of their owners.

The central role of the dog in Arctic travel and survival could not have long been lost on European explorers, but it was not until Parry bought his first ones for a relatively short excursion that any European thought to emulate the Inuit in this. Many others who came later would, for obscure reasons, eschew their use as well—almost always with ill effects.

The *Fury* and the *Hecla* overwintered twice on this voyage on the western shore of Foxe Basin, farther south than Melville Peninsula, so there was more sunlight and, for some at least, a different kind of entertainment, provided by the Inuit people there. Parry would later write (with classic nineteenth-century hypocrisy):

> I fear we cannot give a very favourable account of the chastity of the women, nor of the delicacy of their husbands in this respect . . . it was not uncommon for them to offer their wives as freely for sale as a knife or a jacket. Some of the young men informed us that when two of them were absent together on a sealing excursion, they often exchanged wives for a time, as a matter of friendly convenience; . . . the behaviour of most of the women, when their husbands were absent from the huts,

plainly evinced their indifference towards them, and their utter disregard of connubial fidelity. The departure of the men was usually the signal for throwing aside restraint, which was invariably resumed on their return. For this event they take care to be prepared by the report of the children, one of whom is usually posted on the outside for the purpose of giving due notice.

George Lyon, the second in command, also harrumphed in print about Inuit morals, writing that it "is considered extremely friendly for two men to exchange wives for a day or two, and the request is sometimes made by the women themselves. These extraordinary civilities, although known, are never talked of, and are contrived as secretly as possible. . . . Divorced women and widows, and even young and well-looking girls, are equally liberal of their persons."

A later explorer, Charles Francis Hall, would have a conversation with an elderly Inuit woman from this region named Erktua who claimed to have been the lover of first Parry and then Lyon, and said that Lyon additionally had left two Eskimo sisters pregnant. It is well established now that the later Arctic explorers, Peary and Stefansson among them, also left descendants in their wake.

Parry made another Arctic probe on the same two ships and with much the same commission: to pass through the strait he had named for the *Fury* and the *Hecla*. But they were beset by ice immediately on entering Lancaster Sound and obliged to spend ten months on the northwestern shore of Baffin Island—a barren, desolate, and deserted region, and one without the comfort provided by friendly Inuit. Freed from the ice near the end of July, Parry was proceeding down the eastern shore of Somerset Island when he ran into a gale that drove the *Fury* ashore at a place still known as Fury Beach, where she was abandoned, lying heeled over in the ice under an enormously high rocky cliff. Stuck again for the winter, Parry kept the men busy with music, performances, scientific observations, and school classes. Thus they avoided ennui and the fact that all around was "dreary monotonous whiteness. Not merely for days or weeks, but for more than a half a year altogether. Which-ever way the eye is turned, it meets . . . inanimate stillness . . . a deadness with which a human spectator *appears out of keeping*." Indeed, Parry was often preoccupied with the "dreary solitude of this wintry desert."

The high cliffs kept the Sun from melting the pack ice until later than usual. Early in July 1825 Parry ordered the men to saw a passage through the pack ice, and the expedition returned to England with both crews on the one ship, the *Hecla*.

Still the hero, Parry gave up on the Northwest Passage but made one final probe in 1827, this time going due north of Svalbard in an attempt to reach the North Pole across what he understood was a good deal of pack ice. Ever the innovator, he had two sledge boats built that could be either hauled overland or launched in the sea. As with the cart he had used before, he hitched the sledge boats up to twelve men each, but they encountered none of the hoped-for smooth ice. Instead, they ran up against the high walls of pressure ridges as well as ice hummocks—the rugged frozen terrain that would frustrate Arctic explorers until well into the twentieth century. Parry's progress was excruciatingly slow, and after more than a month on the ice, he perceived that the southward drift of the ice was nearly offsetting whatever northward progress he was making. He reached as far as 82° 45′ N, a record that would last another fifty years, and spent more overall time on the ice (sixty-one days) than has anyone else to date. He returned, still not quite forty years old, with four Arctic expeditions under his belt, one of the most proficient (and engaging) of the men who led people north to the Ultima Thule.

There were rumors at the time, and since, that Parry's voyages were not all harmonious. The ship's surgeon, for example, pointed out darkly that after Parry's second voyage he refused to take the same officers along from one trip to the next (except for a lieutenant named James Clark Ross, who was the nephew of the disgraced John Ross). There may also have been jealousies based on class between the several officers of Parry's ship and the others. And the old Inuit woman Erktua reported that when she switched her attentions from Parry to Lyon, Parry was irate and wildly jealous. But of course the Admiralty, to which all the records of these voyages were given, was tight-lipped about such matters, and one can imagine they saw to it that any memoirs of the trips were not an embarrassment to His Majesty's Royal Navy.

After Parry's fourth effort, the attempt on the Pole, however, the navy lost interest in Arctic exploration for a while, and the initiative fell once again to private hands. John Ross persuaded a Londoner named Felix Booth to finance an expedition that would follow up on Parry's third voyage, finding the passage through Prince Regent Inlet to the coast of North America and thence to the Pacific. Booth was a philanthropist whose fortune presumably arose from both of his professions—he was at once the sheriff of London and one of the nation's major distillers, producing Booth's gin, still a favorite—and he wanted his name affixed to some Arctic features. Ross would reward him handsomely, putting Booth's name on the longest peninsula in the Canadian Arctic and its biggest gulf, along with attaching his Christian name to a harbor and his office of sheriff to another. This aggrandizement of expedition benefactors was done both before and after Booth, but never with greater flair than by the American explorer Robert Peary in the late nineteenth and early twentieth century (though a later commentator on the Arctic, the writer and fabulist Farley Mowat, found the practice reprehensible).

John Ross appointed his nephew, James Clark Ross, as second in command, and in May 1829 they sailed from London on the *Victory,* a ship of only 165 tons and a total complement of just twenty-three men—as opposed to Parry's third expedition, on two 375-ton ships with 128 men. The streamlining would prove fortuitous. The *Victory* bore the first steam engine to be used on a polar expedition (which proved a bit troublesome, as such new inventions often do, and was later beached) and the hopes of John Ross for the rehabilitation of his reputation. They reached Baffin Bay without much incident, entering the Lancaster Strait on August 6 and Prince Regent Inlet five days later. While there they visited the site of the wrecked *Fury* and its stores at Fury Beach and entered a gulf that Ross dutifully named Boothia, in the process sailing past a strait that was, in fact, the outlet from Prince Rupert Inlet to the Northwest Passage. This strait would later be found and named Bellot Strait.

With winter closing in, they put in at a place Ross named Felix Harbor, on the southeast shore of Boothia Peninsula. There Ross scuttled the steam engine, which was by then a useless "encumbrance." Ross and his nephew spent most of the next two years on land, venturing several times onto the peninsula. The next summer (1830) the ice pack allowed them to sail but a few miles from Felix Harbor to another, which they named Sheriff Harbor, and they again made exploratory trips across Boothia Peninsula when the weather allowed. Nephew James discovered King William Island (which he thought was part of the mainland) and—on June 1, 1831, at 8:00 A.M.—became the first European to stand on the north magnetic pole, which was then on the west coast of Boothia Peninsula. There, in what was otherwise a trackless frozen waste, he erected the British flag and claimed the surround in the name of Great Britain. (A hundred fifty years later this pole was in western Greenland; it is constantly on the move and can thus be regularly "rediscovered.")

In the winter of 1833 Ross decided to abandon the *Victory* to the ice and trekked to Fury Point, where he and the crew spent the next winter in a rude shelter, surviving on the provisions that had been left behind by the *Fury* expedition under Parry. The next summer, in 1833, they sailed and rowed the small boats of the *Fury* out into Lancaster Sound and Baffin Bay, where they had the astonishingly good fortune to encounter a homeward-bound British whaler, *Isobella,* which took them back to England. Perhaps even more astonishing, *Isobella* was coincidentally the same ship that John Ross had captained on his first (and disastrous) expedition to the Arctic.

This expedition was the longest in duration of any known Arctic expedition before or since—four years, from 1829 to 1833, with four over-winterings. It returned with twenty of the original twenty-three men, a considerable accomplishment that was owing to several factors. Their first three winters had been in Inuit country, and the natives supplied them with furs to replace their navy-issue wool clothing. The Inuit also provided them with fresh meat, particularly seal blubber, which we now know is rich in vitamin C, making it an excellent scurvy preventative. Without the Inuit, the explorers would almost surely have perished. Also, they were a small party with the flexibility to move in a coordinated manner as they trekked from the *Victory* to Fury Beach. And finally, they were just plain lucky to have a cache of boats and provisions available to them for the eventual escape. (It would be decades before Europeans had a true picture of the nature of the Arctic environment. In such a place, relatively few species of creatures exist—be they oceanic plankton, plants, or animals—although populations are typically large. But the individuals tend to be spread out far and wide or else are found in dense congregations that are either migrating or in the few areas that will support them at the right time of year. Similarly, Inuit bands were relatively small and typically moved far and wide. A single band of Inuit hunters might comprise about fifty men, women, and children, annually patrolling an area of some 30,000 square miles.)

Though the Northwest Passage still remained unnavigated, John Ross returned after four years in so challenging a region as a hero, his honor restored, and was knighted. More than a decade later, another Sir John went in search of a bracing victory over the Arctic to restore *his* honor. This was Sir John Franklin, who had sailed as second to Buchan in the quest for a straight shot at the North Pole. Before that, this career navy man had served at Trafalgar and other important moments in the British conquest of European navies. And subsequent to the failed attempt to sail across the Open Polar Sea to the pole, Franklin would soon lead two more Arctic expeditions for the English Admiralty—strangely enough, on foot.

Franklin's new expedition began in 1819 and lasted three years—years of frustration and ultimately catastrophe for a naval leader unaccustomed to the lubberly world of land exploration. Sir John had not hiked, canoed, or hunted anywhere in the Arctic, but he was assigned the task of traveling north from Great Slave Lake in northern Canada to the coast of Victoria Island, in order to map the coast west to Alaska. This land was still plied by French-Canadian voyageurs and other north-country habitués in search of furs on behalf of major entrepreneurs such as the Hudson Bay Company and the North West Company. Why the Admiralty would have engaged in such a mission and, even stranger, would send someone with only a landsman's experience is not at all clear.

The expedition made about 150 miles and then was forced to return, for they were near starvation and unable to kill sufficient game such as musk oxen for food. (The Inuit way of hunting herds of musk oxen was to chase them up to high ground, where the animals would form a protective circle. The hunters' dogs would hold the animals at bay while their masters picked off the oxen with arrows.) As Franklin's expedition trekked back toward Great Slave Lake, they were reduced to eating old shoes and other scraps of leather. Finally they were obliged to break up into three parties, one of which consisted of those men too weak to go any farther. Franklin's closest associate on the expedition, Dr. John Richardson, agreed to stay behind with these men. The second group of four men couldn't go much farther, and all but one of the four perished, the survivor—a French-Canadian voyageur named Michel Teroahaute—returning to Richardson's camp. (The third group, with Franklin, made it back to the lake.)

Two days after reaching Richardson's camp, Teroahaute went hunting and returned with some fresh wolf meat, a reprieve against the killing hunger. All hands welcomed the meat, but it had a strange taste, and Richardson began to wonder if it was indeed the meat of a wolf, as Teroahaute said, or that of a missing crew member. A few days later, while Richardson and a colleague were out gathering lichens to eat, they heard a shot from back in camp. They returned to find Teroahaute standing and the only other man of that group who had survived up until then dead with a bullet hole in his forehead. Teroahaute said it was a suicide, but Richardson concluded that instead Teroahaute had executed him . . . for the sustenance of the survivors. Richardson reasoned that he himself might be next and took preemptive action, shooting Teroahaute. The party, now considerably reduced in number, was eventually rescued, but Richardson was never brought to trial for killing Teroahaute.

Eleven of the nineteen men who had set out with Franklin in 1819 returned alive—not a good record but evidently not enough to stigmatize Franklin as an inadequate overland Arctic leader. He was sent out again in 1825, again accompanied by Richardson. They and the rest of the expedition traveled by boat down the Mackenzie River from Great Slave Lake to the Arctic Ocean and then split up. Franklin headed west and mapped the Canadian and Alaskan shore for 500 miles; Richardson went east the same distance. Both parties fared well—for such expeditions—and returned along the Mackenzie River.

At one point, Franklin would later write, with starvation stalking his party, they encountered a herd of musk. They sent out the best hunters, who took two hours to get within gunshot range of these unpredictable beasts. Their very lives depended on killing one of them. "In the meantime we beheld their proceedings with extreme anxiety, and many secret prayers were, doubtless, offered up for their success." The hunters opened fire; one cow fell and was promptly butchered. "The contents of its stomach were devoured upon the spot, and the raw intestines, which were next attacked, were pronounced by the most delicate amongst us to be excellent."

It was clearly a more seasoned John Franklin who embarked on this second overland expedition. Upon returning to England two years later in 1827, he was knighted—at the same time Edward Parry was knighted for his maritime explorations of the Arctic.

Now in his fifties and a widower, Sir John married a beautiful and intellectual London woman, Jane Griffin, just as his career was heading into eclipse. The Admiralty was reluctant to find a commission for him, finally offering him a year on a frigate in the Mediterranean. Nothing followed for a year after that, but then they offered him the governorship of Antigua, which he, and particularly his wife, found insulting. Soon the Admiralty offered him the governorship of Van Diemen's Land (Tasmania), which was bigger than Antigua, more populous, and white, even if the population was mostly members of a penal colony. When young Lady Jane agreed that this was acceptable, Sir John took the position and for six years proceeded to make a hash of things. He was unable to deal with the politics of the place, which were too subtle for a forthright military officer, a man of action; his wife did not help, being considered by most on the island an insufferable busybody in a day when women were supposed to be ladylike, quiet, and submissive. Eventually Sir John resigned amid a flurry of complaints, complaining himself that he was cut out only for a naval commission, and went home to seek one.

Then in 1843, out of the blue, the Admiralty again took up the notion of navigating the Northwest Passage. The way west halfway through it was well known by now, and the way north and east from the Bering Strait well along the coast of North America was also well known. Thus it was thought that this expedition, which would actually navigate the passage, could be little more than routine. At the time John Barrow, second secretary of the Admiralty and long the sparkplug behind the navy's attempts in the Arctic, was eighty-two and near retirement. It would be a crowning achievement for the old man. A list of possible leaders was drawn up and, with a good deal of lobbying (no doubt urged on by Lady Jane), Sir John got his name on the list, albeit last. First, of course, was James Clark Ross, who, after probing about in the Arctic with the best of them, had also spent many successful years exploring the Antarctic, but he asked not to be considered. Others on the list were eliminated—either they did not want the assignment or they were thrown off for political reasons of one sort or another, mostly internal Admiralty politics. The process of elimination finally left Sir John Franklin, now fifty-nine years old, as the leading candidate.

Evidently Lord Haddington, First Lord of the Admiralty, objected to Franklin on the grounds of his age, but Franklin persuaded him that with age came wisdom, calm, and a bellyful of useful experience. And so, on May 19, 1845, Franklin left England in command of a two-ship expedition—the *Erebus* and the *Terror,* manned by 128 men. The orders were utterly straightforward, and the ships were almost overcautiously provisioned for a stay of three years in the Arctic. The stores for the two ships included some twenty-nine hundred books, plenty of scientific instruments, and hand organs for musical performances. The crews would not be bored in the long Arctic winters.

In July two whalers noted the expedition was in Baffin Bay, hooked up to an iceberg, waiting for the wind to take them north. Later it would be pieced together that the two ships entered Lancaster Sound, circumnavigated Cornwallis Island, and wintered at Beechey Island, off the southwest coast of Devon Island. The next summer they sailed south between Somerset and Prince of Wales Islands and were soon beset by ice off the northwest coast of King William Island. There they remained for the long winter of 1846–47. When summer came, they were still unable to get free of the ice, and Franklin and several others died, evidently of scurvy. The remaining men overwintered yet again—their third winter—but by April the two ships had been crushed in the ice. The 105 surviving members of the expedition could do nothing but set out on foot with sledges, carrying whatever might be useful for a long trek south across the icebound sea and land.

They were never heard from again. The wrecked ships were never found. The expedition disappeared into the fog and mist, with no trace of it being found for several years, and then only accidentally.

Meanwhile, having heard nothing of the expedition by early 1847, Lady Jane grew fretful and asked the Admiralty about it. She was told not to worry and reminded that the ships were, after all, provisioned for three years. But by the end of 1847 the Admiralty was itself alarmed and sent out two ships, which promptly were caught in the ice and had to overwinter, returning with no word of Franklin's ships or men. Two more ships were sent the following year, with the same results. In all, some forty expeditions—mostly by sea, though two went overland, and mostly sponsored by the British navy—would go forth in the years following, all to no avail. Some of the search missions flew kites and balloons; others fired rockets. Some left deposits of coal here and there, and one caught foxes and tagged them with directions to the coal deposits. Most of these expeditions were doomed to fail before they set forth, since the Admiralty focused virtually all the search parties west and south of Lancaster Sound, near Banks and Melville Islands, where in fact nothing was to be found. Also, Franklin's ships had sunk, leaving nothing above the water and ice.

For various reasons, Franklin's disappearance in the ice and cold captured the imagination of the English—and the Americans—as no one else who had ever been lost in the Arctic had. British pride was at stake, of course. This was an era of fervent belief in the excellence and power of scientific progress (of which exploration was an important part), and the loss of the Franklin expedition was akin to the twentieth-century losses of the *Titanic* or the space shuttle *Challenger.* The American interest was almost entirely the result of the continuing efforts of Lady Jane, who came to the United States early on. She had an audience with President Zachary Taylor, who promised that all of America would pray for her husband's safe return—which, of course, Lady Jane found a useless and contemptible response, and she demanded more of the president, who managed to get her out of the office, later referring to her as an insufferable bore. She went on a lecture tour and managed to persuade Henry Grinnell, a shipping tycoon, to put up $30,000 to buy two ships, which were put at the disposal of the U.S. government, which in turn was shamed into manning them and sending them off—without success. In all, this was the greatest search for missing men ever mounted before or since, and while all the voyages failed to find a trace of Franklin's expedition, they did succeed in learning more about the unexplored Canadian archipelago than all previous expeditions had done. New channels, new islands, and new shorelines all came to light; landmasses were crisscrossed; and all of the high Arctic south and west of the Parry Islands now could appear with some accuracy on maps and charts.

Half of the Admiralty's £20,000 prize for navigating the Northwest Passage, in the meantime, was given to one of the searchers, Robert McClure, and the men of *Investigator,* who had sailed through the Bering Strait in 1850, overwintered twice at Banks Island, and then proceeded overland to a point just west of where Sir Edward Parry had fetched up. Many felt that the award was inappropriate: the passage had not been navigated in the maritime sense of the word. But it was now known that a northwest passage did, in fact, exist—either through Bellot Strait from the Gulf of Boothia (when it was ice-free) or down Peel Sound between Somerset and

Prince of Wales Islands, and then around the southern portions of King William, Victoria, and Banks Islands to the Beaufort Sea. Whether or not McClure and his crew on the *Investigator* deserved the prize, McClure's original task in 1850 had been, like so many other ships, to find whatever remained of Franklin's last expedition. In this they had no more luck than the others, and they wound up beset in the ice in Mercy Bay along the northern coast of Banks Island. The *Investigator* remained blocked by the ice until 1853 and was finally abandoned, with McClure and his crew rescued by the HMS *Resolute*. One hundred fifty-seven years later, on July 25, 2010, a group of Canadian marine archaeologists peered through the clear cold waters of Mercy Bay by means of side-scanning sonar from a small boat and saw the *Investigator*. Resting in shallow water, she was in excellent condition, with her masts and rigging long since sheared off. Three graves of sailors suspected of having died from scurvy will be left undisturbed, as will the hull of the *Investigator*.

By 1854, the British interest in the Northwest Passage had waned, thanks in part to the Franklin debacle and full realization that the passage had little or no commercial value. At the same time, Englishmen had begun dying in the Crimea, and the attention of the nation was to the south, where a sad and sorry war was being fought for obscure causes.

In 1854, given the utter lack of success in finding anything from the Franklin expedition after some forty attempts, the Admiralty gave up and declared all hands dead. Four months later the first clues came to light, thanks to John Rae, a surgeon, explorer, and civilian employee of the Hudson Bay Company. In 1853 his company had asked him to complete the surveying of a part of Canada's northern shores. In particular, he was to settle the question of whether Boothia was a peninsula, as thought, or an island, and whether King William was an island, as thought, or a peninsula. Rae was familiar with the techniques of traveling and surviving in the Arctic—that is, he knew the ways of the Inuit and other natives who plied these northerly regions. He trekked overland from Repulse Bay on Foxe Island to Pelly Bay on the Gulf of Boothia, where in 1854 he met, talked with, and traded with a few Inuit.

From them he learned that other Inuit, four years earlier, had seen forty white men traveling south over the ice of King William Island, dragging a boat and sledges. None of them spoke Inuit, but they had used sign language to help the natives understand that their ships had been crushed by the ice and they were headed south to find deer to shoot. They were thin and out of provisions, and they bought some seal meat from the Inuit. Their officer, the

Sea and land travels of John Rae, 1853–54 (from Berton 1988)

Inuit reported, was a tall, stout man. At the end of the day they pitched tents, and the Inuit went on their way.

It was not at all uncommon for Inuit who found people lost and starving to feed them and help them along. But forty starving men would have been far too many for the Inuit to assist in any meaningful way without starving themselves. The Arctic is a vast place with a great deal of game, but—as noted—it is spread out very sparsely, for the most part, and no single area can support very many people. The British navy might have understood this from the success of Sir John Ross in making it back from a disaster with a relative handful of men who were helped by the Inuit, but the Admiralty ignored that lesson in the case of Franklin—one of innumerable examples of bad planning that underlay this greatest of polar tragedies. (Adventure, most experts say, is the last thing a professional explorer wants to have occur, but an expedition that goes without a hitch is simply not that interesting. Franklin's failure commands far more words in popular accounts of polar exploring than other, successful expeditions, and of course, in modern times the nearly fatal *Apollo 13* mission is far better remembered than the smooth *Apollo 14* mission that followed.)

In his account of his meetings with the Inuit, Rae wrote that later in the season, but before the ice broke up, the Inuit came across the corpses of about thirty people, some graves, and later, on an island, another five corpses. "Some of the bodies were in a tent or tents, and some lay scattered about in different directions. . . . From the mutilated state of many of the bodies, and the contents of the kettles, it is evident that our wretched countrymen had been driven to the last dread alternative as a means of sustaining life."

Rae went on to explain that there "must have been a number of telescopes, guns (several of them double-barreled), watches, compasses, &c, all of which seem to have been broken up, as I saw pieces of three different articles with the natives; and I purchased as many as possible, together with some silver spoons and forks, an order of merit in the form of a star, and a small silver plate engraved 'Sir John Franklin, K.C.H.'"

Rae carried his news to England in 1854, where he claimed and was given the £10,000 reward that Parliament had established for news of the Franklin disaster. With Rae's information, the Admiralty saw no reason to reopen the search for further information or artifacts—or bodies. But Jane Franklin was not so easily satisfied. After all, Rae's were secondhand reports, hearsay. The few objects Rae obtained could have been traded to the Inuit by members of the expedition. Rae had never visited the actual sites where these corpses were supposed to lie.

From what remained of her own money, and by public subscription, the determined and astoundingly faithful Lady Jane sponsored one last expedition (she had already financed several). It was now known where the search should be carried out: King William Island. And so in the same year (1853) in which Rae had set out to survey the Canadian coast, a British naval officer named Francis M'Clintock would later set out by sledge in search of any remnants of Franklin's expedition, traveling 1,338 miles in 105 days, a record for such treks. M'Clintock was an unusual British naval officer for the time in that he knew and emulated the ways of the Inuit when in Inuit country—something he had learned from James Clark Ross, for whom he had served as second officer. It was M'Clintock whom the Admiralty chose to command the *Fox* in Lady Jane's last attempt to pin down how her husband and his men had died. M'Clintock sailed in 1857, acquired dogs and an Inuit driver in Greenland, and was beset in the ice in Melville Bay in August. He would need to overwinter twice before setting three sledge parties loose on King William Island. There, in various places, they found a cairn with a message from the expedition that all was well, and then another cairn and message that reported the death of Franklin and the abandoning of the ships.

Along the southern shore of King William Island, M'Clintock came across a sledge with a boat on top, in all a weight of some 1,400 pounds, "a heavy load for seven healthy men." He and his men were amazed by what they found in the boat: "portions of two skeletons . . . five watches . . . two double-barreled shotguns—one barrel in each loaded and cocked—standing muzzle upright against the boat's side." They also found a half dozen books, "all of them scriptural or devotional works, except for the 'Vicar of Wakefield,'" along with seven or eight pairs of boots, silk handkerchiefs, towels and soap, toothbrushes, combs, and a gun cover. "Besides these articles we found twine, nails, saws, files, bristles . . . powder, bullets, shot, cartridges, wads, leather cartridge-case, knives, . . . needle and thread cases, slow-match, several bayonet-scabbards cut down into knife-sheaths, two rolls of sheet-lead, and, in short, a quantity of articles of one description and another truly astonishing in variety, and such as, for the most part, modern sledge-travelers in these regions would consider a mere accumulation of dead weight but slightly useful, and very likely to break down the strength of the sledge-crews."

Farther north, some three days' march from the point where the ships had been abandoned, they found yet another cairn and a pile of abandoned stuff the crews had evidently found it impossible to haul, however they might have been bent on leaving no possessions behind. They had abandoned four cooking stoves, shovels and pickaxes, old canvas, a copper lightning conductor, curtain rods, twenty-four phials of medicines, bar magnets, a small sextant engraved with the name Frederic Hornsby, and a four-foot pile of warm sailor's clothing.

One can only imagine that a certain kind of madness had settled into the feverish brains of the survivors, leaving useful material in a heap and pressing on with useless dead weight. It was not the first instance of insanity, and it would not be the last; there are many forms of madness inspired by the Far North.

5 OPEN SEAS AND CLOSED MINDS

The dreams of men come and go, replacing old and worn-out themes and impossible goals with fresh endeavors, new madnesses, or, as we often prefer to call them, challenges. Foolish or not, the quest for the Northwest Passage came to an end for the British Admiralty with the loss of the Franklin expedition, and it never much interested the Americans, whose passage to Cathay started perfectly conveniently in Seattle or San Francisco. And before too many years of the twentieth century went by, the passage so long sought by Spanish conquistadors, French voyageurs, British factors, and other geographic dreamers—an easy, direct route through the Western Hemisphere to the Orient—was built by main force through the Isthmus of Panama. No longer did men think they needed to obey the actual configuration of the Earth; indeed, there was once talk of a new and improved Panama Canal that would be gouged out of the land by nuclear explosions. For a time before the collapse of the Soviet Union, there was a good deal of talk about turning the flow of some of its rivers backward so they would run from north to south, that is, run inland from the Arctic Ocean. Happily, sometimes people wake up before the dream takes hold.

The new, post-Franklin dream of those with an eye on the Arctic was in two parts: (one) reach the Pole (two) by sailing across the Open Polar Sea that was still thought to exist. But governments in Europe and America saw nothing much in it that would justify an expenditure from their treasuries, and so the new dream was left, for the most part, to be fulfilled or not by private citizens. These would turn out to be mostly Americans, encouraged and impelled largely by fledgling nongovernmental scientific institutions. The seeds of organized American scientific institutions were planted about the same time that Franklin's expedition disappeared, with the founding of the Smithsonian Institution in Washington, D.C., in 1846 with a noted physicist, Joseph Henry, at its helm. Before long, science in America was less a case of lone individuals and haphazard networking and more a matter of scientific societies devoted to the advancement of the sciences as delineated fields of knowledge, with centers of scientific research beginning to develop, notably in Boston, New York, Philadelphia, and Washington, D.C.

Many American scientists of good standing—and most Arctic explorers— stoutly insisted that the Open Polar Sea did indeed exist, even though no one had ever come close to seeing such a thing. Today we know, of course, that there is no such thing. So how is it that this notion could hold on in an age more given to science than any before? It has a great deal to do with the very nature of science itself, and also the state of science at the time. At the turn of the millennium, in a world where the technological fruits of science are virtually ubiquitous—where communication, healing, transportation, agriculture, and practically all other aspects of daily life are hastened along thanks to the stupefyingly rich findings of science—it is hard to imagine how very little scientific understanding of the world existed in the late 1840s.

By way of setting the scene, what follows is a very short and selective list of things that no one knew of, had conceived of, or had seen at the time: the principle of conservation of energy, storage batteries, oil wells, anthropology as such, germ theory, the measurement of the speed of light, the connection between electricity and magnetism, dynamite, Cro-Magnon man, the revolver, the periodic table of elements, taking accurate soundings at sea, typewriters, telephones, phonographs, electric light, psychoanalysis, the motion picture camera, rabies vaccine, and radioactivity. And in 1850 no European had been farther north than about 80° N, some 700 miles from the North Pole.

What this means, of course, is that there were no defining data on the matter of the Open Polar Sea at the time. Defining data are those pieces of information that pull a matter of scientific inquiry out of the realm of mostly speculation and into an area where a reasonable hypothesis can actually be put to a test. For example, we know today that carbon dioxide has increased in the atmosphere over the past forty years (1958 to 1998) by 11 percent. The assumption is that a large increase (11 percent is certainly large) in this and other greenhouse gases will lead, as in a greenhouse, to higher temperatures for the terrestrial and oceanic Earth. But the only absolutely certain thing we know is that there was an 11 percent increase; as many a scientist has said, we are going through a global geophysical experiment today the likes of which the Earth and mankind have never seen before. We have amazingly sophisticated computer models of climate into which we can plug a host of variables and play out the future, and they produce all kinds of futures to contemplate. But in the absence of more data—defining data—we simply don't know which, if any, of the models is accurate.

In 1850, the only defining datum available on the polar sea was that north of the Arctic Circle one encountered sea ice. So on the basis of whatever assumptions one wished to make beyond that simple fact, one could conjecture that the Arctic Ocean was solid or liquid, and one could hypothesize the existence, or nonexistence, of landmasses up there. Such conjecturing and hypothesizing can be perfectly logical, perfectly reasonable, according to what is known at the time, but even the most logical progression of thought can go completely awry if you start off with a wrong assumption.

In what are called the hard sciences—mainly physics and chemistry—it is pretty easy to settle such matters. It can usually be done by framing experiments that either prove or disprove the hypothesis. Other people can do the same experiments the same way and see if the results say what the first ones seem to say. When inquiring about matters as messy as the Earth, biology, or human behavior, however, the scientific method is not so straightforward. You can't control all the variables, and in many cases you can't frame an experiment or repeat one that happened before. In such sciences, which in the mid-nineteenth century included a host of data-poor fledgling disciplines such as oceanography, there is plenty of room for speculation. Typically, the more room there is for speculation, the greater the determination to defend one's position against all comers. This is not as extreme a tendency in science as it has been in, say, religion, but it is a matter of human nature, in which almost every scientist shares. And in such instances in the history of science, the opinions that prevail are generally those of the most prominent, best-known persons in the field—at least until new information or defining data arrive to make their position untenable. This was the case in the mid-nineteenth century concerning the nature of the Arctic Ocean.

Just as Mercator was the preeminent cartographer of the sixteenth century, a German named August Petermann was the preeminent cartographer of the nineteenth. He served for eight years, from 1847 to 1854, as the queen of England's physical geographer, and in 1874 a British explorer of Australia, Ernest Giles, named a mountain range there after him. In 1854 Petermann returned to Germany and began producing a yearly series of exquisitely illustrated volumes, *Petermanns geographische Mitteilungen*, which gave the latest geographical findings from around the world. The series continues to this day as a geographical journal with the same title.

In 1852, while England was still involved in the search for Franklin's remains, Petermann held forth on the subject. "It is a well-known fact," he wrote, "that there exists to the north of the Siberian coast, and, at a comparatively short distance from it, a sea open at all seasons; it is beyond doubt that a similar open sea exists on the American side . . . it is very probable that these two open seas form a large navigable Arctic ocean." Until searchers entered this huge basin, he went on to say, there was no hope of finding any trace of the Franklin expedition. Forget for a moment the rhetoric Petermann employed to blitz any nonbelievers: "a well-known fact," "beyond doubt." He also had an answer for the reasonable question of where the heat came from that kept the ocean warm: the Gulf Stream.

A great Arctic current, he averred, that brought drift ice in from Siberian shores relaxed in the summer, and the Gulf Stream, which was hemmed in by ice in the spring and summer, could then head for the Siberian coast, carrying the drift ice with it and clearing the way for "easy navigation." In fact, this is basically correct, but what is wrong is the assumption that the Gulf Stream transfers enough heat to the Arctic Ocean to keep it ice-free.

Petermann also went on to suggest that there were two "poles" of cold (not associated with the North Pole) that moved around seasonally, in a sense creating an annulus or ring of ice around the warmer Arctic Ocean to its north. There was, of course, no data whatsoever to support such a notion. In an 1869 map Petermann did a splendid job of getting the details correct in the northern regions that lie south of the Arctic Circle. But above that, error crept in—for example, the projection of Greenland north across the Arctic to the Siberian coast, beyond the limits then known. Here again, most people didn't notice at the time that the old Spanish cartographers' rule—do not put a line on a map unless you know what's there—was being violated.

Another major supporter of the idea of an Open Polar Sea was a man who might be called the father of oceanography, an American naval officer who led a life that was at times as adventurous as that of any explorer. He was Matthew Fontaine Maury, a Virginian who circumnavigated the world as a midshipman, was promoted to lieutenant, and then was lamed in a stagecoach accident three years later, in 1839. Unfit for active service, he was put in charge of the U.S. Navy's Depot of Charts and Instruments, from which eventually arose the U.S. Naval Observatory and Hydrographic Office. He instructed American captains on keeping certain records at sea, from which he compiled pilot charts of winds and currents, allowing ships to cut the time of various voyages. Eventually, with international information, he prepared wind and current charts of the Atlantic, Pacific, and Indian oceans. He profiled the Atlantic Ocean bottom, showing that a transatlantic telegraph cable could be laid across it, and in 1855 he published the first modern oceanographic text, *The Physical Geography of the Sea.*

Map of the North Pole (Petermann 1869)

When the Civil War erupted, Maury went home and joined the Confederate Navy, serving as head of shoreline and river defenses and attempting to invent an electric torpedo. He was then sent as a special agent to Mexico, and after the war he remained there as Emperor Maximilian's commissioner of immigration, hoping to establish a Confederate colony. When this scheme fell apart, he eventually returned to Virginia as a professor of meteorology at the Virginia Military Institute. He was, in short, a man of action and of learning, someone above all to be respected when he spoke of matters oceanographic.

Part of Maury's thesis about the Open Polar Sea referred to observations of wind directions that indicated a lowering of barometric pressure toward the Pole, which he thought had to be the result of the liberation of latent heat. He asked, "Whence do those vapors come which liberate all this heat . . . if not from that boiling, bubbling pool of Gulf Stream water, which my observations show," and so forth. So convinced was Maury that he called chapter 7 of his masterwork on the oceans "The Open Sea in the Arctic Ocean," beginning it by recounting observations of harpoons from whaling ships in Baffin Bay that were found in whales in the Bering Strait. Being a careful observer, he admitted that this "did not prove the existence of an open sea there; it only established the existence—the occasional existence, if you please of a channel through which the whales had passed." His main argument, like Petermann's, had to do with the transfer of heat from the Gulf Stream to the Arctic Ocean, noting that a relatively warm undercurrent passes through the Davis Strait from the Atlantic. There must be a place, he wrote, where the undercurrent stops flowing north and turns south as a surface current bearing huge quantities of salt. In fact, there is such a current—the Norwegian Current—which keeps the coast of Norway free of ice, but it is not warm enough to take care of the entire Arctic Ocean.

Maury also brought in what was then understood about the migration of birds and mammals in the Arctic, postulating that there had to be a warmer climate "somewhere in that inhospitable sea," because the birds and mammals were found at various seasons migrating north, "evidently in search of milder climates. The instincts of these dumb creatures are unerring," and the only thing that would make it milder to the north was a large open ocean. Of course, we know now that those migrations do not continue out into the barren Arctic ice pack. But thus, on the basis of wholly inadequate data and considerable exercise of logic, was it demonstrated that there was an Open Polar Sea.

This kind of argument would be offered for several decades after the search for the Franklin expedition was called off—and of course, not everyone agreed. Others adduced equally excellent logic from the assumption that there was no Open Polar Sea and that the climate grew colder as you moved north to the pole—again, in the face of no defining data. Neither view, it should be pointed out, was absurd.

One of those who held with the notion of the Open Polar Sea was the first American to make an actual attempt to reach the North Pole, a remarkable man named Elisha Kent Kane. Born in 1820, Kane died when he was only thirty-seven years old, one of the earliest celebrities in a nation that would eventually turn celebrity into an industry. But unlike most of today's celebrities, who are created out of whole cloth, Kane deserved his renown (and notoriety), if for no other reason than that he accomplished more in his short life than most other men dream of.

Stricken at an early age with rheumatic fever, he lived with the forecast of a shortened life and reacted with the conscious decision to live his life to the fullest. He sought out a medical education and became a naval surgeon, and before he was thirty Kane had explored a volcano in the Philippines and traveled to other foreign lands from Brazil to Borneo, Nubia to China, Greece to the West Indies, and Persia to boot. In the course of these travels he contracted various other diseases, including tetanus and bubonic plague. During the Mexican War he was assigned by President Polk to carry a message to General Winfield Scott in Mexico City, a job that put him into contact with Mexican guerrillas, one of whom wounded Kane with a lance. By 1850 he had settled down to a mundane and comfortable job with the Coast Survey in Mobile, Alabama.

This was when much of the English-speaking world was abuzz with the ongoing attempts to find the remains of the Franklin expedition, and it was the year that Lady Jane Franklin persuaded Henry Grinnell to buy two ships for the purpose and offer them to the U.S. government. This put the expedition under the aegis of the navy, and when Elisha Kane heard about the expedition, he wrote asking to be included; he was selected as surgeon for one of the ships. Led by a naval lieutenant, Edwin De Haven, the ships entered Lancaster Sound in that same year, eventually drifting with the ice out into Baffin Bay. Attempting to sail north again in 1851, they were thwarted and returned to New York that September. This nondescript voyage, one of forty that all failed, would have been merely a footnote to history but for its effect on the young naval surgeon onboard.

Elisha Kane had caught a different kind of bug, the Arctic bug. He wrote a book about the expedition, a well-written account that sold well. For two years after the return, he lectured and solicited funds for a second expedition. Meanwhile, he heard about a British navy captain who in 1852 sailed into Smith Sound and reported there was no problem with ice, and that he could have sailed even farther north except that he ran out of time. Here, then, Kane reasoned, was the way through the ring of ice that surrounded the Open Polar Sea. And if he were to sail to Smith Sound in search of Franklin, he could take the time to become the first man to reach the North Pole. He let on to his backers that, given the lack of success in finding Franklin west of Baffin Bay, the place to search now was to that bay's north. But he kept his plan for a polar dash to himself.

Kane persuaded Henry Grinnell to put De Haven's brig, the *Advance*, at Kane's disposal, and the navy agreed to provide ten men. The recently founded American Geographical Society, whose first president was also Grinnell, supported the mission (and Kane as its leader, though he had no experience heading any sort of expedition). The *Advance*, a 140-ton brig (that is, a two-masted square-rigger), was originally designed for carrying loads of iron, and it had been strengthened yet more for the Arctic ice floes, which could crush less-solid craft like flies. Cornelius Grinnell, Henry's son, was put in charge of outfitting the ship, since Kane was recovering from a bout of rheumatic fever at the time. With not enough volunteers to make up a full complement of seventeen (seven plus the ten navy men), Cornelius scoured the waterfront and came up with, among others, a couple of unsavory characters named William Godfrey and John Blake, along with a sailing master, John Wilson, who had no experience in the Arctic. Cornelius also provisioned the expedition with enough food for about a year, but not for two winters.

Kane would prove to be a brave and dogged explorer. He came close to death on several occasions, the result of scurvy and other illnesses, not to mention exposure and near starvation, but always managed to recover and forge on. Kane's dauntlessness can be perceived in a single diary entry for December 15:

> We have lost the last vestige of our midday twilight. We can see no print, and hardly paper; the fingers can not be counted a foot from the eyes. Noonday and midnight are alike; and, except a vague glimmer in the sky that seems to define the hill outlines to the south, we have nothing to tell us that this Arctic world of ours has a sun. In the darkness, and consequent inaction, it is almost vain that we seek to create topics of thought, and, by a forced excitement, to ward off the encroachments of diseases.

At the same time, he was no seaman; he was chronically seasick, nearly to the point of debility, whenever the ship was under way. And (it would turn out later, long after the journal of this voyage had been published and cemented Kane's position as a major American hero) he wasn't all that effective as a leader. In fact, it seems he was a bit of a snob, taking a patrician's stance throughout much of the voyage. This was not the sort of thing to endear him to his men; nor was the favoritism he showed for William Morton, the personal servant he brought along. In fairness, Morton was possessed of great endurance and was a valuable man in a pinch, of which there would be a great many.

The expedition left New York on May 30, 1853, and made its way slowly into Baffin Bay and then north into the basin that now bears Kane's name. They encountered extremely dangerous ice floes and huge icebergs as the weather began to close in on them. Kane wrote on August 20 of the nautical nightmare of ice floes pressing, hurricane-force winds howling, and the ship's lines, anchored to an iceberg for protection, breaking loose:

> The manilla cable was proving its excellence.... We could hear its deep Eolianne chant, swelling through all the rattle of the running gear and moaning shrouds. It was the death song! The strands gave way with the sound of a gun; and we were dragged out by the wild sea, and were at its mercy.... At seven in the morning we close upon the piling masses of ice ... Down we went with the gale again, helplessly scraping along a lee of ice seldom less than thirty feet thick.... One upturned mass rose above our gunwale, smashed our bulwarks and deposited a half a ton of ice in a lump upon our decks. Our staunch little brig bore herself through all this wild adventure as if she had a charmed life.

Geography of region investigated by Elisha Kent Kane (from Berton 1988)

Subsequently the *Advance* found itself among towering bergs, and the gathering floes shoved the craft up a sloping berg and heeled her over on her side. The crew could do nothing. Eventually, her timbers groaning, she settled back into the water. There was a deep silence, Kane wrote, before "the clamor of congratulation and comment could burst forth."

They were most fortunate to have with them two men of Inuit extraction, and the experience of one of them, Hans Hendrik, in navigating these hazards was essential. They overwintered at Rensselaer Harbor and spent the days in frigid tedium. As Kane would later write of the miserable hours:

> We could keep no note of time and except by the whirring of the drift against the roof of our kennel, had no information of the state of the weather. We slept and cooked coffee, and drank coffee, and slept and cooked coffee, and drank again; and when by our tired instincts we thought that twelve hours must have passed, we treated ourselves to a meal—that is to say we divided impartial bites out of the raw hind-leg of a fox, to give zest to our biscuits spread with frozen tallow.

When spring came, Kane sent out several sledge parties (powered mainly by humans, since most of the dogs he had obtained died during the winter) to seek out the Open Polar Sea that he was convinced lay ahead. These sorties proved unsuccessful; two men died in the effort, and the others returned suffering from the onset of scurvy. Kane, normally an optimist, was covered with doubt, acutely feeling that he had failed; a year had passed and he had absolutely nothing to show for it. But then in early July his manservant, William Morton, returned from an excursion onto the Humboldt Glacier, along the northwest coast of Greenland. He told Kane that on June 24 he had stood upon the shore and seen "not a speck of ice." As far as he could see, he reported, "the sea was open, a swell coming in from the northward and running crosswise, as if with a small eastward set. The wind was due N—enough of it to make white caps,—and the surf broke in on the rocks in regular breakers." Morton had stood, he said, at 80° 30′ N, the farthest north achieved by any white man, his feet upon the northernmost land on the face of the planet.

So here was success for Kane's expedition. He believed that if he was able to get his ship or perhaps just some seaworthy boats to that point, he could possibly achieve the Pole. But it was then that the expedition began a downward spiral. It became clear during the summer that they would not be able to free

William Morton's Open Polar Sea (from Kane 1856)

the *Advance* from the ice in Rensselaer Harbor. They would be stuck there for at least another winter, because it was also too late in the season to try to escape south by boat. The crew, already fed up with the hardships of the voyage, grew mutinous. Kane called a meeting on August 24 and let everyone know that he would provide boats, provisions, and equipment to any who wished to leave and head south, however foolish an idea that was. To his astonishment and dismay, eleven of the seventeen men voted to go (only nine eventually left the ship). Among those who wanted to leave was the ship's surgeon, Isaac Israel Hayes.

Kane had lost control; his command was meaningless. In the book he would eventually write (*Arctic Exploration: The Second Grinnell Expedition in Search of Sir John Franklin, in the Years 1853, '54, '55*), Kane made little of this mutiny, but to his journal he confided: "I have washed my hands of them as a man and a Christian. . . . They have left the expedition and God's blessing go with them, for they carry not the respect of good men." Later he wrote in his journal that he expected some of them to return, seeking refuge, and he would provide it. But, he wrote, "but—but—but—If I ever live to get home—home! and should meet Dr. Hayes [and the others], let them look out for their skins."

The deserters fared poorly, returning to the *Advance* some three months later, exhausted and in poor health. In their travails, they had been watched and sometimes aided by the Inuit, who coveted the mutineers' knives and other equipment but feared their firearms. In an uneasy arrangement, the

Inuit would barter food, enough to keep the deserters dependent on them. When the deserters finally realized that the Inuit were simply waiting for them to die off so that they could take their equipment, the sailors took matters into their own hands and forced the Inuit at gunpoint to sledge them back to the ship, where Kane took them back—but without forgiving them.

They survived the winter largely because of a verbal treaty with the local Inuit, known then as the Etah Eskimos, wherein they gave the expedition enough fresh meat to avoid starvation and the worst of scurvy. This treaty, which Kane took credit for arranging, was more likely the work of the part-Inuit Hendrik, whose expertise in Arctic ways may well have made the ultimate difference between survival and doom for the entire expedition. Meanwhile, they were forced to dismantle the oak sheathing from the hull of their ship to use as fuel for fires against the ferocious cold, and finally the structural parts of the ship were burned as well, leaving enough wood to construct a couple of sledges long enough to carry the ship's boats.

Kane later wrote of the time when all the ship's timbers were burned and they used lamps for heat, like the "Esquimaux," whom they were imitating in all else as well: "Counting those which I have added since the wanderers [the mutineers] came back, we have twelve constantly going, with grease and soot everywhere in proportion.... Our beds and bedding are absolutely black, and our faces begrimed with fatty carbon.... I found an overlooked godsend this morning—a bear's head, put away for a specimen, but completely frozen. There is no inconsiderable quantity of meat adhering to it, and I serve it out raw [to the men who were sick with scurvy]."

In the course of the winter one of the mutineers, the troublemaker Godfrey, slipped off to go live with the natives. One day he returned to the ship with a dog sled loaded with fresh walrus meat, a most welcome gift. Kane, seeing the man as a deserter, ordered him to stay, but Godfrey simply turned tail and ran off across the ice. Kane ordered an armed companion to shoot the man, but the rifle misfired. Kane raced back to the ship, snatched another rifle from the gunstand, fired at the receding Godfrey, and missed. Not about to let Godfrey escape, he went to the Inuit camp at Etah and forced Godfrey to return at gunpoint.

On May 20, 1855, Kane and the crew abandoned the skeletal remains of the *Advance*, leaving a "memorial" pinned to its mast in which Kane wrote for any explorers who later happened upon the ship that he hoped "we have done all that we ought to do to prove our tenacity of purpose and devotion to the cause which we have undertaken." Escape by sledge across the southern ice was "an imperative duty—the only means of saving ourselves and preserving the laboriously-earned results of the expedition."

In fact, the results of the expedition were mostly chimerical except for the loss of three members of the crew and the crippling of several others from surgery for frostbite and the aftereffects of scurvy and other hardships. They did finally make it out, leaving in three boats from Rensselaer Harbor, reaching civilization on the southwest coast of Greenland.

Elisha Kent Kane returned to the United States in the fall of 1855 to a hero's welcome, a major outpouring of public celebration. His first book had come out, and he was already famous, even before he returned from the expedition. Though he had found no trace of Franklin (and indeed it was now clear he never had any intention of looking for Franklin), he could say he had achieved a major first, a stupendous prize: he had found the Open Polar Sea.

It is difficult from this distance in time to appreciate the intensity and breadth of the popularity Kane enjoyed. Some two hundred thousand people bought his book, which was published in 1856. That is equivalent to two million people today, the kind of instant audience that greets a new Tom Clancy or Danielle Steel novel. The nation's most prominent historian, W. H. Prescott, called Kane's book "one of the most remarkable records I have ever met with . . . No man has probably done more than Dr. Kane to lift the dread veil of mystery which hangs over the Arctic regions." The orator Edward Everett enthused that the book would "secure him an abiding-place on the rolls of honest fame among the heroes of humanity." The statesman and antislavery spokesman Charles Sumner said it was possessed of "all the attractions of romantic adventure elevated by scientific discovery."

Kane's book made him a small fortune, which, unfortunately, he had very little time to enjoy. On a doctor's advice, Kane moved to Cuba to try to recover his failing health, but he died there of a heart attack on February 16, 1857. The nation's grief was enormous. The funeral procession was more elaborate and longer than any in the young nation's history and would be exceeded in the nineteenth century only by that of President Lincoln some eight years later. Kane's casket went from Havana to New Orleans by ship and then by steamboat up the Mississippi and Ohio rivers to Cincinnati, with people in mourning on the levees and wharfs of every town along the way. The body went by train from there to Philadelphia, again with mourners crowding the tracks at every town and small city where the train stopped. It lay in state briefly at the larger cities en route, among them Columbus, Louisville, and Baltimore, and was finally buried in Philadelphia on March 14.

Only later would the more unseemly parts of Kane's expedition be revealed—the mutiny and other avoidable difficulties. And what of Morton's sighting of the Open Polar Sea? In the first place, he was not near 80° N when

New-York Daily Times.

DR. KANE HOME AGAIN.

The Second and Third Arctic Expeditions Safely Ended.

Arrival of Propeller Arctic and Bark Release at New-York.

THE ADVANCE LEFT IN THE ICE.

NEW LANDS FOUND.

A Bridge of Ice from Greenland to the Continent.

AN OPEN SEA FOUND.

NO TRACES OF SIR JOHN FRANKLIN.

LATITUDE 82° 30′ N. REACHED.

LIFE IN THE FROZEN REGIONS.

ON SLEDGES FOR THIRTY DAYS.

Detailed and Interesting Account of the two Expeditions.

DR. KANE'S OWN ACCOUNT.

Dr. KANE, the intrepid Arctic navigator, after having been given up as lost, has returned safe home, with the loss of but three men on his whole expedition. He left his brig frozen up in the Arctic Sea, on the 24th of May, 1855. went three hundred miles over the ice to the sea, and then in open boats thirteen hundred miles to Upernavik in Greenland. After waiting for

New

VOL. V.....NO. 1269

from the fact, that the entire circuit of Smith's has been effected, and its shores completely cha

THE OPEN POLAR SEA.

But the real discovery of the Expedition open Polar Sea. The channel leading to the sea was entirely free from ice, and this feature w cored more remarkable by the existence of a r solid belt of ice, extending more than or dred and twenty-five miles to the southward. sea verifies the views of Dr KANE, as expre the Geographical Society before his departure

The lashing of the surf against this frozen t ice was, we are assured, impressive beyond tion. Several gentlemen with whom we hav versed, speak of it with wonder and admiratic

An area of three thousand square miles wa entirely free from ice. This channel has been after Hon. JOHN P. KENNEDY, late Secretar Navy, under whose auspices the Expedition wa

The land to the north and west of this chan been charted as high as 82° 30′. *This is the land to the Pole yet discovered.* It bears the Mr. HENRY GRINNELL, the founder of the ex which bears his name.

THE WINTER OF 1854–'55.

The extreme severity of the previous season evident that the brig could not be liberated be Winter set in. She was fast imprisoned in th of a large field of ice. The provisions, a abundant, were not calculated to resist scur the fuel, owing to the emergencies of the p Winter, was deficient in quantity.

Under these trying circumstances Dr. KANE party of volunteers, on an attempt to reach th of Lancaster Sound, in hopes of meeting the expeditions, and thus giving relief to his axs passed in an open boat over the track of B travel, riding out a heavy gale. They found a terrupted barrier of ice, extending in one grea shoe from Jones' to Murchison's Sounds, ar forced, after various escapes, to return to the b

Front page of the *New York Daily Times*, October 12, 1855 (from Corner 1972)

he saw whatever he thought was that much fabled phenomenon, but much farther south. And he may have seen a polynya, a Russian term for a large area of open water in a sea of ice, and somehow—out of exhaustion or the delirium that was not uncommon among Arctic trekkers, especially if they were ill and underfed, or perhaps out of the faithful servant's desire to please the boss—expanded it into an ocean. But in 1857 there were "scientific" reasons to think the Open Polar Sea existed, and now it had been seen.

All that remained was to cross it. The idea of being first to reach the North Pole, now clearly thought of as accessible, became something of a fixation for Americans, and later for the British as well.

The next person to try just that was Isaac Israel Hayes, the surgeon aboard the *Advance* who had deserted. He had lost some toes to frostbite, but his enthusiasm for Arctic adventuring was intact. Less persuasive than the heroic and dashing Kane, he was unable to get the aging Henry Grinnell to come up with two ships and had to settle instead for a 133-ton schooner he named the *United States.* Convinced along with "many learned physicists that the sea about the North Pole cannot be frozen," he set out in 1860 with the plan to push his little schooner to the 80th parallel through Smith Sound and then haul a boat over the ice to the open sea, whence the Pole beckoned.

Of course, it was not so easy. At one point they anchored to an iceberg, which promptly began to disintegrate and then to plunge and heave, seeking a new equilibrium and threatening the *United States* with disaster. They ran into blizzards, fogs, gales, and rapidly forming ice, finally reaching Etah, where they had to overwinter. Hayes sent sledge parties out north across the ice cap of Greenland, and things began to go wrong. A man froze to death when he fell through the ice. The sled dogs they had picked up earlier from Upernavik died in an epidemic. Hayes claimed to have reached as far north as 82° 30′ N before he had to turn back. Although he didn't actually see the Open Polar Sea, he maintained it was just beyond the final point reached by his expedition, and he titled the book he wrote several years later *The Open Polar Sea.* In it he wrote:

> Suffice it here to say that I stood upon the shores of the Polar Basin, and that the broad ocean lay at my feet; that the land upon which I stood, culminating in the distant cape before me, was but a point of land projecting far into it, like the Ceverro Vostochnoi Noss of the opposite coast of Siberia; and that the little margin of ice that lined the shore was being steadily worn away; and within a month, the whole would be as free from ice as I had seen the north water of Baffin Bay.

Hayes's book would not appear until 1867, long after his return from the Arctic. His predecessor, Kane, returned to instant national acclaim, but Hayes's *United States* sailed back into Boston Harbor on a foggy day to the notice of practically no one, as the Civil War had begun. Hayes would spend the war as an army surgeon in a hospital in Philadelphia, and his book, as well as any sort of Arctic adventuring, was put on hold. Meanwhile, in 1862, one of the scientific backers of the expedition, Alexander Dallas Bache, wrote

Hayes asking for the return of the scientific instruments lent to the expedition. Hayes was forced to reply that he had expected lectures to pay for the remaining costs of the expedition, but the war had intervened and he was forced to hock the instruments in order to pay his crew their accumulated wages. Worse yet, later expeditions would find that many of Hayes's physiographic descriptions were inaccurate, and his claim of a farthest north at 82° 30′ N was no farther north than 80° 10′ N, an error of 140 miles.

In the days when searching for Franklin's expedition was almost an Anglo-American obsession, an odd figure determined that he wanted to become part of the scramble, but he could not raise the funds for an expedition ship. He was Charles Francis Hall, a high-school dropout with no scientific background, no knowledge of navigation, and no other naval skills. But he had read virtually everything in print about the Arctic. He was in the newspaper business in Cincinnati at the time, with a family to support, yet he came to believe that he had been called north by God. This insistent and often prickly man left business and family behind and, after spending months in the eastern United States trying to raise money to outfit his own expedition, wangled a free berth on a whaler to Baffin Island, where, in Frobisher Bay, he disembarked. His plan was to live alone, with only the support of the local Inuit, and eventually sail to King William Island in a small boat bought with funds supplied by polar angel Henry Grinnell. But while still on the whaler, writing in his cabin, he heard a female voice behind him.

"Good morning, sir," the voice said.

He turned and to his amazement found an English-speaking Inuit couple standing in the doorway. Their names, he learned, were Tookoolito and her husband, Ebierbing. In the 1850s a whaling captain had taken them to England, where they thrived, even to the point of having dinner with Queen Victoria and Prince Albert, and eventually returned to Baffin Island. They took Hall in hand, and through them he heard Ebierbing's grandmother tell stories that she had heard as a child about ships that arrived many years before—first one ship, then next year three, and then in the third year, fifteen ships. She spoke of coal, bricks, and iron that had been left behind. Here, of course, was an oral history of the Frobisher expeditions. He went to the specific locations the old woman had mentioned and there rediscovered—three hundred years after the fact—the remains of Frobisher's gold-mining venture. In 1862 Hall returned to the United States with relics from the Frobisher encampment and with Tookoolito and Ebierbing, who would come to be known to Americans as Hannah and Joe. He settled his Inuit friends in Groton, Connecticut, with a small grant from Grinnell, saw his family in Cincinnati for two weeks, and returned to the East Coast to seek funds for a second trip. And before too long, Hall would head back north.

At this same time, a Finn named Adolf Erik Nordenskiöld began visiting the Arctic.

Trained as a geologist and chemist at the University of Helsinki, in 1855 he was fired from his junior position at the university and at the state mining administration for seditious promotion of the reunion of Finland with Sweden. The Russian authorities in Finland branded Nordenskiöld a "dangerous rabble-rouser," and he was forced to emigrate to Sweden in 1857, where he obtained a similar junior position at the University of Stockholm and a year later was appointed chief of mineralogy at the National Museum of Natural History, a position he held for the rest of his life.

In 1858, the Swedish government sponsored—and local businessmen supported—an expedition into the Arctic; Nordenskiöld was among the scientists on board. It was chiefly a scientific voyage, designed to make detailed geographic surveys as well as studies and collections related to geomagnetism, geology, botany, zoology, and marine biology. It would be the first of many voyages to the Arctic for this promising young mineralogist, and he, like Charles Francis Hall, would one day attempt to reach the Pole. But if Hall was one in the growing lineage of American amateurs in the Arctic, Nordenskiöld would, in a sense, be the father of a lineage of supreme professionals, most of them from the nations of Scandinavia. Before long, English eyes would take note of such efforts and find that the pride of Britannia was again at stake; the Arctic was, after all, really a British preserve, wasn't it? And several other nations of Europe, notably Germany and Austria, would see fit to join this new international competition: the race to reach the North Pole.

ANYTHING IS GOOD THAT DON'T POISON YOU

While the American Civil War was raging to its bloody conclusion, Charles Francis Hall headed back into the Arctic, leaving in 1864 to stay again among the Inuit, along with his companions and mentors, Ebierbing and Tookoolito. In 1865 his book *Researches and Life Among the Esquimaux* was published in the United States, having appeared the year before in England. He remained in the Arctic for five years, an accomplishment unequaled in the annals of Arctic exploration, and he journeyed some 3,000 miles by sledge. During this long sojourn he came upon and collected a few relics of the Franklin expedition and traversed the shores of the Gulf of Boothia and King William Island.

One unfortunate incident cast a shadow over this second expedition. In July 1868 Hall hired five men from a whaler to help him, and he soon got into a heated argument with one of them, a man named Patrick Coleman. Coleman had questioned the Inuit about one thing or another; Hall believed that conversing with the native people was his exclusive bailiwick. In the course of the argument, Hall came to believe that Coleman had threatened his life, so he went to his quarters, fetched a revolver, and shot Coleman dead. Like several men before him, from Henry Hudson facing his mutineers to Elisha Kane, Hall got off scot-free, in his case without even a trial. It was not so much that the Arctic was lawless as that it seemed ordinary laws didn't apply to so strange and remote a place.

One of Hall's accomplishments on this second sojourn was to prove to everyone's subsequent satisfaction that no members of the Franklin party were still wandering about in the frozen north among the Inuit. On returning to New Bedford, Massachusetts, in September 1869, again with Ebierbing and Tookoolito in tow, he handed over his Frobisher and Franklin relics to the Smithsonian Institution. In 1870 his book was reissued with a simpler title, *Life with the Esquimaux*; it detailed the lifeways of the Inuit in greater detail than anything before it had done. And herein lay Hall's chief contribution to Arctic exploration. He showed that someone from Europe or America could survive perfectly well in the Arctic if he was willing to take on the lifeways of the people who had lived there for millennia. He learned not only to live like an Inuit and eat what the Inuit ate, but to like it. He felt at home there—more so, it would seem, than with his family in Cincinnati. Had others before him (and several after him) learned the same lesson, easily available in his writings, a great many lives would have been saved.

By the time Hall returned to the United States, another expedition had been launched—this for the Pole, by a consortium of European adventurers under the German flag. Two ships were to break through the girdle of ice by sailing north from northeastern Greenland. The two vessels were separated quite early, with one sinking in the ice pack. The crew drifted about on the ice through the winter and made it to southeastern Greenland the following summer in the ship's boats. The other ship made it as far north as 75° N, where it languished until they could launch a sledge expedition, which made its way to 77° N before turning back.

The group accomplished little in the way of establishing the Germans as first-rate Arctic explorers, but its effort did focus yet more American attention on the Arctic and especially the felt need to be first among the civilized nations to reach the Pole. And thus came about Charles Francis Hall's third Arctic journey, in 1871. In the annals of Arctic exploration it would be downplayed by historians and others with sensitive noses, since it resulted in a mysterious death, which has since been shown to be a murder, and a case of scandalous betrayal, as well as one of the most terrible (and unnecessary) voyages of escape in all the history of humankind.

With congressional funds flowing for another attempt at the Pole, Hall was chosen to lead the expedition, and a 380-ton former tugboat was outfitted and renamed (with great expectation) the *Polaris*. Steam-propelled, she could also proceed by sail. The screw, or propeller, was arranged so that it could be withdrawn to protect it from battering by the ice, and the hull was reinforced with oak planking. Among its amenities was an organ, presented to the expedition by the Smith Organ Company to be used in Sunday services. Hall had hoped to sign on as sailing master a seasoned captain named George Tyson, but he was otherwise committed, so Hall chose Sidney Budington, a whaler who had dropped Hall off at Baffin Island back in 1861. Then Tyson became available and signed on as second navigator. Most of the officers were Americans but the crew was mostly German, as was the chief scientist, a young physician and naturalist named Emil Bessels. William Morton, Kane's servant, was along, as were Tookoolito and Ebierbing.

The *Polaris* sailed from New London and made for Upernavik, Greenland, where they added the seasoned Inuit sailor Hans Hendrik (plus his wife and three children) to the roster. From there Hall pushed on through Kane Basin toward the place where both Morton and Hayes had previously reported that the Open Polar Sea gave onto the north. They proceeded to 82° 11′ N, the farthest north for a ship, before being forced to turn back by the massive and solid ice that covered the Arctic Ocean. They overwintered at Thank God Harbor on Greenland, and Hall determined then that when spring came they would head for the Pole by sledge. Other members of the crew—especially Captain Budington and Bessels—thought that, having met so awesome a barrier, they should return home. Unpersuaded, Hall set out with Hendrik and Ebierbing to reconnoiter the ice pack, returning to the *Polaris* on October 24, One of his first acts upon his return was to ask for a cup of coffee, and on drinking it, he became violently ill. Over the next days he would seesaw between apparently good health and bouts of illness that included stomach pains, vomiting, dehydration, vertigo, and dementia. At times he confided to Tyson that he thought he was being poisoned by crew members who were hostile to his plans. On November 8, two weeks after his return, he had a final relapse and died. He was given a solemn funeral and buried on shore at Thank God Harbor in a shallow, frozen grave.

Budington was now, by prearrangement, in charge of the expedition, and he was determined to go home. But the ice kept the *Polaris* locked in place until August 1872. Meanwhile he armed the crew (except for Tyson), and they managed to get by on the ship's stores and the occasional seal they were able to shoot. Once free, the ship began to drift south, attached to one of the ice floes. On October 15, the engineer came on deck with the cry that the ship was leaking badly and was being crushed by the ice. Eighteen people, including Tyson and the two Inuits, went onto the ice while the others hurled all readily available provisions and food supplies to them. It appeared that the ship's crew would have to spend the winter on the ice. But then the *Polaris* suddenly broke free and drifted off. To those stranded on the ice floe, it appeared that the men in command of the ship were not making much of an effort to retrieve them, and soon they set about facing a most uncertain and perilous future. With the help of Ebierbing and Hendrik, ice shelters were made in the snow, the Germans having one to themselves. In addition to the provisions they had off-loaded, they also had two of the ship's boats. Their drifting island was some five miles by one mile in dimension and thus an ample platform—for the time being.

Route of *Polaris* and Charles Francis Hall to the north, and drift of George Tyson to the south (from Berton 1988)

Theirs would be a long and harrowing voyage, drifting helplessly from Ellesmere Island south past Baffin Island all the way to the coast of Labrador over a period of half a year. Temperatures were regularly –40°F or lower, and many on the floe developed frostbite; one man lost both feet and most of both hands to this insidious enemy. Tyson, nominally in charge, kept everyone on short rations (most of the men grumbled bitterly about this), but finally the ship's provisions ran out, and they had to rely on the two Inuit men to catch seals or dovekies (small seabirds). When all else failed, everyone was

The *Polaris* at 82° 11′ N on September 1, 1871 (U.S. Naval Historical Center, Washington, D.C.)

forced to chew on sealskin thongs and eat the burned seal blubber from the lamps. "Anything is good," Ebierbing remarked to Tyson (or so the much-repeated story goes), "that don't poison you."

The German members apparently were reluctant to move out of their sleeping bags; nor did they want to allow the exhausted Inuit hunters a larger share of the seal, foxes, and other creatures they killed. Dissension was rife, and Tyson was largely powerless to enforce any regimen against the armed crew. The Inuit children were constantly crying from hunger, the world was increasingly gloomy, and people began dropping off, racked by scurvy and other ailments, the cold, and starvation. Five men died (usually quite peacefully, Tyson reported, once they accepted that they had no future). Tyson, often delirious himself, simply entreated the men to die like men, not beasts—this in response to numerous instances of food theft. In spite of all they were doing to keep the crew alive, the Inuit knew full well that the German members of the crew were eyeing them as the first to be cannibalized, if it came to that.

With the coming of warmer weather, the ice floes began breaking up. The expedition's ice island was fragmenting under their iglus and tents, finally leaving them with a platform so small that they could not all lie down at once. Gales brought huge seas washing over the floe, and the weakened, dying men nonetheless had to stand for hours in this weather, hoping to keep the one remaining boat, their only hope of reaching the land that was always just out of sight, from being washed away. They never did get to use it; instead, on April 29, they were finally rescued by a steamship within sight of the Labrador coast—after a voyage of horror that traversed at least 1,800 miles. It was one of the most astonishing episodes in the history of the Arctic or elsewhere.

Meanwhile, Budington and the others on board the *Polaris*, having in fact made no effort to rescue the people stranded on the ice floe, made for Greenland and reached the friendly Inuit settlement at Etah, where they were sustained through the winter by Inuit kindness. They set off in two boats in the spring and subsequently were rescued by a whaler.

Later a Naval Board of Inquiry looked into Hall's death and the other unfortunate aspects of the expedition. It came out that as early as October 1871 Budington and Bessels were openly hostile to Hall and his plans. Budington was dead set against going farther north, and young Bessels considered Hall to be incompetent. According to testimony given by others, Budington had said of Hall's death, "There's a stone off my heart." Bessels was reported as saying, "Captain Hall's death was the best thing that could happen for the expedition." Such comments notwithstanding, the board of inquiry had little to go on and finally concurred with Bessels that Hall had died of "apoplexy," or what we call a stroke, and not poisoning.

One of the German officers on board gainsaid Tyson's reckoning of how far north *Polaris* had reached under Hall, further diminishing Hall's accomplishments, which in fact included taking a ship straight through the waters between Ellesmere Island and Greenland and reaching the edge of the polar sea. Hall had established that it was icebound and not open, as so many had believed for so long.

The navy evidently wished to avoid the sort of scandal that would have ensued if Tyson's version of events had been believed. Later a great Scandinavian explorer, Vilhjalmur Stefansson, would point out that the continuing rumors of Hall having been poisoned, probably with arsenic, could easily be resolved by digging up the corpse, no doubt still frozen in Thank God Harbor, and testing its hair. But the suggestion was greeted with an icy silence, until a century passed and an English professor at Dartmouth, Chauncey Loomis, undertook a biography of Hall that he entitled *Weird and Tragic Shores*, published in 1971. He took on the process of solving the mystery surrounding Hall's death and obtained permission from the Danish government's Ministry of Greenland to uncover the grave and take hair and fingernail samples for analysis. (Hall's body had mummified in the permafrost, with the skin having the texture of leather.) The samples were sent to the Centre of Forensic Sciences in Toronto, which reported that they revealed "an intake of

considerable amounts of arsenic by C. F. Hall in the last two weeks of his life."
So Hall died from arsenic poisoning, not a stroke, and there is little doubt
where the arsenic came from: in the form of arsenious acid, it was a standard
part of medical supplies in the 1870s for the treatment of headaches, ulcers,
cancer, gout, and syphilis.

Hall, had he lived and not been so badly discredited, could have let subsequent explorers know that there was no Open Polar Sea. But it would have to
be proven again. In the meantime, the oceanographer Maury had been replaced
as the U.S. Navy's man in these affairs by Silas Bent, who stoutly defended the
concept of the open ocean. But, unimpressed by the man's credentials or his
arguments, Charles P. Daly, president of the American Geographical and
Statistical Society, took Bent on in his presidential address of 1870. He said
loftily that he was not about to comment on Bent's "deductions" from the laws
of ocean currents, because "our knowledge of these laws is imperfect," and also
because they were hypothetical and best left to those "who have made
hydrographical studies a specialty"; beyond that, he added, what was called for
were actual "facts and not theories." He pooh-poohed Bent's idea that the Gulf
Stream and Japanese current were warm-water gateways to the Pole, saying that
no one knew for sure where the Gulf Stream went beyond the coast of Norway
but that it was known to diminish and weaken in the Arctic, making it unlikely
that it reached the Pole or had sufficient heat in it to affect the climate of the
polar basin. Daly was not, by the way, a man of science; he was a judge.

Two years after Daly's skeptical address, the Austrians mounted an expedition under the leadership of Karl Weyprecht and attempted the Northeast
Passage, but they became beset by ice, spending two winters in the Arctic and
returning without much to show for it besides the discovery of a new land,
which they called Franz Josef Land. Later, in 1875, Weyprecht would urge
upon a group of scientists the idea of a synchronous international exploration
of the Arctic for scientific purposes, and not the inflated and unimportant
stunts of finding new islands and racing one another to the Pole. What, he
asked, is the nature of the Arctic climate? What drives it? How does it affect
the weather of warmer latitudes?

Neither Hall nor Daly (nor Weyprecht) would be taken seriously by the
British, whose national pride had been significantly piqued. The British believed
that the Americans, despite little in the way of official backing on inadequate
equipment, had gotten rather far north in their quest for the Pole, Hayes and
Kane having actually come across the Open Polar Sea before returning. Surely
the English boosters of an expedition, which included the leaders of the Royal
Geographical Society and the British navy, could do better.

On May 29, 1875, flags fluttered in Portsmouth Harbor and people cheered. Sir George Nares was about to set out for the Pole, the plan being to pass between Ellesmere Island and Greenland, breach the annulus of ice, and sail triumphantly to the Pole. The *Times* of London burbled that the enthusiasm of the assembled multitude "indicate[s] pretty clearly that a true chord has been struck, and that the sympathies of all, from the Queen downwards, go with" the expedition. Indeed, the crowd was aware that "the crews were about to enter upon a battle with Nature in her sternest aspects, and that it was the honour for the country that this should be so."

Nares was one of the few remaining men alive who had served in the Franklin rescue efforts. He was a seaman of unquestioned ability and had been called back by the Admiralty to take on this Arctic expedition from the ship *Challenger*, the first vessel to be equipped specifically for oceanographic science. Sir George was not a scientist but a close observer; he had earlier noted on the *Challenger's* oceanographic expedition that the distribution of temperatures in the Atlantic showed the ocean was divided down the middle by "one of a chain of banks with less than 2000 fathoms of water over them," this being the first mention anywhere of what we now know to be the Mid-Atlantic Ridge, where two tectonic plates are moving apart, with upward-flowing lava filling the gap. On his polar expedition, Nares was served by eager volunteer officers, "the Royal Navy suffering," as one historian put it,

The Nares expedition, 1875–76 (from Berton 1988)

"from a slump in sea warfare," making an Arctic voyage the best game in town for obtaining promotions.

They all set out in two ships, the *Alert* and the *Discovery,* and before long both were beset in the ice, the *Alert* in Floeberg Bay at 82° 27' N, the farthest north any ship would go under her own power until the age of icebreakers in 1948. The other ship was beset in Lady Franklin Bay. Nares sent out several sledge parties from both ships, and one of them achieved a farthest north of 83° 20' N, the best effort to that date in the Arctic. Even with such achievement, the expedition was doomed—and it had been doomed from the start. Inexplicably, the Royal Navy had learned nothing from its own failed expeditions of the early 1800s; nor had it learned anything from people, such as John Rae (in England at the time), who had thrived in the Arctic. The Nares expedition was allowed to leave port with inadequate navy-issue clothing, improper food to prevent scurvy, and inadequate sledges to cross the hummocky terrain of the northern ice. They took no snowshoes and had no experience building houses out of ice; none of Nares's officers had ever even seen an iceberg. And, of course, seeking help from the locals was out of the question.

The result of all this was that by spring Nares had some sixty cases of scurvy on his hands, and several in the sledge parties died. Though equipped to spend a second winter in the Arctic, Nares prudently returned early, reaching Portsmouth on November 2, 1876. The expedition was widely judged a disappointment among the English, who had been oversold in the beginning. A board of inquiry later took the expedition and its planners to task for all the lapses that had led to such a sorry conclusion, pointing out, among other things, that two dogs can do the pulling of one man but eat less and require no clothing. However, they did achieve one thing: a bit redundantly, they proved that there was no Open Polar Sea, but instead a great frozen ocean.

Yet it was still possible (though barely) for diehards to believe in an Open Polar Sea, thinking that Hall and Nares simply had not been looking in the right place. One possible way to the sea was still untried: the route of the Bering Strait between Alaska and Siberia. This was the route championed by Silas Bent, the navy's chief hydrographer, in the face of the skepticism of Judge Daly as announced in 1870. The idea was that the Kuroshio, a Pacific current that is the equivalent of the Atlantic's Gulf Stream, split near the Kamchatka Peninsula, with a northern branch proceeding through the Bering Strait—"a thermometric gateway to the Pole."

Amid the polar passion of the Americans and, however briefly, the English, an altogether dispassionate expedition took place designed to resolve a matter of Arctic exploration that was not so romantic as the Pole, but perhaps more commercially useful. We noted earlier that Adolf Erik Nordenskiöld began voyaging to the Arctic on scientific missions in 1858. He made five more such expeditions and was the leader of the last four; on two occasions he attempted to reach the Pole but was turned back by the ice. Even so, by 1868 he was well known by a world that was hungry for daring heroes. In times of relative peace, such adventurers were comparable to the first waves of astronauts and cosmonauts in our era. In Sweden Nordenskiöld was indeed not unlike John Glenn, being elected a member of the parliament, a position he would hold until 1893.

In 1875 and 1876, Nordenskiöld made two more Arctic trips, to the Barents and Kara Seas, expeditions designed to dredge for biological specimens and also to determine the feasibility of trade between Europe and Siberia via a northern ocean route. With ships powered by steam as well as sail, they were able to improve on the records set by others in quest of the Northeast Passage and pass south of Novaya Zemlya and up the Yenisey River.

Then in 1878 the Swedish Northeast Passage expedition left port, sponsored by the government and financed by a Swedish businessman, Oscar Dickson, and a Siberian counterpart, Aleksandr Sibiryakov. Its purpose was simple: navigate the Northeast Passage from the Norwegian Sea to the Bering Strait. Nordenskiöld was in charge of the entire expedition (which also had a scientific component, as did all such voyages); the *Vega* was under the command of Captain Louis Palander. On July 28 they passed south of the Novaya Zemlya, and on August 19 they passed south of Severnaya Zemlya, the northernmost part of Asia usually affected by ice. Nordenskiöld and company were the first to pass from the Kara to the Laptev Sea. On September 28 they were obliged to stop and overwinter at Kolyichinskaya Guba, a mere 200 miles from their ultimate destination. The only unexpected complexities they encountered were some minor fracases with the local native population.

Ten months later, on July 18, the ice let them out, and the *Vega* reached Yokohama, Japan, on September 2. From there they made their leisurely way back to Sweden, passing through the Indian Ocean, the Suez Canal, and the Mediterranean. Regaled by well-wishers all along their journey, they reached Stockholm on April 24, 1880, acclaimed as heroes. Their expedition had been superbly planned and professionally carried out, without anything that could be considered a serious mishap. Such expeditions, unpunctuated by Sturm und Drang, do not usually make for very exciting reading, but Nordenskiöld wrote a two-volume account of the voyage that was financially successful enough that he could buy a country estate and add to his collection of maps.

(A footnote to a pleasant bit of Arctic history: the Swedes intended to celebrate the fortieth anniversary of the *Vega*'s expedition in 1920. Someone

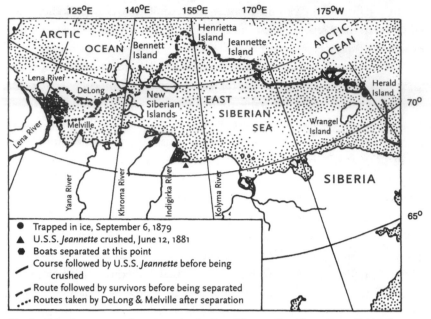

Track of the *Jeannette* and survivors in the East Siberian Sea (from Caswell 1956)

had the idea of inquiring about Sibiryakov, the Russian merchant who had helped make the voyage possible. It was found that he had fled Russia after the Communist Revolution and was living in poverty in the southern coast of France. The Swedish government voted him an annual pension that sustained him comfortably until his death in 1933.)

In 1879 people could look at the great European cartographer Petermann's map of the north and see a final west-stretching arm of what he took to be a much larger, pole-crossing Greenland. This arm, which we know now is an island, was called Wrangel Land. One person who took this map at face value was James Gordon Bennett, owner of the *New York Herald*, which had enjoyed a splendid surge in circulation when its man Henry Morton Stanley found Dr. David Livingstone in darkest Africa. Bennett had grown interested in the Arctic and the race for the Pole. He bought a small yacht called the *Pandora*, renamed it the *Jeannette*, and persuaded the U.S. Navy to man it on a dash to the Pole via the Bering Strait. The leader of this voyage was a young lieutenant, George Washington DeLong, who was instructed to sail as far north via the Bering Strait as possible, proceeding along the coast of Wrangel-Greenland, and to go overland by sledge along that arm of land to the Pole if necessary. Thus would Bennett bag the Pole for the United States of America.

But by the autumn of 1879 the *Jeannette* was trapped in the ice, and she drifted about aimlessly in its clutches for eighteen months.

By then a disillusioned DeLong was convinced that Wrangel Land was an island, perhaps an archipelago. He believed, along with others, that warm ocean currents do not regulate the northern ice but vice versa, writing that "if any warm current came through Bering Strait it would be the Kuro Siwo [Kuroshio], and our sea temperatures indicated no such fact." He was, he realized, on a fool's errand. "No matter what the difficulties, or troubles, or accidents," he wrote in his journal, "the failure to do the specified thing stands out in bold letters. So with us. We started for the Pole; we are beset in the pack in 71 plus; we drift northwest; our ship is injured . . . : we drift back southeast."

In a cry of pain and disappointment, he wrote: "We have failed, inasmuch as we did not reach the Pole; and we and our narrative together are thrown into the world's dreary wastebasket, and recalled and remembered only to be vilified and ridiculed."

On June 12, 1881, the *Jeannette* was crushed in the ice and sank the next day. The crew escaped onto the floes near the New Siberian Islands and attempted to maneuver over ice, water, and land to the Lena River. They made their way overland to a land mass called Bennett Island and from there went south to the delta. A storm intervened, and one party was lost, never to be seen again. Others, in two boats, separately made it to safety—but DeLong was not one of them. Of thirty-three men on the expedition, only thirteen survived.

The *Jeannette* sinking (U.S. Naval Historical Center, Washington, D.C.)

Three years later, on June 18, 1884, three Inuits out on the ice floes on the other side of the world, off southern Greenland, picked up a torn checkbook, a broken box, and a pair of oilskin trousers. The boxes bore the name *Jeannette*, and the oilskin trousers bore the name of a survivor of that ship. This bit of serendipity would later give a great Arctic explorer one of his greatest ideas.

Word of the DeLong fiasco didn't reach America until 1881, and by then the United States had embarked on another ill-starred Arctic expedition, this one under the command of Adolphus Greely, who was a lieutenant not in the navy but in the army. Several nations of Europe and the United States had taken up the idea originally offered by the Austrian Weyprecht for an international year of polar exploration. The U.S. Army had leaped at the idea and agreed to send a ship fully outfitted for scientific observations to one of eleven stations, the American station to be the farthest north of all. Greely evidently also was given secret instructions to make a dash for the Pole, which had until then been the navy's province.

The plan was to leave in 1880, but the navy held things up, refusing to sanction the use of the ship, the *Proteus*. In the ensuing interservice quarreling, a fed-up Greely resigned, only to be rehired when the feud was resolved the next year, just two months before departure. The *Proteus*, as planned, dropped off the men and their equipment at Discovery Harbor (where Nares had overwintered), and the squabbles broke out almost immediately, with one officer resigning over his disgust at being asked to rise in the morning at the same early hour as the enlisted men. (The *Proteus* left before this man was officially relieved, so he remained in an unofficial capacity—never something welcomed in a military situation.) A supply ship was supposed to arrive the following year, and a relief expedition the year after that, 1883. Greely named their encampment Fort Conger and that winter sent out dog sledge parties toward the Pole; one of them bested the record from the Nares push by four miles, reaching 83° 24′ N.

More squabbles broke out after the resupply ship didn't show up. Greely never was completely in charge and seemed to be what today might be referred to as a minor-league martinet. The physician on board thought further sledge trips were a bad idea, using needed food supplies, and in a rancorous argument with Greely he refused to sign up for another year. Greely arrested him, which seems an idiotic solution given the remoteness of their situation.

As the long Arctic winter set in, Greely cast about for some means of amusing the men. He had no musical instruments, no library, and (we can assume) none of the theatrical bent of Edward Parry more than two centuries earlier. He decided to give "daily, a lecture of from 1 to 2 hours in length upon the physical geography and the resources of the United States in general; followed later by similar talks on each state and territory in particular." He spoke of grain and fruit production and gave an hour to mineral production, reporting that it "was interesting to note the lack of interest shown by the party regarding the production of gold and silver."

When no relief ship appeared by August 1883, they finally abandoned the *Proteus* and left in the ship's boats, which, it being too late in the season, were hemmed in by the ice. Plagued by indecision and storms (which destroyed much of the scientific equipment and records), they overwintered on Cape Sabine, 33 miles across the water from the Inuit village of Etah on Greenland. There, on diminishing rations, they squabbled and fought through the three months of sunless days; several men died. The rest desperately netted krill from the sea, hoped to nab the occasional fox, and harvested lichens from rocks. Jens Edward, one of the two Inuits capable of hunting down seals, died when his kayak capsized—a major loss. In June one of the crew spotted Private C. B. Henry taking meat from some abandoned winter quarters; they claimed it was human meat. Greely had him shot. People continued to die of starvation and the cold; the physician ingested narcotics from his medicinal stores and died, apparently a case of suicide.

Eventually the few remaining men were rescued by Newfoundland sealers commissioned by the U.S. Navy, and Greely went on to lay pipelines in the Philippines and help oversee the cleanup of San Francisco after the 1906 earthquake leveled the city. Meanwhile, in America, the polar passion ebbed away for a decade, so calamitous and even macabre had the last three efforts been—those of Hall, DeLong, and Greely. But if the Pole seemed beyond the reach of mere men, and if the achievement of yet another "farthest north" hardly seemed worth the expense in lives lost or ruined, there were other challenges remaining in the Arctic, and there were men interested in taking them on.

III   RACING FOR THE POLE

7 THREE FACES OF AMBITION

By 1880 it was generally and, at last, assumed that there was no Open Polar Sea. Instead, the North Pole and much of the Arctic Ocean were understood to be covered with ice year round. There could be only two ways to achieve the Pole: by slogging over the ice with sledges, or by air (airplanes were decades away, of course, but there were hot-air balloons). After Greely's aborted effort, the polar urge ebbed for about a decade. Everybody knew where the Pole was and could imagine what it looked like. No new and important knowledge would be added to the world's wisdom by actually reaching the Pole; no strategic advantage would accrue to the nation that first placed a citizen on it; and the patenting of the first zipper in 1893 would have a far more profound economic effect than any successful expedition to the Pole. It simply lurked up there as a challenge by which some individuals would one day again choose to measure themselves.

Along with the first navigation of the Northwest Passage, another more modest (though highly perilous) goal remained unreached: no one, or at least no European, had crossed the Greenland ice cap, which crouched atop this large island. Here on Greenland, three of the most remarkable men in the history of Arctic exploration would try out their survival skills from 1886 to 1892 in a prelude to their great race for the North Pole. One would die a clouded hero, one would do time for fraud in a federal penitentiary, and one would go on to win the Nobel Peace Prize.

In 1886, when polar exploits resumed, Robert Peary was thirty years old, a civil engineer in the U.S. Navy with the rank of lieutenant. His father had died when he was but three years old, and he was raised by his mother, to whom he wrote at age twenty-four: "I don't know whether it is my fortune or misfortune, or whether it is the sign of an ignoble spirit, but I cannot bear to associate with people, who, age & advantages being equal, are my superiors. I must be the peer or superior of those about me to be comfortable, not that I care to show my superiority, simply to know it myself."

From this curiously introspective young officer would eventually rise the most driven, even fanatical, Arctic explorer of all time. He would be a life-long member of the navy, winning extensive leaves of absence for his much-publicized Arctic trips, of which he made eight—more than anyone else (Table 7.1). His first one, in 1886, was quite modest: an attempt to cross the Greenland ice cap. He borrowed funds from his mother to travel by ship to the southwest coast of Greenland and headed north to Disko Bay, where he attempted to cross the big island from west to east along with a young Dane whom he had met, Christian Maigaard, and two Greenlanders. On foot, they got about 90 miles inland and reached an elevation of almost 3,000 meters, the highest to date and the farthest north, but they were forced to return by foul weather.

Peary reported having penetrated the ice cap farther than previously achieved; this, it turns out, was an exaggeration. Five years earlier, some Lapps on an expedition across the ice cap, led by Nordenskiöld, had gone farther inland. But even with his actual achievement, not to mention his claim, Peary was well on his way to the fame he so desired. He wrote his mother soon afterward, confiding that the trip "has brought my name before the world and my next will give me standing in the world." His exploits would lead to "an enduring name &. honor" and "social advancement . . . powerful friends with whom I can shape my future instead of letting it come as it will."

Table 7.1 **Chronology of the Eight Arctic Expeditions Under the Leadership of Robert Peary**

Years	Other personnel	Region
1886	Christian Maigaard	Greenland
1891–1892	Frederick Cook, Eivind Astrup, Matthew Henson	Greenland
1893–1895	Eivind Astrup, Matthew Henson	Greenland
1896	Matthew Henson, John Bartlett	Greenland
1897	Matthew Henson, John Bartlett	Greenland
1898–1902	Matthew Henson, Thomas Dedrick	North Pole
1905–1906	Matthew Henson, Robert Bartlett	North Pole
1908–1909	Matthew Henson, Robert Bartlett, Donald MacMillan	North Pole

He went on, writing emphatically, "Remember Mother I *must* have fame & I cannot reconcile myself to years of commonplace drudgery & a name late in life when I see an opportunity to gain it now & sip the delicious draught." Surely such was the motivation of most of the men who sought to triumph over the Arctic, not to mention most adventurers in general. In any event, Peary immediately began to lay plans for a return trip and another attempt to cross Greenland. But two years later, before he could get under way, his hopes were dashed to pieces.

Enter Fridtjof Nansen, a Norwegian man for all seasons and, indeed, a hero several times over. As a youth, he grew tall and strong, an excellent skier, skater, hunter, and fisherman. At the university in Oslo (then called Christiana), he elected to study zoology, in part because it would keep him outdoors. In 1882 he shipped aboard a sealer for a voyage into Greenland waters and saw the ice cap from afar, thinking it should be possible to cross it. In 1887 he announced his plan, which stood on their heads the notions of other such explorers—notably Nordenskiöld and Peary, both of whom had sought to cross Greenland from its inhabited west coast, thus having the option to return to some modicum of civilization if things went awry. Nansen, on the other hand, who had the most profound faith in his stamina and planning, decided that he could start from the uninhabited and barren east coast and, cutting off any useful line of retreat, force himself to press on. The major task in such a plan would be to get up over the ice-covered east coast mountain range. From its top, at an elevation of 8,920 feet, it would be downhill skiing all the rest of the way, with a wind from behind to boot. So he reasoned, but others thought the idea suicidal. And indeed, if Nansen was somehow wrong, his party could easily perish in the attempt.

Having completed his work for a doctorate in zoology, he left Norway aboard a sealer with five companions in May 1888 and arrived, after some difficulties with the weather, on the east coast of Greenland on August 15. Amid severe storms, the party snowshoed up the eastern mountain range, arriving at the top on September 5, and skied down the western slopes and across the ice cap, arriving on the west coast at Ameralik Fjord three weeks later, on September 26. Nansen had, among other things, answered a previously unanswered question: Did the ice cap extend all the way across Greenland? For this venture, Nansen developed some light and flexible sledges with which dogs could haul provisions; these vehicles were based on both Inuit and Norwegian designs, came to be known as Nanseny sledges, and were used by subsequent explorers for decades to come. The party was forced to overwinter at the settlement of Godthåb, where Nansen spent his time learning more of the ways of the Inuit there.

It was a flawless expedition, with little drama or melodrama. Later, in 1891, Nansen would write a book titled *Eskimo Life* about this journey, in which he included an odd incident, the sort of coincidental meeting that so often would occur in the vast Arctic region. The first European he met after reaching the west coast in Ameralik Fjord was a Dane who was wearing a tam-o'-shanter but otherwise dressed in the manner of the Inuit. The fellow asked him if he was English or spoke English. Nansen replied in Norse and revealed that he was Fridtjof Nansen.

The Dane then said, "Allow me to congratulate you on taking your doctor's degree." Nansen wrote that, "to put it mildly, it struck me as comical that I should cross Greenland to receive congratulations of my Doctor's degree, which I happened to have taken just before I left home. Nothing, of course, could have been more removed from my thoughts at the moment."

The party returned to Norway in May 1889, and Nansen was acclaimed as a national hero. He had placed Scandinavia in ascendancy over the polar explorers of North America and the rest of Europe, and confounded the experts by going east to west. He was appointed curator of zoology at the university in Oslo, but without specific responsibilities. He was free, in other words, to do whatever he wished. He was already developing a far more ambitious and innovative plan. He had read about the discovery of some of the relics of the failed American expedition under the leadership of George Washington DeLong in Baffin Bay, all the way across the world from the location of the wreck. They must have been carried there by the drifting ice, Nansen reasoned.

Meanwhile, Robert Peary was in the midst of planning his second attempt to cross the Greenland ice cap when the world heard about Nansen's splendid performance. Peary was furious and accused Nansen of stealing his plans and preempting him in a way that was inappropriate. Nevertheless, needing to shift gears quickly, he chose a new objective: to determine the northern limit of Greenland. In 1888 no one knew how far it extended to the north or the east. Petermann's map was still in use, showing it reaching virtually to the Pole and its western arm being Wrangel Land near the Bering Strait. So Peary announced an expedition to cross northern Greenland from west to east to chart its unknown northeastern shoreline and determine, if possible, its northern extent. Set to get under way in 1891, this would be a grander expedition than his first, and he obtained the sponsorship of the Philadelphia Academy of Natural Sciences and the American Geographical Society. Under the aegis of these august organizations, he was more easily able to raise the money for the voyage. Peary, as was the custom, put notices in newspapers that he was engaged in outfitting his U.S. North Greenland Expedition and seeking crew members for it.

Enter Frederick Cook, an American who had just (and barely) passed his examination to become a physician in 1890 after graduating from New York University. He was raised in a poor family in Brooklyn and worked, among other places, in a dairy to put himself through medical school. He set up a practice in Brooklyn and then saw Peary's notice; he immediately volunteered to serve as surgeon without pay. He was accepted and thus began his polar career, one that would eventually put him on a collision course with Peary himself. Nansen, Peary, and Cook would all in due course be (at least figuratively) at each other's throats. Nansen was already among those pointing out that Peary exaggerated the extent of his initial trek onto the Greenland ice in 1886.

Peary's new expedition included Cook as surgeon; a Norwegian named Eivind Astrup, who had, like Cook, responded to the newspaper notice offering to volunteer his time; Peary's black manservant, Matthew Henson; and Peary's wife, Jo. The ship *Kite* left them off in the vicinity of today's Thule Air Force Base, on the northwest coast of Greenland at the head of Baffin Bay, where they were to overwinter and be picked up the following year by the *Kite*. Cook's presence on the expedition came in for early appreciation when Peary broke his leg on the voyage and needed medical attention. At this juncture, the two men gained a great respect for each other.

During the summer of 1892, his leg now healed, Peary, along with Astrup, made a tremendous overland traverse to the northeast, across 500 miles of unrelieved ice, finally reaching a promontory that Peary named Navy Cliff. That, plus the return of another 500 miles, was the longest such trek ever undertaken in the Arctic and was a notable achievement in itself. Peary reported later that from Navy Cliff he saw a body of water to the east, which he called Independence Bay. Thus he had reached the northeastern coast of Greenland. Looking north, he saw a landform that he called Peary Land, separated from the mainland by a channel he called Peary Channel, thus determining the northern extent of Greenland. Peary Land was apparently an island, perhaps part of an archipelago that extended farther north.

It is impossible at this remove in time to determine what it was that Peary saw (or didn't see). Independence Bay was not a bay—which is defined as a broad indentation immediately adjacent to a coast—but a fjord, which is an elongated inlet with its head as much as a hundred miles or more distant from the coast. Independence Bay is now known correctly as Independence Fjord. Overlooking this fjord, Peary was still some 200 miles from Greenland's northeast coast.

Sketch map of "Independence Bay," east coast of Greenland (from Peary 1898)

Also, there is no Peary Channel, and Peary Land is part of the mainland; no archipelago extends north. In his own report to Norwegian geographers, Astrup made no mention of the Peary Channel and said that no conclusion could safely be drawn as to what body of water extended to the east from Navy Cliff. The *American Geographical Society Journal* later reported the commentary of European geographers, one of whom found it "at least surprising" that Astrup made no mention of the discovery of the northern end of Greenland, "as if it were a matter of secondary importance." Another said, "The Norwegians are for the most part truthful observers. The American Polar voyagers, we regret to say, do not always inspire the same confidence, since the exaggerations of [Isaac Israel] Hayes."

Immediately on his return to the United States in September 1892, Peary began planning another expedition for the following year, and Frederick Cook was offered and accepted the position as surgeon. But then a breach between the two men occurred. On returning, Cook lectured to medical societies about the lifeways of the Inuits and decided to write a book on the subject. In this endeavor, he asked if Peary would let him use photographs Cook himself and others had taken. Peary reminded Cook that he had agreed not to publish anything about the expedition of 1891 until a year after Peary's narrative appeared, and he refused to allow use of the photographs. After all, the financing of Peary's next expedition depended on the success of his lectures and narrative; indeed, Peary was an indefatigable lecturer, giving 165 of them in the 103 days after his return. Reasonable as the refusal was, Cook saw it otherwise. Deeply annoyed, he decided not to accompany Peary on his next expedition.

But Cook had the Arctic ambition. He spent the better part of the next two years on what were essentially frivolous expeditions. In the summer of 1893 he was hired by a Yale University professor to take his son on a sightseeing trip to the Arctic, so Cook chartered a ship and crew and they traveled to Newfoundland, Labrador, and the west coast of Greenland. In 1894 he organized a hunting expedition of some fifty sportsmen to travel to northwest Greenland, chartering a ship called the *Miranda*. On July 17 the ship struck an iceberg and had to return to Labrador for repairs. Then, heading for Greenland, she struck a submerged ledge and eventually had to be abandoned. The crew and passengers were soon rescued by a fishing schooner and taken to Newfoundland. Not

Map of northern and northeastern Greenland; cross marks the Peary and Astrup Navy Cliff site

to be discouraged, on the return trip to the United States the assembled sportsmen decided on the basis of their shared experience to form a club. It was called the Arctic Club, and it would play an important role in Arctic exploration in the future. (That august group exists to this day, meeting in New York City.)

While Cook was acting as Arctic guide in 1893 and 1894, Peary was on his way to what he hoped would be a new triumph. He left the United States for Greenland on June 26, 1893, with a party of fourteen that included Astrup and Henson again, as well as a doctor and nurse for Jo Peary, who was pregnant and delivered the Pearys' first child, Marie, on September 12 at their base camp, slightly north of Thule. Aside from Marie's arrival, the expedition was considered a dismal failure by all hands, including Peary himself. In the summer of 1884 they were able to force a traverse of no more than 128 miles to the northeast, beaten back by intensely bad weather, and Peary sent everyone back to base camp except for himself, Henson, and a young volunteer named Hugh Lee. In 1895 these three made it to Navy Cliff but nearly starved on their return trip, having to slaughter and eat their dogs. Peary was able to add nothing to his previous expedition, much less find a convenient route to the Pole.

For Peary, as for any other explorer, such a wholesale failure simply wouldn't do. He knew that many years earlier John Ross had mentioned the existence of three nickel-iron meteorites from which the Inuit made iron implements. So Peary went south to Cape York, found them, and brought the two smaller ones back with him by sledge. *Small* is a relative term, of course; one weighed 300 pounds, the other 6,000.

Nevertheless, Peary felt himself to be at the nadir of his career. Indeed, he saw his dreams disappearing, his polar career at an end. On his return, he told the *New York Times*: "I shall never see the north pole unless someone brings it here. I am done with it." He went on to explain that such ventures required a younger man than he, "a trained man, a thorough athlete, and that I am not." He was in his forties at the time, "not an old man, as age is reckoned here, but I am too old for that sort of work."

Even so, Peary would soon recover his élan and his Arctic dreams. Perhaps the success of his rival Nansen had something to do with it.

In 1893, with the full financial backing of the nation's parliament and its king, Nansen set off on an extraordinary voyage, a passive reconnoiter of the Arctic. Based on the reported discovery of DeLong relics on the "wrong" side of the world, Nansen concluded that if he had the right sort of ship, he too could drift with the ice across the Arctic Sea. No one had ever even contemplated such a hazardous venture, but Nansen had the utmost confidence in his own abilities, his careful planning, and (of extreme importance) the scientific precision he brought to analyzing the situation he would face. Rather than refitting an existing ship, he needed a new ship with a totally new design—it should have a bathtub-shaped cross section so that it would ride up on the ice rather than being squeezed and crushed. But a ship with a flattened bottom was hardly oceanworthy. Nansen soon found a man who had designed maneuverable harbor pilot boats, and the two of them came up with a design that would permit the ship to sail to the ice margin and also to be carried upward and along with the floes. Once built, it was a compact ship with a displacement of 800 tons, a length at the waterline of 113 feet, a width of 34 feet across the beam, and a depth of 17 feet. Nansen named it—a sailing ship with an auxiliary engine—the *Fram*, which means "forward." She can still be seen in refurbished condition at the Fram Museum outside Oslo.

The *Fram* left Oslo on June 24, 1893, with a crew of thirteen, including its expedition leader. If Nansen had been at all wrong in his assumptions, he likely would have gone down in history as vain and foolhardy—and perhaps prematurely dead. The British humor magazine *Punch* saw fit to make some fun at Nansen's expense:

> So Dr. Fridtjof Nansen's off!
> Cynics will chuckle and pessimists scoff,
> What a noodle, that Norroway chap,
> Who'd drift to the Pole to—complete our map.

Designs for the *Fram* (from Nansen 1898)

The *Fram* followed the same route Nordenskiöld had with the *Vega* to the New Siberian Islands; then, in late September, she became frozen fast in the ice. Drifting with the ice, she took a zigzag path to the northwest and then to the southwest, where she was released from the ice in July 1896— what amounted to three years in the ice. Along the way, there were scientific measurements and observations to be made (aside, of course, from confirming that the ice drifted from the New Siberian Islands to Spitzbergen). For example, the expedition established that the Eurasian side of the Arctic Ocean was a deep basin and not a shallow sea. Indeed, even Nansen had assumed the Arctic Ocean was relatively shallow throughout, and the cables he had brought along to sound its depths were nowhere near long enough, a problem he solved by unraveling the individual cables and stringing the pieces together. A six-volume scientific report, compiled at the voyage's end, contained information that is of value still on the oceanography, bathymetry, and bottom deposits of the Arctic Ocean; the natural history of Arctic birds, crustaceans, and plankton; astronomy; terrestrial magnetism and gravity; and meteorology.

Partway along, Nansen realized they were not going to pass near the North Pole, so he left the ship on March 14, 1895, with a companion, Hjalmar Johansen, twenty-eight dogs, three sledges, two kayaks for crossing open water, a tent and stove, skis and snowshoes, and provisions for a hundred days. They were to attempt a dash for the Pole. As it turned out, the two men would be on the ice for nearly fifteen months.

At first the going was easy, but by March 29, only a couple of weeks into their trek, they were confronted with "great ridges of piled-up ice of dismal aspect," as Nansen wrote later. The following day they were stopped by "ugly pressure ridges of the worst kind, formed by the packing of enormous blocks," and the following day Johansen fell into the water as the ice broke under him. The open lead widened, and they had one man and a sledge on one side, two sledges and a wet man on the other. Later the lead froze over and they pressed on; after some level areas, they were again confronted with pressure ridges, and Nansen began to realize that the ice was moving south under them. By April 8 Nansen realized that "there is not much sense in keeping on longer; we are sacrificing valuable time and doing little." They were at 86° 13′ N, the farthest north of any expedition so far. They headed south.

For almost the next three months they traveled south across the pack ice, sighting land on July 24. By now their twenty-eight dogs had dwindled to two, the weaker ones being fed to the others along the way. The sledges were being pulled by one man and one dog each. Now it was time to abandon the

Nansen on a pressure ridge near his Farthest North (from
Nansen 1898)

sledges and kayak across the water to what was Franz Josef Land. There was no
room in the kayaks for the remaining two dogs, so they were killed. On
August 24 the two men went into winter quarters on Franz Josef Land, essentially hibernating until the following May, surviving like Inuit in a hut of
stone covered with walrus skins, eating the meat of seals, walruses, and polar
bears they hunted, and using the blubber for fuel. After nine months they set
out again in the kayaks. It was May 19. But where were they to go?

Spitzbergen, the nearest inhabited land, was more than 100 miles away, an
absurdly long journey by kayak. Perhaps Nansen thought he might have been
able to make it, but fortunately he never had to try such a journey. Still on
Franz Josef Land on June 17, he and Johansen happened on a British Arctic

expedition led by Frederick Jackson. Nansen's astonishingly good luck had held. As Jackson wrote later, "A more remarkable meeting I never heard of. Nansen did not know I was in Franz Josef land . . . and I had not the slightest idea he was within hundreds of miles of me; in addition, Nansen was very uncertain as to what part of the world he was in." Jackson pointed out that there were now 160 miles of practically open sea between Nansen and the nearest known land, not the kind of environment for "leaky canvas canoes," and he reported that "Nansen repeatedly remarks that nothing will ever induce him to undertake such a trip again."

Nansen and the *Fram* returned to Norway to unprecedented acclaim. He went on a lucrative lecture tour through Europe and the United States. His book on the expedition, *Farthest North*, became an instant best seller. Scientific societies on both sides of the Atlantic showered the man with gold medals and prizes. He was suddenly independently wealthy, as well as the darling of Norway. He did not make another polar attempt or another major Arctic expedition, though he thought hard about it at one point. Instead he moved gracefully back into the world of the academic scientist, writing much of (and editing all of) the six-volume report on the *Fram* expedition.

Here we detour from the main story of Arctic exploration and follow the amazing trajectory of Nansen's life, since he was clearly the most extraordinary and variously accomplished of all men who ever sought adventure and knowledge in the Arctic region. Soon after the turn of the century, Nansen

Drift of *Fram* through the Arctic ice and traverse of Nansen and Johansen across the Arctic ice (from Nansen 1898)

found himself in the thick of national politics, as a supporter of the movement (begun by Norwegian shipowners) for a peaceful separation of Norway from Sweden. For the previous century, the two countries had been both separate and one, in that each had its own parliament, but both had the same king as supreme monarch, and foreign policy was run out of Stockholm. Norway, though, was a maritime nation, and her foreign interests were quite different from those of Sweden.

Negotiations were under way in 1905 when Sweden suddenly broke them off. Nansen began writing a series of provocative newspaper articles, which, given his hero status as well as his persuasive pen, revitalized the national spirit. He was sent abroad to convince the great powers of Europe and the United States to encourage Sweden to resume the negotiations. This finally happened, and a peaceful dissolution of the union was accomplished in that same year.

The new Norwegian government then sent him to be their first ambassador to the Court of St. James, in London, where he convinced England to sign the Integrity Treaty, guaranteeing the newly obtained independence of Norway. Following that, in 1908, he returned to Oslo, where he again took up the university life, now as a professor of oceanography. Up to World War I, he made numerous oceanographic cruises and invented the Nansen bottle for collecting samples of water at various depths in the ocean. A wire with a weight on it is lowered over the side of a ship by winch. At intervals along the wire, cylindrical bottles, initially open at both ends, are attached to the wire. When the bottles are at the desired depth, a weight called a messenger drops along the wire and hits the top attachment of the first bottle, which flips over onto the bottom attachment, closing off the bottle itself with a sample of water from that depth. At the same time, a second messenger is released from the first bottle and falls down the wire, repeating the process, and so on. In addition to inventing this device, Nansen also wrote and illustrated a book, *In Northern Mists*, a history of the early northern explorations of the Greeks, Vikings, and others, published in 1911 and still a classic. And if that were not enough, Nansen also illustrated the book.

He came to the attention of the world again after World War I when he was appointed the Norwegian delegate to the Assembly of the League of Nations. Given his prominence (and the fact that he was from a neutral nation), he was then appointed by the league in 1920 to facilitate the return of prisoners of war—German and Austrian prisoners held in Russia, and Russian prisoners held in Germany. The Bolshevik government in Russia did not recognize the league, so he negotiated with them as a private citizen. Having arranged with

A sketch of Fridtjof Nansen by himself (from Whitehouse 1930)

both governments the return of these men, he then had to arrange through private sources for the money to pay for their return. In all, some half a million prisoners of war were thus repatriated under his aegis.

Meanwhile, thousands of Russians had fled their country after the Communist takeover in 1917, and they now were living abroad without permission and without the documentation necessary for civil functions or for travel. In 1921 the League of Nations appointed Nansen high commissioner of refugees to deal with just this problem, and his solution, agreed to by fifty-four nations and the league, came to be known as the Nansen Passport. It did not confer nationality; it simply gave the holder a title to existence. The concept of statelessness was, for the first time, enshrined in international law. By ensuring reentry, the document removed the main barrier to crossing borders, and the refugee was in effect under the protection of the high commissioner, a kind of international consul. Nearly a million Nansen Passports were issued in those years; among their holders were Igor Stravinsky, Marc Chagall, Anna Pavlova, and Sergei Rachmaninoff.

In that same year, Nansen would see to the raising of enough money to buy and transport grain to twenty to thirty million starving Russians, saving a great number of lives (but incurring some opprobrium as a result of accusations of being soft on Communism, since many of the starving were Red Russians, along with White Russians whose anti-Communist cause most of Europe supported). In the following two years, his main task was to resettle peacefully another one million displaced persons, the result of Greco-Turkish hostility that was of centuries-old standing. Nansen was able to arrange with both governments that the Moslems left in Greece would settle in Turkey and the Orthodox Christians in Turkey would settle in Greece. In 1922, during these negotiations, Nansen was awarded the Nobel Peace Prize. The citation said, in part:

> Work of an international character carried out by Mr. Nansen during these past years has brought him the Peace Prize. I might especially mention his work in the repatriation of prisoners of war, his work for the Russian refugees, his work in aiding the millions in Russia struggling against famine, and now his work for the refugees in Asia Minor and Thrace. Although this activity has been in progress for only a few years, its extent and significance are such that the Nobel Committee has felt it worthy of the great distinction of the Nobel Peace Prize.

Nansen died in 1930, a man of astoundingly diverse achievements and countless distinctions. Among these, he had also set a standard for grace and excellence in the exploration of the Arctic that would never be matched.

AMATEURS, PROS, AND CONS

The years following Nansen's *Fram* voyage, Peary's second expedition, and the beginning of the falling out between Cook and Peary—that is, from 1896 to 1909—would see an unprecedented flurry of Arctic probes as well as Antarctic ones, some successful, some tragic, some almost tragicomic.

There is, after all, a bit of comedy about the notion of setting off in a balloon with the hope of reaching a specific destination hundreds of miles away. Anyone who has ever ridden in one knows that balloons are notoriously at the whim of the winds. A stiff breeze can send the balloon scudding off far too fast to make a safe landing, as well as simply send it in the opposite direction from the one desired. No breeze at all leaves the balloon becalmed, able only to rise or fall in place. There may be no mode of travel that is less reliable. But this did not deter a Swede named Salomon Andrée, who was almost surely the first to have the idea of reaching the North Pole by air. Certainly he was the first to try it.

Evidently he was aware that the Arctic winds blow away from and around the Pole, not toward it. He planned to counteract this by retarding the balloon's motion through dragging ropes on the ground and then somehow "sailing" the balloon in a direction counter to the wind. He was a dreamer like Nansen, but Andrée's dream had little basis in reality. Even so, he was able to persuade several notable countrymen (including Alfred Nobel) to finance his venture. In the summer of 1896 he took his balloon to a small island off the northwest coast of Spitzbergen, where he intended to fill it with hydrogen produced on the spot with a chemical generator. He needed a favorable southerly wind, and so he waited for several weeks; but it never came, and he had to abandon the venture for that season.

By another of the many, almost standard, coincidences that brought strangers or acquaintances together in the Arctic, Andrée met a Norwegian explorer, Otto Sverdrup, who was passing through

Spitzbergen on his way home after spending three years aboard the *Fram* on her first voyage (1893 to 1896). Almost totally unsung in the years to follow, Sverdrup would spend more time in the Arctic than any of his fellow countrymen, including Nansen, and would discover more new Arctic land than all the combined discoveries of the forty Franklin search parties. Sverdrup is an example of how well-planned exploratory missions that go without a hitch do not make memorable legends.

The balloonist Andrée returned to his island off Spitzbergen the following summer, plans unchanged. A favorable wind blew, and on July 11 his balloon, carrying him and two companions, rose into the Arctic air. He kept a diary documenting the flight. At first they drifted to the northeast, but the next day the drift changed to the west, and then to the east. A heavy fog weighed the balloon down, keeping it from gaining altitude; soon the cab was simply bouncing along the ice pack. By the end of this second day "aloft," Andrée realized they had no chance of reaching the Pole. He opined in his journal that they could have thrown some ballast overboard and made it to Greenland but instead decided to land and get some rest. Andrée, however, knew the adventure was over. "How soon, I wonder, shall we have successors?" he wrote. "Shall we be thought mad. . . . I cannot deny that all three of us are dominated by a feeling of pride. We think we can well face death, having done what we have done. Isn't it all, perhaps, the expression of an extremely strong sense of individuality which cannot bear the thought of living and dying like a man in the ranks, forgotten by coming generations. Is this ambition?"

On July 14, the three men abandoned the balloon, heading south on foot with the hope of reaching Franz Josef Land and then setting a course for Spitzbergen. In early October, at a camp on White Island, the diary entries end. The men were not seen until thirty years later, when a Norwegian expedition came across their remains and Andrée's diary, still intact.

In 1898, the tireless Sverdrup was back aboard the *Fram* on an exploratory and scientific mission that left on June 24 and would be at sea for four years, until September 1902. Three hundred years earlier, William Baffin had noted three waterways out of the northern end of the bay that came to have his name: Lancaster Sound, later plied by Parry, Ross, Franklin, and others; Smith Sound, explored by Kane, Nares, and Hall; and Jones Sound. It fell to Sverdrup to penetrate Jones Sound. He and the fifteen members of the crew went on to explore and map the south and west coasts of Ellesmere Island and the north coast of Devon Island. He discovered and mapped new lands west of Ellesmere, in particular Axel Heiberg Island, Amund Ringnes Island, and Ellef Ringnes Island, collectively known now as the Sverdrup Islands

(Heiberg and the Ringnes brothers were the financial support of this expedition). In all, Sverdrup discovered more than 100,000 square miles of new territory in this four-year expedition, most of it traversed in two-man, dog-drawn sledges during the spring and summer months.

Of the three ambitious explorers—Nansen, Peary, and Cook—only Peary would continue in the early part of these years with a single-minded focus on the Arctic. His next two expeditions were, once again, in aid of interplanetary salvage: he sought the third meteorite at Cape York, this one weighing 33 tons. His expedition in 1896 failed, but the following year he succeeded, returning with this huge chunk of nickel-iron. He lent all three meteorites to the American Museum of Natural History in New York, and much later his wife, Jo, sold them to the museum. The largest of the three has been for many years a stunning attraction just inside the door of the Hayden Planetarium, where generations of students and tourists hand-polish it to a high sheen. In 1897 Peary petitioned his employer, the U.S. Navy, for another leave of absence, five years in all, to continue his polar explorations. It was duly

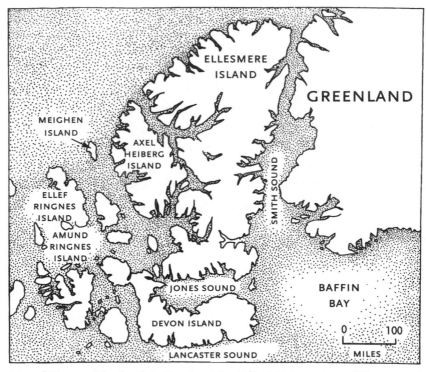

Map of Ellesmere Island and the Sverdrup Islands (Axel Heiberg, Amund Ringnes, and Ellef Ringnes (from Central Intelligence Agency 1978)

granted, the navy deciding that even though the Spanish-American War was brewing (or being deliberately brewed), their purposes would be better served in this largely naval campaign if Peary could attain the Pole under the navy's flag.

Meanwhile Nansen was, as noted, off on scholarly pursuits, and Frederick Cook, the doctor, shipped as medical officer and surgeon for an expedition to the other end of the world: Antarctica. The ship was named the *Belgica*, and this was the Belgian Antarctic Expedition of 1897–1899, under the leadership of a Belgian named Adrien de Gerlache. De Gerlache had spent three years raising the funds for the expedition, largely from private sources but also, in the end, from the Belgian government. The crew was half Belgian and half Norwegian, and one of the Norwegians who signed on as mate was named Roald Amundsen.

The purpose of the expedition was to put a four-man scientific party ashore on Victoria Land to make various measurements. But the ship was almost immediately locked in the ice in the Bellingshausen Sea, a long way from Victoria Land, where it remained for nine months.

Young Amundsen would recall that the highlight of the voyage was meeting and working with Cook, whose previous polar experience with Peary on Greenland in 1892 put him in the position of teacher to the pupil Amundsen. Together they made numerous trips into the Antarctic highlands using Nansen-type sledges. The Belgians had provisioned the expedition with, among other things, canned meat, but Cook knew what the result of that would be: scurvy. He insisted that the crew eat fresh seal and penguin meat, finally prevailing over the protestations of the ailing commander, de Gerlache. Later Amundsen would recall of this trip that Cook won the respect and devotion of all hands, and deserved it: "From morning to night he was occupied with his many patients, and when the sun returned it happened not infrequently that, after a strenuous day's work, the doctor sacrificed his night's sleep to go hunting seals and penguins, in order to provide the meat that was so greatly needed by all."

Long afterward, Amundsen's affection for the genial and dedicated doctor would put him into a most precarious position.

Peary's next expedition was to set out in 1898, while Cook was hunting and doctoring in the Antarctic. Peary was spurred on by reports in the fall of 1897 that Otto Sverdrup and the *Fram* were going to make an attempt on the Pole via the west coast of Greenland. In fact, Sverdrup had no intention of going to the Pole; he planned to map the north coast of Greenland. As we have seen, he did not even do that, but instead went west to Ellesmere and beyond. In any event, Peary wrote Sverdrup in November 1897, drawing attention to information in the newspapers about his forthcoming attempt on the Pole and saying that Peary had already announced similar plans to the American Geographical Society, his preparations were well advanced, and he wished Sverdrup "to give me the authority to deny the statements." He ended the letter by saying, "With sincerest regards and the highest admiration for the masterly way in which you brought the Fram home, I am," and signed it.

A month later Peary got a letter from Sverdrup that said, "I beg to tell you that you are in a mistake when you mean, that I intend to reach the pole. My expedition has only a scientific purpose and is going to make scientific explorations in the north of Greenland and to study the paleocrystal [ancient] ice." Sverdrup then congratulated Peary on his intention of reaching the Pole "by that way, which I do not think difficult."

Peary wrote back some time later, saying that "I cannot believe" Sverdrup's intention to do science in northern Greenland when Peary's own presentation to the American Geographical Society the previous year had included such scientific work as part of its mission. "I am sure you will pardon me if I remind you that such action on your part, in entering a field in which I have been at work for several years and assuming objects which I have formally proposed for my own work, will be without precedent in the annals of Arctic Exploration."

Indeed, Peary had so far devoted his professional life to mapping and other discoveries in northern Greenland and to finding a route to the North Pole. It was, in fact, considered ungracious of one to burst in on someone else's turf and reap potential rewards on the basis of that person's groundwork. Explorers and exploration scientists still feel this way, whether the turf in question is a piece of the ocean bottom, the East African highlands, or space. As it turned out, Peary's and Sverdrup's paths would cross, but their aims and accomplishments would not overlap.

In 1898, what would eventually become known as the Peary Arctic Club came into being—not to be confused with the Arctic Club, which had arisen on the sportsmen's voyage led by Cook. The new group was relatively small and exclusive, made up of wealthy and influential individuals who elected to support Peary's efforts and in the process see their names affixed to various pieces of Arctic geography. Prominent among the members was Morris Jesup, president of the club and a noted philanthropist, a founder of the American Museum of Natural History, and a president of the American Geographical Society. The club also included Thomas Hubbard, vice president of the group and a prominent New York lawyer; Herbert Bridgman, the club's secretary, who was business manager of the *Brooklyn Standard-Union*; and George Crocker, a substantial contributor to Peary's efforts and a director of the Southern Pacific Railroad. Peary had parlayed his exploits into the friendship and admiration of the finest in society. The club financed the bulk of Peary's final expeditions, with Jesup, Crocker, and Hubbard putting up $120,000 (almost $2 million in today's dollars) for a properly built and outfitted ship.

Peary's sixth expedition left New York on Independence Day, 1898, aboard the *Windward*. They made their way to a winter base all the way north to Cape D'Urville on the east coast of Ellesmere Island, where they were frozen in. Slightly south of Cape D'Urville was Cape Sabine, and it was here that Sverdrup on the *Fram* had to put in for the winter. One day in December Peary arrived at the camp on a sledge with an Inuit driver. He gave Sverdrup a terse hello and immediately left, suspicions swirling through his mind. He was now convinced that Sverdrup was planning to one-up him in an attempt at the Pole, so he immediately instituted a forced march north to the Fort Conger site to establish a base camp there before Sverdrup could. Fort Conger was 200 miles north of where Peary was, it was now the season of nearly total darkness, and the temperatures along the way were below −50°F.

Even so, with Matthew Henson, a doctor named Thomas Dedrick, and four Inuit, Peary left Cape D'Urville on December 20 and reached Fort Conger on January 6, 1899, On the way Peary fell, and his right arm and hand were partly paralyzed by the impact. But worse, his legs had become frozen up to his knees. Upon their return to the *Windward*, Dr. Dedrick had to remove seven of Peary's toes because of frostbite; eventually an eighth was removed as well, leaving Peary with only his two little toes.

The pain of frostbite and of amputation was extreme. Peary could ski or snowshoe only with great difficulty, and then only for short distances. Most men would have given up, gone home, and rested on their laurels, but Peary, with almost superhuman willpower and endurance, stayed on for the three remaining years of the expedition (and later carried out two more). In the annals of Arctic exploration, there are numerous examples of astounding fortitude, and Peary's is near the top of the list.

For understandable reasons, little was accomplished during the exploration season of 1899. Peary returned to Fort Conger, attempted to cross Robeson Channel but couldn't, returned to the *Windward*, and completed a survey of Princess Marie Bay. Then he sailed to Etah, where his summer supply ship, the *Diana*, met him. In August both ships sailed for home, leaving Peary and his party to overwinter in Etah. In 1900, explorations were more successful. Peary undertook a major sledge journey along the north coast of Greenland to its northernmost point, which he named Cape Morris Jesup, and from there he traveled north of the Arctic ice to 83° 50′ N. He arrived back at Fort Conger in June and overwintered there.

Earlier Peary had sent a letter describing his physical condition, including the loss of his toes, home to his wife with the departing *Diana*. Jo Peary decided to go north and bring her husband home, setting out during the summer of 1900 on *Windward*. The ship became locked in the ice in Cape Sabine, where she spent the winter of 1900–01 while her husband remained at Fort Conger to the north. She was conditioned to spend a winter in the Arctic, but she was not prepared for what happened in another of those chance encounters that so often took place in the vast Arctic expanse—this one a meeting that Peary surely wished would not happen.

An Inuit woman named Allaksingwah boarded the *Windward* one day that winter. Jo Peary immediately recognized her as the nude woman lying on the rocks in a photograph in Peary's 1898 book, *Northward over the Great Ice*. The photograph bore the strange caption, "Mother of the Seals."

The woman was the mother of more than seals. Allaksingwah boasted that she was Peary's wife, and she had a baby with her to prove it. (She meant no real harm; she was utterly unaware of the differences in mores between Eskimo and American cultures.) Jo, on the other hand, had lost her second child at seven months and now had this staggering blow to deal with as well. She wrote her husband a letter, dated August 28, 1900, in which she said, with restraint that one cannot imagine today: "You gave me three years of the most exquisite pleasure that can be had; after that the pleasure was pretty evenly divided with the pain until now is all pain, except the memory of what has been." Peary and his wife would meet briefly in August 1901, and they remained married. But both Peary and Henson fathered children in Etah, and their descendants still live there.

In 1901 the Peary Arctic Club resolved that it needed to act. It had heard nothing from either Peary, and so it sent out a second relief ship, the *Erik*, with Harry Bridgman aboard, along with Frederick Cook, now seasoned by Arctic and Antarctic experience. At the end of August both ships left for home, and Peary, Henson, and Dedrick were left to overwinter at Cape Sabine. The next spring Peary and Henson went north to Cape Hecla, on the northern coast of Ellesmere Island, their progress hampered by polynyas and hummocky ice, and halted by a final barrier that would plague Peary on his next two expeditions as well: what he called the Big Lead. The Big Lead is a shear zone between continental shelf ice to the south and Arctic Ocean ice to the north—a channel of gray-black water that is ice free for much of the summer and some other times as well, but otherwise frozen like the sea beyond. One needs to cross it in the early spring, when it is frozen, and return before it opens up, lest one become stranded on the Arctic Ocean ice.

On April 12, 1902, Peary reached a personal farthest north of 84° 17′ N before being turned back. It was short of Nansen's personal record by almost 2° of latitude and, he would later learn, more than 2° short of a new record claimed for 1900 by an Italian explorer, Umberto Cagni.

So for four years in the Arctic, Peary had little to show except for acts of heroic personal endurance. He had not come close to the Pole; he apparently had no prize to bring home. But in 1899, in his surveying of Princess Marie Bay, he did reach the top of the adjacent Ellesmere glacier. From its summit he saw Greely Fjord, which had been discovered previously, and a new fjord, which he named Cannon Bay after Henry Cannon, a founder of the Peary Arctic Club and president of Chase National Bank. As shown on his original sketch map, he also saw a landmass off to the northwest of his position, which he labeled Jesup Land. But in a written report to the club in August of that year, he made no mention of Jesup Land. Then, in late 1902 and early 1903, Sverdrup's findings began to see the light, and on Peary's 1903 map of the area Jesup Land got moved to the *west* of Peary's site atop the glacier—which is to say that Jesup Land was now located where Axel Heiberg Island is, thus giving Peary a prior claim to the discovery of the island.

Was this self-deception or sleight of hand? In any event, the international geographic community didn't take Peary's claim seriously. Jesup Land vanished, and the island became known by the name Sverdrup gave it.

Peary returned to America in 1902 and immediately began planning his next expedition. The planning was meticulous. He decided his next assault on the Pole would start from Cape Hecla, with a fresh group of people and fresh supplies. He wanted to avoid the exhausting sledge trips up the northeast coast of Ellesmere from Cape Sabine to the Arctic Ocean. And he wanted a special ship with which he could plow his way through the Kennedy and Robeson channels to Cape Hecla. The Peary Arctic Club happily put up the money for the expedition as well as the ship. It was named the *Roosevelt*, after that great adventurer and outdoorsman (and president of the United States), Teddy Roosevelt. Other than the *Fram*, it was the only ship specially built for Arctic work; like the *Fram*, the cross-section of its hull was U-shaped, so it would be able to ride up on the ice.

The expedition left New York on July 16, 1905, with a twelve-man company, stopped briefly at Etah to pick up several Inuit families and their dogs, went through the Kennedy and Robeson channels, and overwintered at Cape Sheridan, on the northeastern tip of Ellesmere Island—a promising beginning. The

Sketch map of Princess Marie Bay region, including "Jesup Land" (from Rawlins 1973)

Map of northern Greenland and Ellesmere Island, with cross marking the Peary glacier site (from Central Intelligence Agency 1978)

following year, on March 6, 1906, several sledge parties set out for the Pole, but they were slowed by the many pressure ridges that barred the way and forced lengthy detours. On March 26 they reached the Big Lead, at a latitude of 84° 38′ N, having traveled 124 statute miles at an average rate of 6 miles per day. Peary had taken no longitudinal measurements along the way but instead had simply headed north. On March 26 when he got out his instruments, he discovered that he had been offset to the west by 80 *miles*. The ice drift to the west had been almost as great as his northward progress. Why Peary had imagined he could operate without his instruments and by dead reckoning is anybody's guess.

He was delayed at the Big Lead for more than a week, waiting for the temperature to drop sufficiently to attempt to cross the young ice. Then at 85° 12′ N, at a location he appropriately named Camp Storm, he was pinned down for another week by a blizzard. Above the Big Lead, the ice drifted in the opposite direction, and during the week of the blizzard Peary drifted 62 miles to the east. Finally, on April 13, he could start north again, having lost seventeen valuable days. He had hoped to set up advance supply depots, but these plans were torn asunder. Nor did he have enough time to get to the Pole and back across the Big Lead before it opened up for the summer months. It seemed that all he could do was seek another farthest north.

He sent everyone back except Henson, six Inuit, and two sledges with dogs.

Peary was next seen at Cape Neumeyer on Greenland on May 9, four weeks after he had left with his small and mobile team. He reported that in the interval, on April 21, he reached a farthest north of 87° 06′ N and then made a beeline back to Camp Storm and thence to Cape Neumeyer. At one point he and his party were blocked by a lead a half-mile wide and were finally forced to eat their dogs and burn their sledges. Eventually, where the lead was 2 miles wide, it began to freeze over, and the party could wait no longer, even though the ice was so thin it could be crossed only with snowshoes, if at all. Twice Peary's snowshoes broke through and he thought he was a dead man, but he shuffled on, and everyone made it safely across.

In all, Peary would have made this round trip of 404 miles in twenty-six days, less the two days he reported being delayed—meaning an average speed of 18 miles per day over a region strewn with pressure ridges that had to be climbed or detoured around, and open leads that had to be avoided. Eighteen miles per day is three times Peary's normal speed of 6 miles per day, and far in excess of speeds registered by any other Arctic explorers of that era. This in itself makes it difficult to conclude that Peary actually reached very far north of Camp Storm, or that he achieved a new farthest north. Circumstantially, his claim is not made any more credible by the fact that during the entire trip of twenty-six days from Camp Storm to Cape Neumeyer he recorded only the one statement of latitude; he made no other detailed observations for the northernmost point he said he reached, and no latitude or longitude observations for any of the rest of the trek. For explorers of this era, such behavior was unheard of.

Meanwhile, other explorers were in the Arctic, seeking other goals. Frederick Cook wanted to be the first person to climb Mount McKinley, which, at 20,320 feet, is the highest peak in North America. And the Norwegian he had met and become friends with in Antarctica, Roald Amundsen, had his eye on being the first person to actually navigate the Northwest Passage.

On returning from Antarctica, Amundsen set about getting the backing of some Norwegian shipowners for his expedition. He left Oslo on a rainy night in June 1903 in a small fishing sloop 70 feet in length and equipped with an auxiliary engine. He had six crew members with him and was provisioned for five years. (He left port surreptitiously, to avoid a merchant who was threatening to stop the expedition for lack of payment for supplies he had rendered. Amundsen was plagued by financial problems throughout his life, his ambitions always outrunning his ability to pay for them. In this he closely resembled his American friend Frederick Cook.)

Amundsen was, however, what we would call a professional. He had wanted the Northwest Passage since he was seventeen years old (he was twenty-nine when he set out in 1903). He was in superb physical shape, was a regular long-distance skier, and had read every book and journal on the Arctic, noting two common problems in Arctic exploration that caused discord

One of Peary's sledge teams crossing a pressure ridge (from Peary 1910)

and often failure. First, the commander typically had no navigation experience, so Amundsen went to sea and soon gained his captain's license. And since there had often been dissension between the scientific staff and the crew, he went to Hamburg and studied the theory and practice of magnetic measurements.

He knew that a small expedition could live off the land, whereas a large one couldn't; that eating seal prevented scurvy; that loose-fitting Inuit-type clothing prevented exposure. He would, in fact, survive two winters on the southern shore of King William Island and grow fat in the process—at the exact location where the Franklin personnel had perished. His expedition was without much by way of incident; he arrived on the southeastern shore of King William Island in September 1903 and built a shelter there for his magnetic and meteorological equipment, carrying out measurements for two years while living among the local Inuit. The following year, in 1906, he completed the Northwest Passage, arriving at the mouth of the Mackenzie River, where he overwintered, sailing the next year around the Alaskan Peninsula, and reaching San Francisco in October.

He returned home to the expected hero's welcome—and to a pile of debts. Immediately he petitioned Nansen for use of the *Fram* for an attempt on the North Pole, using Nansen's proven technique of drifting with the ice. His idea was to sail around South America and north to the Bering Sea, setting the ship in the ice off Point Barrow, Alaska, and when the *Fram* drifted near the Pole he would make a dog-pulled sledge dash for it. Nansen initially had other plans for the *Fram*, believing that the South Pole was a simple goal for someone with his skill in Nordic cross-country skiing; given his duties as Norway's ambassador to England, however, he gave up his South Pole plans and let Amundsen take the *Fram*.

In 1903, the same year that Amundsen set out for the Northwest Passage in his little sloop, Frederick Cook made a reconnoitering trip to the base of Mount McKinley. It was not until 1906 that he undertook the climb, thanks to a promise of $10,000 (more than $160,000 in today's dollars) made by Henry Disston, an heir to a Philadelphia saw manufacturing business, on the condition that Cook would arrange to take him hunting near the mountain in the autumn, after Cook's attempt on the summit. The expedition included two men, Belmore Browne and Herschel Parker, who would become eminent mountaineers, and Edward Barrill, a blacksmith and horse handler. They left for Alaska in early summer and spent two months on the mountain without finding an accessible route to the summit. In August they repaired to Seldovia, Alaska, to meet Disston.

Disston was not there, and after two weeks of waiting for him they received a message on August 25 saying he wouldn't be coming at all. Of course, Cook was in hock. He had made purchases of equipment, contracts for horses, and promises of salaries to some in the party, all on the assumption of getting funds from Disston. He was broke, headed straight for bankruptcy.

On August 27 Cook announced that he and the blacksmith, Barrill, were returning to the mountain to explore the foothills for the following year, but not to climb the mountain. On September 22 the two men returned to camp and Barrill said, "Go back and congratulate the Doctor. He got to the top." Later Cook produced a photograph of Barrill standing on the summit. Despite this triumph, Cook was still in hot water. A lawsuit in Seldovia for breach of contract on horse rentals kept him there for another month. He was found in default and obliged to pay $600 (about $10,000 today), an amount he had to borrow, sending him yet further into debt.

But on returning to the mainland United States, he was widely and enthusiastically feted. He lectured at the Explorers Club and was elected its next president. He was a guest of honor at the American Alpine Club and spoke at the national dinner of the Arctic Club. On December 15, 1906, the National Geographic Society put on a gala dinner attended by four hundred guests, including President Roosevelt and Washington's elite, to honor both Robert Peary's return with a farthest north of 87° 06' N and Cook's summiting of Mount McKinley.

In 1907 an article in *Harper's* magazine by Peary and his book *Nearest the Pole* both appeared, in which he recalled the day on his last expedition when he stood on the peak of Cape Colgate (named after another member of the Peary Arctic Club) 2,000 feet above sea level. From there he saw the western land he had called Jesup Land, "though Sverdrup has later given it the name of Heiberger [*sic*] Land." From there, to the northwest, "it was a thrill that my glasses revealed the faint white summits of a distant land."

Crossing over to Axel Heiberg Land (his Jesup Land), he saw the snow-clad summits more clearly. "My heart leaped the intervening miles of ice," he wrote, "as I looked longingly at this land and in fancy trod its shores and climbed its summits, even though I knew that this pleasure could be only for another in another season."

He named this new and distant land Crocker Land, showing it on his map at the latitude 83° 40' N and at a longitude of 103° W, with a lateral dimension of about 60 miles. This, he said, was the second most important result of his 1905–06 expedition. Yet curiously, he made no mention at all of this mysterious land in his field journal or in any telegrams sent back to the

Peary Arctic Club. In cairns left at the two sites from which he said he had viewed Crocker Land, which were discovered later, he made no mention of this land. Indeed, there is no Crocker Land.

That same year, 1907, Peary was all set to head out on another voyage; a farthest north and a new piece of territory was not enough. He needed the Pole, the big prize. But he ran into a problem: money. His principal financial supporter, Jesup, had died (without an island to call his own, it should be remembered). *Nearest the Pole* flopped, selling only 2,230 copies instead of reaping the vast sum in royalties he had anticipated. The lecture tour that he and Robert Bartlett, captain of the *Roosevelt*, took on raised little money, and Bartlett went back to Newfoundland to go seal hunting. Peary's exploration plans had to wait.

In 1908, he would finally obtain commitments for funds to pay off his debts if he reached the Pole. If not, he would be bankrupt. Peary was fifty-two years old, hobbled by the loss of his toes and by his financial burdens, but determined.

Here, then, were Peary and Amundsen, two of the most prominent seekers of the North Pole, facing what was surely to be bankruptcy if they didn't pull off the big one.

In 1907, while Peary was rounding up conditional promises of funding, Frederick Cook was invited by a professional gambler and co-owner of a casino (the Beach Club, in Palm Beach, Florida) to accompany him on a hunting safari to northwestern Greenland. This was John R. Bradley, a millionaire from very successful gambling, who had just returned from hunting in northern Mongolia. He bought a ship (which he named for himself), engaged a crew, and put his guest, Cook, in charge of the outfitting. Cook, of course, had more than a hunting trip in mind; he envisioned a try for the Pole. He broached the idea to Bradley, and Bradley agreed to supply the extra equipment with the admonition not to say anything to anyone about it.

On June 3, 1907, they left for the Arctic. In September, after the hunting, Bradley and the crew left for home, with Cook remaining at Etah in northwest Greenland. On February 19, 1908, he left on his polar dash with two Inuit, two sledges, and twenty-six dogs. The party crossed Ellesmere Island, traveled northwest along Axel Heiberg Island, and thence to the Pole, which Cook reported reaching on April 21. Via the Ringnes Islands, he reached the north coast of Devon Island, where he overwintered, arriving back in Etah on May 20, 1909. The Pole was his!

While Cook was en route south to Etah on the last day of February 1909, Robert Peary and his party started out across the ice from northern Ellesmere

Island. The Big Lead held him up from March 5 to March 11, and twenty days later he reached a new farthest-north site, called Camp Bartlett, at 87° 47′ N. On April 1 he took off across the ice with Henson and four Inuit, reaching 87° 57 N, which is essentially the Pole. The Pole was his! He was back in Camp Bartlett on April 9.

A month after that, as noted, Cook pulled into Etah, where he ran into a man named Harry Whitney, who had traveled north as a guest of Robert Peary and stayed behind to do some hunting. Cook told Whitney that he had reached the Pole and left with Whitney a cache of instruments and, Cook said, notes. Then, triumphantly, he left by boat and sledge for Upernavik, Greenland, and thence by ship to Copenhagen, where he arrived on September 4, 1909. News of his achievement had run ahead of him, and he was greeted with enthusiastic acclaim. The Royal Geographical Society awarded him a gold medal on September 7, and the Danish university gave him an honorary degree two days later. Cook dined with the king before taking ship for the United States, where he arrived on September 21. A hundred thousand people cheered him as he passed by in a parade organized for him in his native Brooklyn. A reception followed, attended by five thousand admirers, and two days later the Arctic Club threw a grand dinner for more than a thousand guests to honor him.

The Arctic Club of America's banquet to honor Dr. Cook at the Waldorf-Astoria, September 23, 1909 (Library of Congress, Washington, D.C.)

By now Peary knew of Cook's claim. He had arrived in Etah on the Roosevelt on August 17, where he got the news. He was utterly convinced that Cook could not have reached the Pole, given his limited resources. But he also knew that Cook would be widely acclaimed and that he himself would be relegated to the role of also-ran—which was unthinkable. He would have to establish his own claim and destroy Cook's. On September 6 he sent out a telegram claiming the Pole.

The battle was joined. Each man had his supporters. Later in September the *Pittsburgh Press* took a poll of more than 76,000 of its readers. Only some 2,800 believed that Peary discovered the Pole in 1909 and that Cook hadn't actually gotten there the year before. More than 73,000 believed that Cook's prior claim of discovering it in 1908 was authentic, and of those, about 58,000 believed that Peary had never reached the Pole. No respondent thought both claims were invalid.

Polls, of course, are merely matters of opinion—in this case, uninformed opinion. But doubts about Cook's veracity began to loom on the horizon like thunderheads. Encouraged by Peary's financial supporters, Edward Barrill, the blacksmith companion of Cook's on the climb of Mount McKinley, made a sworn statement that he and Cook had never reached the summit. Further, he swore, his diary entries for September 9 through September 18 were left blank at Cook's insistence and then dictated to him by Cook after the fact.

But which Barrill was one to believe: the earlier version or the later one? Then the other climbers, Browne and Parker, weighed in. Both had doubts from the outset and vacillated between support of Cook and censure. They went to the Explorers Club with their doubts, which were based on the extremely short period of time Cook had been away from base camp, and on the nature of the photographs made at the summit. The club arranged a confrontation for October 17, 1909, which Cook attended, but he declined to testify and instead asked for a delay. Then, a month later, he disappeared from New York and was not seen again for ten months, until he turned up in Munich, Germany.

The McKinley claim was easily settled. Browne and Parker returned to Mount McKinley under the auspices of the Explorers Club, carrying with them copies of Cook's photographs of the summit. They did not attain the summit but instead, on June 28, 1910, reached the place where Cook had photographed Barrill at the "summit." It was a rock ledge located less than 6,000 feet up the mountain, which they named Fake Peak.

The McKinley claim was clearly a fake, and Cook, in his absence, had nothing to say about it. His polar claim came under fire also, with people noting he had claimed speeds over the ice of 17 miles per day when the conventional pace was more on the order of 6 miles per day. Peary advocates made a great deal of this, until it was pointed out that Peary himself had claimed speeds in excess of 17 miles per day on his final dash. But there was more that damaged Cook's claim. According to his narrative of the achievement, he sighted Peary's Crocker Land on his trek north; but there is no Crocker Land. Cook said he sighted a new landform he called Bradley Land, but there is no Bradley Land. Near the Pole itself, he said, he sighted a submerged island, but there is no land or ice island, submerged or no, near the Pole. All of these locations, however, were shown on Cook's sketch map.

And another island was missing. In 1916 a small island west of Axel Heiberg Island was discovered; it is called Meighen Island. No one had seen it until then, and it does not appear on Cook's map of his traverse in 1908. But if we are to take Cook's map at face value and believe that it shows his return route, he would have passed close enough by Meighen Island to see it. Yet he makes no mention of sighting the island.

The principal thing that dashed Cook's claim, however, was that he never could produce any data showing he had made the trip from Axel Heiberg Island and back. For eighty-eight days there are no notes showing that any celestial navigation was done. They were asked for in both Copenhagen and New York, but to no avail. Cook claimed in the newspapers after his return to New York that he had left navigational equipment and his "proofs" (that is, his measurements) with Whitney at Etah, and a year later the equipment was found in a box at Etah, but there were no papers, no measurements, no proofs. Then in November 1909 an insurance agent named George Dunkel approached Cook with the proposition that a Norwegian sea captain named Loose would supply Cook with a fake set of astronomical observations for $4,000 ($64,000 in 1990 dollars). Loose dutifully delivered the calculations, and Dunkel went up to Bronxville, New York, where Cook was staying, to pick up the $4,000. But Cook did not pay him, and he disappeared two days later, eventually fetching up in Munich. In December 1910 Cook came back to the United States and told a reporter, "I still believe I reached the Pole although I am not sure I did." Later still he reverted to his previous position, insisting he had bagged the prize in 1908. But very few could continue to champion him, and most explorers put as much distance as they could between themselves and Cook. He was once a founder and president of the Arctic Club, a member and president of the Explorers Club, and a founding member of the American Alpine Club. By the end of 1910 he had been expelled

Sketch map by Cook of his attainment of the Pole (from Cook 1913)

Frederick A. Cook (from Cook 1913)

from all three organizations, with his polar and Mount McKinley claims judged fraudulent.

A tragic event occurred in 1908, the year before Peary's dash to the Pole, the result of some misinformation about the nature of northern Greenland that arose from Peary's account of his expedition there back in 1887. A 1908 Danish expedition to Greenland was to proceed up its east coast and then across the southern shores of what Peary had seen as Independence Bay and the Peary Channel, to the north coast of Greenland. When they reached the latitude of Peary's sightings, they found to their dismay that the land went off to the east, not the west, as Peary had it. They trekked along the shore of what is now called Crown Prince Christian Land until it finally turned west, but no clear route emerged. Instead they ran into two uncharted fjords. They turned back but perished. The following spring a relief party found the body of one of the Danes, a detailed map of their journey, and a commentary that the other two had perished in the fjords.

In a report on this tragedy, Adolphus Greely, now a major general in the U.S. Army and onetime polar expedition leader (however unsuccessful), wrote that the Danes' "explorations conclusively show, however, that Peary was mistaken, and his point of view at Navy Cliff was on a waterway a few miles wide and not on the sea, there more than a hundred miles distant, while Greenland extended to the east twenty-two degrees of longitude, or about a hundred and ninety miles."

To this day, people still argue about which of the two Americans made it to the Pole, and Peary usually wins out. He had many distinguished, wealthy, and very influential supporters both while he was alive and after his death, and he has come down in the public mind as the man who discovered the North Pole. (One of the few who would support Cook's claim even into the latter half of the twentieth century was the Canadian adventure writer Farley Mowat, best known for his book *Never Cry Wolf*.)

Today there is no reason to believe Peary reached the Pole. In the first place, in the interval from April 1 to April 9, when he, Henson, and the Inuit made their push, there is no navigational data of any sort—no latitudes and no longitudes—except for the latitude note for the Pole itself. No one can navigate to the pole by latitude alone. Additionally, the distance from Camp Bartlett to 89° 57′ N is 150 statute miles, which gives Peary an average speed of 38 miles per day. No one has ever achieved such speed over the ice before or since: the fastest was a 1968 polar achievement by snowmobile that averaged 11 miles a day.

Peary's field journal raises severe doubts as well. On April 6 he makes no mention of attaining the Pole, and for the next two days he made no entries. Instead, a loose page was inserted (on clean paper and clearly not something written at the time) with the lead statement: "The Pole at last!!! The prize of 3 centuries, my dreams & ambition for 23 years. *Mine* at last."

This is not illusion or self-deception. It is sleight of hand. Here was a man who insisted that he achieved the goal of his lifetime, his dream and ambition, but he said nothing about it until September, when he learned of another man's claim. On April 6 he did not share his single latitude observation with Henson, which he usually did. It was normal for Henson to note such positions in his own diary, but not this time. There was no great hurrah back at the *Roosevelt*, no triumphant telegram sent off to the Peary Arctic Club.

For Peary, ambition always seemed to be one step ahead of his accomplishments, and in most cases the accomplishments eventually caught up. In 1886 he claimed the longest trek across Greenland, which was not the case; on the next trip he made the longest trek across Greenland. On that expedition, 1891–92, he claimed to have reached Peary Land and the northernmost part of Greenland, which was not the case; on the next expedition he found Greenland's northernmost point. On the 1898–1903 expedition he sighted

Jesup Land, which in fact was not a new land but instead merely a part of Ellesmere Island; on the next expedition he mapped the northwestern coast of Ellesmere. On the 1905–06 expedition he claimed a new farthest north of 87° 06′ N, which is difficult to accept; on the next expedition, he did reach a farthest north of 87° 47′ N at Camp Bartlett.

On his last expedition he claimed to have reached the Pole, which we have no reason to believe he did. But there would be no further expeditions. He died in 1930 after nine years of retirement from the navy, a man venerated by many but haunted by a particular kind of loneliness, walking through the last thirty years of his life without eight toes, forcing a peculiar gliding shuffle. He evidently grew tired of the version of himself that came through from his lectures. He began to close down, becoming dyspeptic and tyrannical.

Robert Peary in London, 1910 (Rauner Special Collections Library, Dartmouth College)

Peary's actual Arctic accomplishments, however achieved, were in fact the greatest of any American explorer. "His determination," as author and Arctic trekker Barry Lopez would write in the 1990s, "the depth and power of this man's obsession, absolutely stills the imagination of anyone who has looked upon the landscape he traversed." What drove Peary to cripple himself in the quest for the Pole? As another polar trekker, a physicist and playwright named David Fisher, wrote in his book about a trip through the Arctic on a Russian icebreaker, it was not so much jingoistic patriotism. It was not a desire to have the Stars and Stripes be the first flag planted there, though Peary spoke of this. Nor was it Peary's determination not to be beaten out by the hated Cook. It was, Fisher writes, "the passion Joan of Arc knew for God, the passion Paris and Menelaus knew for Helen, the passion of Faust for knowledge and power . . . simply *passion*: blind and unreasoning, indefatigable and ultimately irresistible."

As others have pointed out, however, it is an especially haunting and lonely feeling to wonder when one's untruth will be found out, and both Peary and Cook no doubt experienced this. As for Cook, he tried going into business, failed twice, and then formed a stock company called the Texas Eagle Oil and Refining Company with some other partners in 1920. Using his name for its celebrity, they mailed out a massive appeal that raised $800,000. But this effort soon failed as well, and Cook formed the Petroleum Producers Association, designed to salvage other failing or defunct oil companies. In 1922 postal authorities began an investigation that found the company had issued bogus stock. Cook and his partners were indicted in 1923 and tried later that year; Cook was sentenced to fourteen years in prison. The presiding judge sneered at Cook's "persuasive hypnotic personality," compared him to Machiavelli, and said, "I know the men who defended you, defended you with their handkerchiefs to their noses. It smelled to high heaven."

In 1930, after seven years in Fort Leavenworth, Cook was paroled, and in 1940 President Franklin Roosevelt granted him a full pardon at the request of Cook's family and other explorers. But he was by then a sick man. He died in August of that same year.

9 FROM POLAR LARKS TO CANARY WATCHING

If there were only four truly important firsts to be achieved in polar exploration, they would be the achievement of the two poles, north and south, and the navigation of the two passages, northwest and northeast. In 1910 both passages had been navigated, but neither pole reached. Neither of the two great American explorers, Peary and Cook, can be given the honor they both claimed with such fervor, with such wholesale lack of proof, and with claims of overland speed never before or since attained or even closely approached. The two passages were achieved, in each case by a Scandinavian, and it was one of these, Amundsen, who would lay legitimate claim to the South Pole, while the North Pole would remain untrodden for decades.

In 1909 Roald Amundsen, with Nansen's backing, was in the midst of raising the money and laying detailed plans for his own attempt on the North Pole, a journey he hoped to achieve by drifting nearby on an ice-bound *Fram*. But on September 1 of that year, while he was well along in his plans, with a sailing date only four months away in January 1910, the local papers announced that Frederick Cook (Amundsen's old friend from the Antarctic) had reached the North Pole the year before. And a week later he read in the same newspaper that Robert Peary had also recently reached the North Pole. His own effort would be utterly redundant— nothing more than a footnote, if it were successful.

What did he do?

In July 1910 he sailed south as planned—the original idea having been to enter the Arctic via the Bering Strait. But Amundsen had an entirely different goal in mind now, about which he said nothing to anyone. He was now headed for the other end of the planet, the South Pole. He kept this a secret from Nansen, his mentor; from the Norwegian government; from his financial backers; and from his crew. The latter were informed of the new destination only when the *Fram* stopped at the island of Madeira off the coast of Morocco on September 9, from where he also sent a telegram to the English explorer Robert Falcon Scott, who had long since announced his plans to make a scientific expedition to Antarctica and try for the South Pole.

Amundsen, of course, had announced *his* original plans as a purely scientific expedition to the Arctic, keeping the dash to the North Pole secret from his backers. Now he decided to make a nonscientific, purely exploratory dash to the *South* Pole, later justifying this intrusion into Scott's announced business by saying that Scott had announced to *his* backers only the intention of doing some science in Antarctica. In fact, Amundsen was, without much question, a sneak, but he would also reach more polar goals than anyone else in history, because, in an almost wholly uneventful trip, he reached the South Pole, thus bagging his second of the four big polar achievements. And he eventually bagged a third as well, though with an asterisk.

The *Fram* arrived in the Bay of Whales on January 14, 1911. After establishing depots along the way, Amundsen and a party of four others on skis with dog-powered sledges set out for the South Pole on October 19. They reached it on December 14 and, after spending three days there, returned to the ship. The only difficulty the skiers encountered was the ascent of the Axel Heiberg Glacier to the Polar Plateau, where the geographic South Pole is located. On his departure he left a tent with a thirteen-foot center pole on which the Norwegian flag fluttered, and a letter for Scott.

Scott arrived a month later with a party of four; on their return without skis and with man-powered sledges, they all perished.

The British, of course, howled with cries of poor sportsmanship. No "gentleman explorer" would act as Amundsen reportedly had, usurping Scott's right of first shot at the Pole by changing his plans and rushing off to Antarctica—a cowardly deceit that, some opined, had forced Scott to speed up his planning, thus leading to fatal error. Scott's heroic death and his diaries, discovered a few months later, moved all of England. Amundsen's achievement and his careful planning counted for nothing in Albion; Scott had *also* reached the Pole, after all.

And there was the matter of the dogs. Had Scott used dogs and not crew members to pull the sledges, his party would almost certainly have survived. Amundsen had, in another ungentlemanly action, used sled dogs on his return and then *eaten* them. Scott himself, on the other hand, had earlier expressed the British attitude to the grand game of exploration: "To my mind," he wrote, "no journey made with dogs can approach the fine conception" of men facing hardships unaided. "Surely in this case the conquest is more nobly and splendidly won."

In all of this the English were content to ignore the fact that Scott had used ponies on his trek to the Pole and killed and eaten them at the foot of Beardmore Glacier. In any event, the English never were at all comfortable acknowledging Amundsen's great first; nor were the Americans. By 1926 the geographic establishment in the United States had ruled that Robert Peary's claim to the North Pole was legitimate and that Frederick Cook's was not. Cook was by now, of course, languishing in federal prison for mail fraud. And in that year Amundsen, in financial troubles as always, was on a lecture tour in the United States.

After his success (acknowledged with great fanfare by the Scandinavians while the British and Americans sulked), Amundsen achieved sufficient wealth to establish a successful shipping business and, for once, not live in financial difficulty. He grew enamored with the notion of flying to the North Pole, a feat that at the time had not been accomplished, and in 1925 he ordered two Dornier flying boats from Germany and went to the United States in an effort to raise money to pay for them. He had the good fortune to meet Lincoln Ellsworth, who was not just an explorer but an explorer from a rich family. Amundsen received financing for the planes and the expedition, which left Spitzbergen on May 21, 1925. They flew northward for eight hours and landed on an open lead big enough for both planes, which they reckoned was the North Pole, but unfortunately they discovered they were 120 miles off. Then the lead froze up before they were able to leave, so they had to spend three weeks constructing a runway on the ice before they could take off. They had to leave one of the flying boats behind.

The following year Ellsworth put up the money to build a dirigible capable of flying across the Arctic from Spitzbergen to Alaska. The *Norge* was built in Italy and piloted by the Italian Umberto Nobile, with the overall expedition under the command of Amundsen. It left Spitzbergen on May 11, 1926, arriving in Alaska three days later, having circled the Pole several times.

It was a far-from-satisfying victory, and for two reasons. One was Richard Byrd, who would become one of the most celebrated explorers in American history. The other was Amundsen's expedition mate, Nobile.

On May 9, 1926, two days before Ellsworth and Nobile cast off for the North Pole in the dirigible, Byrd, with pilot Floyd Bennett, cranked up the engine of a Fokker trimotor aircraft and at 12:37 a.m. left King's Bay, Spitzbergen, expecting to be in the air for twenty-four hours, returning with the first overflight of the North Pole.

Roald Amundsen on arrival of the dirigible *Norge* in
Alaska (from Amundsen and Ellsworth 1927)

Byrd was from a prestigious Virginia family; the Byrds virtually owned
Virginia politics for much of the twentieth century, with Richard's brother
Harry being a U.S. senator from the commonwealth for decades. Richard
Byrd served with distinction as a pilot in World War 1 and was on a flying
expedition over the Arctic ice when he determined to be the first to fly over
the North Pole. The flight took less than sixteen hours, not twenty-four, since
the plane had to return to King's Bay at 4:07 p.m. with a troublesome oil leak
in the right engine. Byrd, who traveled as observer/navigator on this flight, as
on others to come, and his pilot, Bennett, became the first to claim to have
flown over the Pole. Returning to a ticker-tape parade in New York City and
awarded the U.S. Congressional Medal of Honor for this achievement, Byrd
would later become the first also to fly over the South Pole, and in his lifetime
he did perhaps more than any other person to encourage and stimulate the
exploration of Antarctica. When he died in 1957, at age sixty-nine, holding
the position of officer in charge of U.S. Antarctic programs, he was an international hero. He was buried with military honors in Arlington Cemetery.

But he never actually made the North Pole.

King's Bay, Byrd's departure point for that attempt, is 660 nautical miles from the North Pole, making a round trip of 1,520 *statute* miles, which Byrd covered in fifteen hours and thirty minutes—an average speed of 98 miles per hour. The Fokker trimotor, outfitted with skis for landing gear rather than wheels, had a top speed of 80 miles an hour, meaning Byrd would have had to enjoy a tailwind of 18 miles an hour from the *south* while headed for the Pole and a corresponding 18-mile-an-hour tailwind from the *north* on the return to King's Bay. Or he needed a tailwind of 36 miles per hour on the way to the Pole and no tailwind on the return, or some other combination of changing winds. None of those meteorological conditions existed at the time—a fact since established from weather records.

Later Floyd Bennett confessed to fellow pilot Bernt Balchen that they didn't make the Pole. And in a 1979 book, *Antarctica, My Destiny*, by Finn Ronne, a captain in the U.S. Navy and a noted Antarctic explorer after World War II, the story came out that Byrd himself had admitted his fraud. Apparently Isaiah Bowman, then president of the American Geographical Society, had doubts after Byrd's return in 1926 that he had ever flown over the Pole. He asked for Byrd's compilations and navigational aids, but Byrd was "evasive" and claimed that no one should question his truthfulness. Bowman told Captain Ronne that he got his answer in 1930 after Byrd's successful return from Antarctica and the South Pole. "It was raining," Bowman said, "and after lunch we went for a walk . . . for almost four hours around the blocks of Broadway and 156th Street. By that time I managed to break down Dicky-Byrd, and the time it took was worth it. Byrd confessed . . . that he had not reached the North Pole, but had missed it by about 150 miles."

Bowman, who later served as president of Johns Hopkins University, explained to Captain Ronne that if he made this confession public no one would believe him, so thoroughly was Byrd a national hero by then. But the arithmetic was confirmed, meaning that another feat by another American explorer turns out to have been a nonaccomplishment—in fact, a lie. This is a dreary way to have to end the tales from the heroic period of Arctic exploration—in particular the feats of the Americans, Peary, Cook, and Byrd, all three hoaxers. As a recent historian of such false claims, David Roberts, wrote:

> One thing became clear to me about these men: the decision to fake an exploratory achievement determined almost everything about the rest of their lives. . . . The world was reduced to allies and betrayers . . . we cannot envy these men their declining years. They lived out their natural spans in bitterness and proud isolation, even when surrounded by

the worship of a credulous public, even when decorated with honors. Exposure, one suspects, lurked like a wolf at the door.

Sadly, there is yet more, an unraveling in the life of even the most successful of the Arctic dreamers. Amundsen, it is now known, was the first to fly over the North Pole with his companions, but it was a bitter victory, for even as his claim appeared to make him second to Byrd, he felt that Umberto Nobile was taking more than his proper share of credit for the feat. Amundsen wrote a vitriolic book attacking Nobile and other real or imagined enemies. He was back in debt and had few friends, no family. He retired from polar exploration a bitter man and a loner, but not until he had made a last lecture tour to the United States, where he took a side trip to visit his old friend Frederick Cook in Leavenworth. Afterward he would attempt to justify the life and efforts of this now wholly discredited man, thus adding to the weight of distaste the American public held for him.

In 1928 his anathema, Nobile, made another Arctic expedition with a new airship, the *Italia*, in part to vindicate himself over Amundsen's aspersions. The airship disappeared. A search began with the Italian government asking for the help of the Norwegian government, but specifically requesting that Amundsen not be involved.

Amundsen chose to ignore this snub and accepted the aid of a Norwegian businessman who offered to buy a flying boat from France for his use. Arriving in Tromsø, Norway, in the French plane, Amundsen discovered that three other search planes were readying themselves for takeoff, from Sweden, Finland, and Italy. Nobile's location on the ice had by then been identified and it was now a matter of sending in a rescue mission, but the weather turned sour and the other three groups decided to postpone the rescue effort. They advised Amundsen to do likewise, but he refused their advice and, in an uncharacteristic action for a man renowned for careful planning, took off. It was Amundsen's last act—and a selfless one.

Nobile was eventually rescued along with seven crew members out of an original twenty-five, but the Italian pilot was publicly disgraced by a commission looking into the disaster. Amundsen's plane was never seen again, adding a coda, albeit a most tragic one, to this most romantic period of Arctic exploration, a period that had bloomed with such heroic promise (and promises) and that in the end turned so tawdry.

By the onset of the 1930s, it was generally accepted that the North Pole had been reached—by Peary on foot and by Byrd in a plane, as well as Amundsen,

Ellsworth, and Nobile in a dirigible. Another trek overland—which is to say, over the ice pack—to the Pole and back was no longer something anyone needed to bother with. Other feats of endurance and exploration remained to be achieved: the summit of Mount McKinley was unclimbed, as was Mount Everest on the Tibetan-Chinese border, the highest place on earth; and K2, the world's second-highest peak, on the Chinese-Pakistan border. Beyond that, the ocean depths awaited human eyes to peer at them, and the Moon still hung tantalizingly in the sky, only 240,000 miles away. And even in the 1930s, which we now think of as so far removed in the past, technology was about to take a front seat in the exploration business. Airplanes having longer range and capable of bigger loads were already flying; submarines were being launched. The first man to try to reach the North Pole by sailing toward it under the ice was an Australian named Hubert Wilkins, now largely unsung and little recalled, but one of the most colorful and accomplished adventurers in the twentieth century.

By the time Wilkins finished secondary school, he had somehow picked up a good working knowledge of both electrical engineering and cinematography, and he took it into his head to see the world. To that end, he simply stowed away on a ship leaving Australia, destination unknown (to him at least). He was eventually caught, worked to pay his way, and was discharged at the ship's first port of call, which was Algiers. There he managed to secure employment with an Italian agent investigating the smuggling of arms. At one point the two of them went to a meeting with some smugglers, were duped and drugged, and ended up as captives in a caravan to Tunis to be sold as slaves. Like a character in a romantic novel, Wilkins was rescued by a young Arab woman, who helped him escape.

Wilkins went on to England, learned to fly, and in 1912 found employment as a photographer and war correspondent, covering the Turco-Bulgarian conflict, a little-known war. At one point he was arrested by the Turks and held as a spy. Three times he faced a Turkish firing squad, but in each case all the others were shot while he was spared, since he refused to confess to being a spy. Finally, when an armistice was signed, he was released.

In 1913 he joined Vilhjalmur Stefansson in an expedition to explore and map the northwestern coast and islands of Canada, remaining in the Arctic under the tutelage of this master until 1916. By the time he returned, World War I was well under way, and Wilkins joined the British army, was wounded nine times, and was awarded the Military Cross and Bar for gallantry. After the war he attempted to win an Australian prize by flying from England to Australia but failed; he was forced down near a Turkish insane asylum—where, some of his friends suggested, he belonged. Next he photographed the starvation conditions in Russia for the Society of Friends, where he crossed Nansen's path, and then he led a biological collecting expedition to northern Australia.

In 1926 the Arctic bug bit him again and he returned to polar efforts, this time by plane. He and Carl Ben Eielson, the most famous of Alaskan bush pilots of that era, made a reconnaissance flight out over the Beaufort Sea in search of new land, but they found none. Next year the two scouted yet farther—some 550 miles—to the northwest and were forced down three times, finally because they were out of gasoline. Thanks to Wilkins's previous experience with Stefansson, however, they survived a walk of more than 70 miles across the pack ice with its pressure ridges, hummocks, and bone-chilling cold. Undaunted, the two of them in 1928 made the first airplane flight all the way across the Arctic, from Alaska to Spitzbergen. Wilkins was knighted for this feat, and the two men went on in that same year to fly all the way across the Antarctic.

By now people had begun to think about the possibility of traveling to the North Pole under the ice. Wilkins and his colleagues Sloan Danenhower, Simon Lake, and Lincoln Ellsworth became the first to do anything about such a notion, obtaining a submarine from the U.S. Navy for the nominal rental fee of $1 for five years. This was the O–12, built in 1918 and scheduled to be scrapped under the London Naval Treaty. They rechristened her *Nautilus*, after Captain Nemo's submarine in Jules Verne's *Twenty Thousand Leagues Under the Sea*. The new *Nautilus*, like all other submarines of that era, was not a true submersible but instead a surface ship that could operate submerged for a few hours, on power generated by batteries. The batteries could be recharged only by running the diesel engines on the surface.

Overhauled and refit, the *Nautilus* had a safe diving depth of 200 feet, sufficient for Wilkins's purposes. At a slow speed of 3 miles an hour, it had an underwater range of 125 miles and enough oxygen in the form of bottles of compressed air to remain below the surface for three days. From his own and others' Arctic experience, Wilkins reckoned that about every 25 miles they would come across open water areas—polynyas or leads—big enough for the sub to surface; the vessel was equipped with an observation area in the conning tower for spotting such open areas. She also had a special auger for boring upward through the ice.

There was a great deal of speculation involved here, of course. The distance from Spitzbergen to Alaska via the Pole was more than 2,000 miles, and little was known at the time about variations in the thickness of the ice in the

Arctic Ocean. If they didn't find the open areas of water and if the auger failed, they would perish.

In the fall of 1931 they proceeded under the ice from Spitzbergen, found no open water, and learned that the auger did not work. They would not be able to surface. After several unsuccessful attempts, Wilkins wisely called off the project; it was a good idea, but about three decades ahead of its time. After this, Wilkins turned his attention chiefly to the Antarctic and served in a civilian capacity during World War II with the War Department. He died in 1958, but not before the first nuclear-powered submarine was launched, yet another *Nautilus,* and this time a true submersible like Captain Nemo's. Here was the technology to take men to the Pole under the ice.

In a nuclear-powered submarine, the atomic reactor is a self-sustaining unit requiring no external fuel or oxygen. Equipped with various life-support systems, it can stay submerged for a month or more and can travel several thousand miles underwater in that time. But if you are submerged under the Arctic Ocean, how do you know where you are? The luxury of surfacing and getting a celestial, satellite, or electromagnetic fix is not available. You need a self-contained navigation system. The first inertial navigation systems were just that, and the earliest ones were installed on the *Nautilus* and its partner in polar probing, the *Skate,* in 1958.

An extraordinarily sophisticated instrument, an inertial navigation system is used for ships and aircraft, and as a guidance system for missiles. Its concept starts with velocity, the rate of change in distance. In an automobile we speak of miles we travel in an hour. If, for example, we drive a car at a fixed rate of speed in a straight line on a desert flat, we can easily know our ending position as a product of the speed and time driven. Even if the speed varies during the drive, we simply add up the time increments spent at various speeds and integrate the speed over time.

Velocity has both a magnitude (speed) and a direction. If we have a meter that can measure both speed and direction, we can integrate each component over time and determine our final destination—that is, where we are—after driving across the countryside by highways and byways.

The next problem is acceleration, which is the rate of change of velocity. We need a device to measure both the north-south and the east-west components of acceleration, and then we can determine our position at any given moment via a double integration that can easily be done by computer. Acceleration is pretty easy to measure in itself, since it is the equivalent of a force exerted; sensitive accelerometers are mounted in gyroscopes to maintain their orientation, and over a distance traveled of a few thousand miles accuracy of less than a mile can be achieved.

The *Nautilus*'s first polar attempt was under the command of William Anderson in 1957, when the ship did not yet have an inertial navigation system (though it was equipped with an inverted echo sounder to tell them, by means of sonic echoes, how far above them the lower surface of the ice was). Anderson had to rely on dead reckoning and gyroscopic and magnetic compasses, but as they achieved 87° N their gyroscopic compass failed and they had to turn back. A year later, now equipped with an inertial navigation system, *Nautilus* undertook the assignment to traverse the Arctic Ocean from the Chukchi Sea to the Greenland Sea and immediately had to confront a major problem: the only deepwater passage into the Arctic Ocean is the Fram Strait, between Greenland and Spitzbergen. Elsewhere the ocean is bounded by a continental shelf with shallow water. Further, the ice beneath some of the pressure ridges extends 100 or so feet below the surface of the water, making formidable obstacles for a submarine passage, just as the pressure ridges held up explorers above on the ice pack. A nuclear submarine at the time was 50 feet high from keel to sail.

In June 1958 *Nautilus* made two attempts but was stymied by the thickness of the continental shelf ice. In July she returned after the ice pack had retreated off the shelf and found a passage into a great valley to the deep basin of the Arctic Ocean. Having submerged off Alaska on August 1, she reached the North Pole on August 3 and surfaced between Greenland and Spitzbergen on August 5. It was an astounding (and uneventful) voyage, and a momentous signal that a new age was upon the world: what used to take months or even years of struggling against the cold, the ice, the weather, and the frailties of the human body and the human spirit was achieved in a few days.

That same month and year, August 1958, the nuclear submarine *Skate*, under the command of James Calvert, was assigned the job of developing techniques to surface in pack-ice areas. It was the Arctic summer, and the open-water areas of the polynyas could be detected by the inverted sounder readings. The sub entered the Arctic basin through the Fram Strait, progressed to the North Pole, and went to the western edge of the basin before turning back and exiting via the Fram Strait. She surfaced nine times during the voyage, once near the Pole. In a sense, Calvert had accomplished just the sort of voyage Wilkins had contemplated back in 1931.

After his 1958 voyage, Calvert gracefully took the time to visit Wilkins and Stefansson, who were then both in their seventies, to bring the old warhorses up to date and seek their advice. And they had some advice, suggesting that the *Skate* go back in the winter to try the same thing. There would be no polynyas but instead regions of recently frozen leads where the ice would be no more than two feet thick. (In December, shortly after Calvert's meeting, Wilkins died, no doubt happy to have been involved to the end.)

With its sail strengthened, Skate returned to the Arctic in March 1959, located regions of thin ice, broke through, and surfaced at several sites, including once again the North Pole, where, at Wilkins's request, Calvert sprinkled his ashes, a tribute to one of the greatest adventurers and explorers of the twentieth century. Indeed, one can say that a sense of honor had finally been restored to America's polar explorations.

At the same time, it should be pointed out that these astounding submarine efforts were undertaken not out of any altruistic interest in scientific exploration nor for any sort of adventurer's glory. They were for military ends, pure and simple. The Arctic is the nearest ocean to a number of targets in the former Soviet Union, and the need to be able to reach those targets was preeminent in the minds of the military as well as the U.S. Congress at this time, as the Cold War raged and the balance of the world hung on both diplomacy and the buildup of the most threatening arsenals in history. The Arctic ice also provided a safe haven where a submarine could lurk for extended periods, undetected by surface ships or aircraft. And with the ability to surface near a specified location in the Arctic, as *Skate* had done, the submarine becomes a convenient platform for launching ballistic missiles. As a result, for most of the remainder of the twentieth century the Arctic—so little known only fifty years before—was an integral component of the Cold War, a region of paramount strategic importance.

But still, no one had accomplished what Robert Peary and Frederick Cook had set out to do: cross the ice on foot and sledge and reach the Pole. After all, why bother? We had planes, submarines, and powerful icebreaking ships as well as all kinds of high-technology equipment to facilitate work in the Arctic. And the Arctic was no longer a place for the frivolity of mere adventure. It was serious business, and even in the 1930s no country was more aware of this than the Soviet Union. The Soviets' northern border was the Arctic and of obvious strategic importance, and the Northeast Passage continued to be of great importance to the commercial interests in Siberia, where weather information and predictions were always vital.

As early as 1937, the Russians established stations in the Arctic to monitor the weather and other physical variables. The first Soviet drift station was flown to the North Pole in May of that year, and designated *SP 1* for *Severnyy Polyus 1*, or *North Pole 1*. It included a party of four: the leader, Ivan Papanin;

two scientists, Eugen Fedorov and Pyotr Shirshov; and radio operator Ernst Krenkel. These were the first human beings to set foot on the Pole. But more important to them, it seems, was that they accomplished their scientific mission with skill and élan, paving the way for more such expeditions.

They remained in shacks on the ice for nine months, until February 1938, during which time the Transpolar Drift System took them across the Arctic to the coast of Greenland, where they were eventually picked up by a Soviet ice-breaker. At the time of their rescue, they were inhabiting a slab of ice 100 feet long and 30 feet wide—shades of George Tyson! Along the way they made daily observations of atmospheric and oceanographic conditions as well as geophysical measurements of gravity and magnetism, and on their return they were welcomed as heroes in Moscow—and justifiably so, being not only the first men on the Pole but the first to man an Arctic drift station for such a length of time, 274 days.

The leader, Papanin, a good Party member, sent off a message to Stalin, saying how pleasant it was to think that "we, four ordinary Soviet citizens, have justified the hopes placed in us by our Party, our Government and our beloved Stalin, who reared us and on whose initiative our Motherland has acquired a new waterway linking up the east and the west of the Union of Soviet Socialist Republics."

In the 1960s, once the *Nautilus* and *Skate* had breezed under the Pole, some people began to realize that the goal of getting to the North Pole via the ice, and not over or under it, had not been achieved. The next attempt to do just that would arise in a restaurant in Duluth, Minnesota, in 1966, where an insurance agent named Ralph Plaisted was drinking a few beers with a physician friend, Arthur Aufderheide. They decided to try for the Pole on snow-mobiles. An indefatigable promoter and planner, Plaisted set about gathering funds and equipment (including the snowmobiles) from corporations, institutions, and private individuals. Undismayed by being turned down by Campbell Soup, for instance, he went around to Knorr Soup and talked them out of ample supplies. He also convinced a crew of five television people, including Charles Kuralt, to join the expedition.

In all, sixteen people departed from Ellesmere Island on snowmobiles in late March 1967, headed for the Pole. There has never been a more amateur expedition. None of them had ever spent even an hour on the Arctic ice; one was an instructor at a winter survival school run by the Royal Canadian Air Force, and another had been stationed for a while at the U.S. Air Force base at Thule, Greenland. Otherwise, like Plaisted, they were all utter greenhorns.

They ran into the usual array of pressure ridges and open leads, including the Big Lead that had so frustrated Peary, and also including what they called the Big Ridge, a pressure ridge of indeterminate length and some 36 feet high, which they had to hack their way through. Even though they were supplied by air drops and landings that allowed shuttling of replacements from base camp to field, they eventually had to abandon the project, stymied by an unrelenting six-day storm. Having reached 84° N, they were airlifted out.

But Plaisted was not about to throw in the towel. He had learned a great deal about what to do and not do in the Arctic, and the following year he returned with a smaller crew aboard more powerful snowmobiles, Ski-Doos, manufactured by Bombardier of Quebec. They set out from Ward Hunt Island in northern Canada, winding through jagged ice ridges in the last weeks of the Arctic winter, traveling 825 miles. Pillsbury had contributed special food cartons, so the trekkers enjoyed 5,000 calories a day, as well as vitamin pills. On April 20, 1968, a bit more than a year before Americans set foot on the Moon, Plaisted and three companions became the first to reach the North Pole by an overland route.

Soon airlifted out, they got home to very little attention. No CBS team had accompanied them this time, and most of the media considered Plaisted's trek more of a stunt than the actual achievement it was. The *New York Times* reported it as a brief item on page 68 of the April 20, 1968, issue. Nevertheless, it was Plaisted, the amateur explorer and insurance salesman from Duluth—and not Robert Peary—who was first to reach the Pole over the pack ice.

The following year a Briton accomplished the same thing, except that he went by sledge and on foot. Wally Herbert had long held what he called an "obsessive ambition" to make a surface crossing of the Arctic Ocean via the North Pole. By 1969 he had logged thousands of miles of trekking in the Arctic, Canada, Greenland, and Antarctica, and spent four years planning his crossing of the Arctic Ocean. His plan was to travel from the Pacific side of the Arctic to the Atlantic side, drifting with the ice as Nansen had done before him. On February 21, 1968, Herbert left Point Barrow, Alaska, with three companions and dog-powered sledges. They got as far as 85° N, 162° W in their first season and set up winter quarters. On February 24, 1969, almost exactly a year after leaving Point Barrow, they started out again, reaching the Pole on April 5 and Spitzbergen on May 29. This was a longer expedition than Plaisted's, but like his it was supplied along the way by air.

Almost two decades later, an American adventurer named Will Steger, who, like Herbert, had spent a lifetime trekking in the Arctic and Antarctic, determined to reach the North Pole in the same conditions under which Peary had made his attempt—that is, he sought to complete the journey without resupply by aircraft. With six other men and one woman (a physical education instructor named Ann Bancroft), he set out from Ellesmere Island on March 8, 1986, with five sledges powered by dogs. Fifty-five days later, six of them reached the Pole—Bancroft became the first woman to try to do so and the first to succeed—and were airlifted out with their equipment and dogs.

Once Roger Bannister broke the four-minute mile, it fell to hundreds of other runners. Since the New Zealander Edmund Hillary climbed Mount Everest and the American Jim Whittaker did the same, people almost routinely climb to that highest of summits; it has been done by hundreds of people now. And since Plaisted, Herbert, and Steger reached the Pole, it is no longer an unusual accomplishment—though no one has yet done what Peary and others set out to do: reach the Pole over the pack ice and return over the pack ice with nothing but human and canine power. Instead people get there by air or by icebreaker. The North Pole, in that sense, has become something of an "extreme" tourist destination. In 1991, for example, the American physicist David Fisher came up with $30,000 to buy a round-trip ticket to the North Pole aboard a Soviet nuclear-powered icebreaker, the *Sovetsky Soyuz*, with about a hundred other people. Along the way they found the hut where Fridtjof Nansen spent the winter on a barren island and saw the last island visited by George Washington DeLong on his doomed expedition. Fisher, like other polar travelers before him, wrote a book about his trip, *Across the Top of the World* (1992), full of amusing episodes as well as polar exploratory history. Once the complement of tourists reached the Pole, many of them proceeded to dance in a wide circle around the Pole, insisting that they were now members of the elite group of people who have circled the globe and passed through every time zone on a single trip—this, much to the annoyance of an extremely abrasive passenger who had bragged repeatedly about circling the globe at lower latitudes.

But the physicist sounded a cautionary note. Visiting the islands that the old explorers described as icebound, the passengers found them to be relatively free of ice. Was this just the kind of climatic variability that has always pertained in the Arctic—extensive pack ice one year, less another—or was this ominous evidence of global warming?

By the year 2010, it was hard to find any branch of science that was not being pursued in or about the Arctic, and only rarely did a day go by without the announcement of a new scientific finding, a new effort, a new insight about this still-mysterious region. Hundreds of groups working on one aspect or another of the Arctic world generated an astonishing (and baffling) array of acronyms. One of the most important of these is IPY, for International Polar Year, of which there have been four. The term is a misnomer, since all four international polar years have extended well beyond the chosen calendar year. The most recent one began in 2007 and drifted to its end in 2009.

The first IPY came about in 1881 thanks in great part to the Austrian explorer Carl Weyprecht, the co-commander of an Austro-Hungarian Polar Expedition in 1872–1874. Thousands of scientific observations were recorded during that expedition, but the scientist in Weyprecht told him that all the information was of limited use. This was because, he wrote later, "They only furnish us with a picture of the extreme *effects* of the forces of Nature in the Arctic regions, but leave us completely in the dark with respect to their *causes.*"

It was time, Weyprecht insisted, that nations stop profitless competition for geographical discovery and instead cooperate in coordinated scientific expeditions, "with instruments precisely alike, governed by precisely the same instructions, and for a period of one year at least, to record a series of the utmost possible synchronous observations." Only such an effort would put scientists "in possession of materials enabling us to attempt a solution to the problems which now lie embedded in the Arctic ice."

That first IPY, which ran from 1881 to 1884, was the largest coordinated series of scientific expeditions to the Arctic in the entire nineteenth century. (Though it was directly inspired by Weyprecht, sadly he was not part of it, having died in 1881.) In all, eleven nations participated, building fourteen main research stations and thirteen others throughout the Arctic. In all, seven hundred men managed the stations, including numerous Inuits. Regrettably, coordination stopped once the data-gathering ended. The data were published independently by the various nations, with no effort at combining the national troves of information into an international analysis. As a result no fundamental insights arose.

The data from that first IPY are now available from the National Oceanic and Atmospheric Administration's U.S. Arctic Research Office, offering scientists today a means of studying the Arctic as it was before the current times of rapid climate change. And so Weyprecht's suggestion not only set a tone for further Arctic research but, 130 years after the fact, may well bear real scientific fruit.

Over the past century and a half, another kind of science has been progressing in the Arctic: the softer social science called anthropology and the related field of archaeology (though the latter didn't begin in the Arctic until well into the twentieth century). The subjects of this research were, of course, the people who were called the Eskimos and who are now known mostly by their own name for themselves, the Inuit. They were the first native people in North America to be seen by Europeans; the Norse have been in their country, on and off, for more than a thousand years, and British and other Arctic explorers ran into them before they reached such places as New England. The early accounts by explorers, however sharply observed, basically fell into the category of travel writing; these men were not by any means trained observers of other cultures.

Anthropological studies per se began about two decades before the turn of the twentieth century, with Franz Boas, an early founder of modern ethnography, visiting the Inuit of Cumberland Sound and east Baffin Island. In this endeavor, Boas traveled some 2,400 miles on foot, by boat, and by dog team, making the first charts of Cumberland Sound as well as describing the culture of the eastern Canadian Arctic in remarkable detail (with the help of travel accounts as far back as Parry). More studies followed throughout the entire 6,000-mile range of Inuit lands from eastern Greenland through the Bering Strait to the northeast coast of Siberia, the longest linear distribution of any single group of people in the world.

World War II and the years after brought numerous incursions of the outside world into the lives of the Inuit. Military bases sprouted like thorns. Oil geologists were followed in some cases by large drilling installations and pipelines. Life was changing rapidly and radically for many of these people, who over the centuries had adapted with such skill to extremely hostile conditions in isolation from the rest of the world. Indeed, so remote were some of these groups that when in 1818 Sir John Ross came across what he called the Polar Eskimos, a group of Inuit living in western Greenland, they believed themselves to be the only people on earth. Their isolation had been for so long that they had given up and since forgotten the use of bow and arrow, skin boats, and salmon spear.

Suddenly the silence of the Arctic was broken by the sounds of internal-combustion engines and jet planes, radio and television. New people brought new wishes, new wants. As early as 1957 the ethnographer Margaret Lantis wrote, "The substance of the situation is that Eskimos are trying just as hard today to adapt as they did 500 or 900 years ago; the difficulty is that they are adapting not to the Arctic but to a Temperate Zone way of living." Today, in fact, there is only one community in the Canadian Arctic, a place called Umingmaktok, where no nonnative people live.

But these people are, of course, the unsung heroes in a book about Arctic exploration. They explored most of the Arctic themselves and learned to live in it, making even physiological adjustments to the climate, not to mention subtle cultural adjustments. And had it not been for their usually benign attention, even more European wayfarers would have perished as they probed these strange and awesome new lands. A few Inuit, as we have noted, received the accolades of the European explorers, and some even had their names recorded for history. But for the most part, the various bands of Inuit go anonymous.

There is considerable justice, then, in the recent action of the Canadian government, which in 1982 held a plebiscite in which 53 percent of the people in the Northwest Territories voted in favor of creating a new Canadian province, and which in 1993 passed the Nunavut Act, giving birth in 1999 to Nunavut (the name means "our land"), a province of 895,000 square miles in the northeastern and eastern part of Canada, including most of the Canadian Arctic islands. In this vast area live some thirty thousand people, the vast majority of whom are Inuit, and they will, of course, have the controlling interest in the national parliament over the affairs of the province. The word *Eskimo* will not much longer be heard in this province; it is a Cree word that means "eaters of raw meat" and is considered derogatory. Inuit will be the name of the people and of the language.

Nearly 60 percent of the people in this new province still depend on hunting and fishing for a living; a total of 12.5 miles of highways stretch across this land. Just as the word *Eskimo* will cease to be used, the map will change as well. Cambridge Bay is now called Ikaluktutiak. The names of some of those old explorers—and the names of their financial angels—will surely become things of the past.

IV CLIMATE CHANGE AND A WHOLE NEW ARCTIC

To this point in the long history of Arctic exploration, the pace has been somewhat leisurely, most voyages relatively slow, and the gathering of scientific data about the nature of the Arctic fairly routine. But three decades ago, it became apparent to the scientific community that the world was about to leave the Holocene and enter what might be called the Anthropogenic Era. Indeed, the activities of mankind had already begun to force the planet into a new existence—a significantly warmer existence that would, among other things, profoundly change the nature of the Arctic, and there at a greater rate than anywhere else on Earth. In response, the pace of Arctic research has multiplied perhaps a hundredfold, and the tone behind the cool lingo of climate science is increasingly characterized by a nearly staccato urgency. The tone of this book, then, changes as well.

THE DEICING OF THE NORTH

To rephrase Frank Sinatra, it was a very bad year.

It was a very bad year for the extent of Arctic ice, and the volume of the ice, and the age of the ice.

In September 2007, climate scientists could see from photographs of the ocean's surface (courtesy of NASA) that the Arctic ice was at its lowest extent since satellite photography began. The ice covered just 1.65 million square miles. September is when local temperatures tend to drop with the lowering of the Sun in the sky, beginning the refreezing of the ice until March when the temperatures begin to rise, eventually melting the summer ice to its least annual extent. By contrast, in September 2005 the summer ice shrank to an area of 2.14 million square miles. In other words, the area covered by ice had dropped by almost one-fourth in a mere three summers—an astonishing change, particularly in such a brief time.

After the minimum of 2007, in the following year, 2008, the ice recovered a bit in extent. This led many climate-change deniers (also called contrarians) to screech that the whole business of global warming was a hoax perpetrated by thousands of felonious climate scientists looking for more and more research money. This would, of course, be the largest group of hoaxers in the history of humanity—larger by probably two orders of magnitude. And, on second thought, a bit unlikely. (In point of fact, 2008 had the second smallest minimum).

It would be fair to say that all the thousands of scientists truly involved in researching climate change make a distinction between weather and climate, but deniers don't. The few contrarians who are actual scientists mostly have degrees in fields other than climatology, and most of them do research paid for by commercial interests such as the oil, gas, and coal industry, which have a stake in not rushing us into the world of sustainable energy.

Weather is what happens from day to day, week to week, even year to year. Like politics, it is local: hot, cold, dry, wet, whatever comes along. For example, people living in much of the United States experienced unusually cold weather in the summer of 2009, bringing out the contrarians, of course. But *the average temperature of the entire globe* in 2009 was the second highest in the long period in which instrumental data have been collected, starting about 1880.

Taking the last thirty years, say, of annual measurements of the Earth's average temperature, one finds the high points rising and falling from year to year . . . with an overall trend headed upward. That upward line on the graph is, in fact, climate change, an unmistakable warming of the globe overall, and over time, regardless of a huge snowfall in Cleveland or a cool summer in Montana. There simply are no rational ifs or buts about it. The world is warming, and the trend will continue even if the nations of the planet come together in miraculous unison this month and take massive steps to stop it. This is because the conditions—chiefly but not only increased carbon dioxide in the atmosphere—are already in play and will remain that way for a long time. Once carbon dioxide gets into the atmosphere, it remains there for centuries. In other words, the world is fundamentally stuck with today's conditions, for an unknown number of decades at the least. The human race has never run an experiment this big, this fast-moving, and this dangerous.

The extent of the summer ice in the Arctic can and does grow or shrink every year. A lot of this depends on local—yes—weather conditions in the Arctic, some of which are brought about by such distant phenomena as El Niños and La Niñas in the Pacific Ocean, and such local forces as changing wind patterns. The extent of the ice is important; among other things, the ice is white and reflects the Sun's heat away from the Earth, while the open ocean is dark and absorbs the solar heat, warming up the oceans in which the ice rests. (The varying reflectivity of the Earth's surface—high with ice and white sand deserts, low with forests and open ocean—is called the albedo effect.) So the ice is being melted from both warmer atmosphere above and warmer water underneath.

How much has warmer water in the Arctic Ocean reduced the ice from below? This was hard to ascertain until recently. For fifty years or so, the U.S. Navy (and presumably the Russian navy as well) developed detailed information about the changing depths of the bottom of the sea ice, and thus its thickness, the better not to bump into it. And of course, the better to find places where a submarine could surface by breaking through the ice. Once the Soviet Union disintegrated and the Russian bear seemed to be less of a threat, these data, secret till then, were released; along with other technologies coming on line, they can give scientists a better notion of the thickness of the ice as it changes over time. It is the volume of the ice that is the important parameter over time.

More subtly, but a major influence on the phenomenon of the deicing of the Arctic, is the age of the ice at any given place. Old ice is the result of several winters' worth of freezing in excess of what melts during the summers. It becomes heavier, thicker, more durable. Young ice, the result of one winter's freezing of open ocean water, is thinner, easier on icebreakers, and far more quickly melted away. As the overall extent and volume of the ice diminish in the summer, winter creates more one-year-old ice. Thin ice. And the volume of ice overall in the Arctic is thus diminished. Although an enormous array of other forces, small and large, are involved in this process (air and water temperatures being still on the rise is the major force), it is not difficult to see that growing regions of new ice can produce a situation where eventually new ice leads inexorably to only new ice, and to a growing area of Arctic Ocean that is altogether ice-free in summer.

This series of events seems to have begun. Since a peak in 1980, the sea ice thickness has declined by a stunning 53 percent, or what Tom Wagner, a cryosphere manager at NASA, called "truly one of the biggest changes in environmental conditions on Earth since the end of the ice age." Multiyear ice has suffered a dramatic drop, and thin seasonal ice is now more widespread than multiyear ice.

The point where ice volume loss is irrevocable by any means known is called a turning point. There are some scientists who speculate that 2007, with the smallest extent of summer ice so far, was in fact the turning point that now leads irreversibly to ice-free summers in the Arctic. According to Jim Hansen, the NASA planetary and earth scientist who is most associated with sounding the alarm but who is also doing some of the most compelling science about climate change, "There is a strong consensus among Arctic researchers that we are faced with a clear and imminent threat to the continued existence of summer ice in the Arctic." The real questions, he goes on to say, "are how fast the ice would be lost and how dramatic the feedbacks on tundra, methane hydrates, and Greenland would be."

The work of feedback loops is another phenomenon to which the contrarians pay little or no heed. There are two kinds of feedback loops: positive and negative. They are not aptly named since most positive feedback is bad news, and most negative feedback is just what the doctor ordered. The simplest example of negative feedback is a thermostat. It is set to turn on the furnace when the thermostat says, for example, 60 degrees. The furnace kicks on and when the heat in the house reaches, say, 68 degrees, the thermostat is told to say "off," allowing the house to remain near 69 for as long as the insulation permits. The house eventually cools off to 60 degrees, and the process starts again.

Positive feedback occurs if the thermostat cannot read the instruction to turn off at 69 degrees and continues to heat the house to some intolerable point.

Climate change seems beset by far more positive feedback than negative. Among the scary positive feedback systems at work, a major one involves permafrost, the ground in the northern tundras of the Arctic that remains frozen year-round to depths as great as a thousand yards. As atmospheric temperatures rise in the Arctic, the upper layers of permafrost are defrosted; how much varies greatly from place to place. Houses, pipelines, and other structures that are built on permafrost will then sink into the newly unfrozen, soft soil. However inconvenient this may be (and a number of native villages have simply flopped over), what is worse is that the permafrost contains a great deal of carbon in the form of frozen organic matter, some of which turns to gas—specifically methane. As the permafrost melts, it expels carbon and methane into the atmosphere. Methane itself is an extremely efficient greenhouse gas, much more potent in this regard than plain old carbon dioxide. That's the bad part. The somewhat better part is that, once in the atmosphere, methane turns into carbon dioxide, a less potent greenhouse gas, so methane exercises its potency for a relatively short time. But on the bad side again, carbon dioxide, once in the atmosphere, is likely to remain there for centuries. This is a positive feedback system, amplifying the initial effect. Another source of methane that may well come into play in the Arctic is known as methane hydrates, or gas located deep in the ocean where it freezes with water. Once the ocean temperature rises sufficiently, the methane is released and rises to the surface and thence into the atmosphere.

Methane is also found in great quantities in coal mining operations, land-fills, and agricultural and waste management installations. It is twenty-three times more potent a greenhouse gas than carbon dioxide, so it is far better from the standpoint of global warming to capture as much escaping methane as possible and burn it (as a form of natural gas) than to let it float free. Turning it into carbon dioxide by burning it, Hansen says, reduces its warming potency by 97 percent. The Arctic Ocean is the major source of methane hydrates, and a number of Arctic nations are avidly eyeing ways of capturing it and selling it.

Many other positive (or amplifying) feedback loops exist in the climate change arena. One is water vapor held in the atmosphere. The warmer the temperature, the more water vapor the atmosphere can hold. Water vapor is a potent greenhouse gas, raising the temperature yet more. One of the most potent nongas substances, called aerosols, that cause greenhouse warming is black carbon—essentially soot—which is produced by diesel engines, the seasonal burning of agricultural waste and manure, and household burning of coal, especially in China and India. Black carbon is also a major pollutant of the air we breathe. Of course, it absorbs heat and is considered a substantial contributor to global warming, but the processes that create black soot also create other aerosols, such as sulfates, that are "white." Thus some of the production of bad black soot creates a cooling effect via other chemicals. On the whole, however, black carbon is a big cause of warming. Conversely, such formerly suspect natural events as changes in the Sun's radiation and volcanic eruptions have now been shown to produce relatively trivial amounts of climate warming.

Even with all of these myriad contributors to climate change, one of the best means so far of tracking global warming is to measure the amount of carbon dioxide in the atmosphere, it being the champion greenhouse gas. It can be tracked back millions of years, it has been directly measured with ever more sensitive instruments since the 1970s, and it can be projected into the future through mathematical models with which the climate-change world now teems.

Soon after the turn of the present century, the United Nations took on the chore of assessing global climate change, creating the Intergovernmental Panel on Climate Change (IPCC). The commission's task was to gather all the plausible scientific studies then available and create the clearest and least ambiguous possible picture of what was driving it, what the results were and would be in the future, and when and what policies needed to go into effect to slow down climate change.

For example, a question arising from the warming up of the Arctic and the visible shrinkage of the summer sea ice is when the Arctic Ocean will be essentially ice-free in the summer. The IPCC concluded that it would occur in or about the year 2050, some forty to forty-five years hence. (The commission's report, by the way, was issued in 2007, before the summer ice reached its least extent on record.) Not surprisingly, there were those who complained that the report was not conservative enough, and those who thought the problems were going to grow more extreme earlier than 2050. It was the latter group whose complaint was borne out in the prediction of an open polar sea in summer.

The World Wildlife Fund joined up with the Catlin Arctic Survey to measure the thickness of the ice (by manual drilling) across the northern part of the Beaufort Sea, a region traditionally characterized by thick multiyear ice. They found that the route is now characterized almost entirely by one-year ice. This led Peter Waldhams of Cambridge University's Polar Ocean Physics Group to say in 2009 that the survey "supports the new consensus view—based on seasonal variation of ice extent and thickness, changes in temperatures, winds and especially ice composition—that the Arctic will be ice-free in summer within about 20 years, and much of that decrease will be happening in 10 years." A turning point may well have been reached.

The Arctic has served as a global air conditioner for thousands of years. As the World Wildlife Fund's Martin Sommerkorn said, the "Arctic sea ice holds a central position in our Earth's climate system. Take it out of the equation and we are left with a dramatically warmer world. . . . Such a loss of Arctic sea ice [could] set in motion powerful climate feedbacks which will have an impact far beyond the Arctic itself—self-perpetuating cycles, amplifying and accelerating the consequences of global warming."

Meanwhile, most climate modelers and others agreed that the amount of carbon dioxide in the Earth's atmosphere was then in the neighborhood of 380 parts per million, which seems to the layman like a ridiculously small amount of gas to produce such large planetwide effects, but climate sensitivity on this order is the reality of nature. At the same time, it could be shown that a couple of hundred years ago, before the onset of the Industrial Revolution, the carbon dioxide level was some 280 parts per million. The IPCC concluded that if the nations of the Earth jointly reduced the amount of carbon dioxide to about 350 parts per million, the worst possible effects of global warming could be minimized and in the very long run, as in a century, significantly reduce the amount of carbon dioxide in the atmosphere. But as matters speed up in the Arctic, Hansen and others believe, carbon dioxide in the atmosphere has to be brought back close to pre-industrial levels lest the world become unlivable. And time is running out.

One of the most feared long-term effects of global warming—especially if it goes unchecked, but even if it can be slowed down somewhat—is rising sea levels. Outside of the loss of the great ice shelves of Antarctica (a process lagging behind the Arctic losses of sea ice), nothing in the world could raise sea level like the loss of the Greenland Ice Sheet. The ice sheet is almost unimaginably immense, second only to that covering Antarctica. The Greenland Ice Sheet is 110,000 years old and covers 660,000 square miles. Almost 2 miles thick at the maximum, it is 1,500 miles long and 680 miles at the widest. In all, it consists of slightly more than 680 cubic miles of ice. Were the Greenland Ice Sheet to melt altogether, it would raise the level of the world's oceans by some 23 feet, enough to drown virtually every coastal city and huge portions of coastal nations such as Bangladesh. Most small island nations, like the Maldives and Tuvalu, would simply disappear beneath the waves.

How long would it take for this unimaginably colossal ice sheet to melt away? Hundreds, maybe thousands of years, scientists have suggested. But some, including Hansen, suggest we have no real idea of how fast it could melt. In his book, Hansen presents a scary photograph that shows a few tiny figures of men standing on the ice next to a huge hole down which melt water is pouring. These holes are called moulins; it is believed they drain water all the way down to the Greenland bedrock. Water, between bedrock and glacial ice, could very likely serve as a lubricant.

One NASA estimate says that in the period between July 2003 and July 2008, the ice sheet lost some 200 billion tons of water every year. As Heidi Cullen of Climate Central writes, "That works out to the equivalent of Lake Erie draining into the ocean every two years." Scientists have confirmed by satellite observations and atmospheric models that this rate is in fact accelerating along the glacial edges. Surface melting began to increase around 1996, but so did snowfall, which moderated the melting, keeping the overall losses of ice to half of what otherwise would have occurred. Even so, the melting is sufficiently rapid that the land beneath the Greenland ice is rising at an accelerated pace. If the current acceleration continues, the rise will be two inches a year by 2020. (Much the same thing is occurring in Iceland and Svalbard.)

When the ice sheets were building, their weight suppressed the land; now it is rebounding, and the fact that the rising is accelerating is yet another indication that Greenland's rate of ice loss is doing so as well. The University of Miami's Yan Jiang, who was a leader of the uplift study, suggested that if this continues, the Greenland Ice Sheet could become the major contributor to global sea level rise.

As these very words were being written, on August 5, 2010, a giant island of ice covering nearly 100 square miles—about four times the size of Manhattan—split off from the Petermann Glacier between Ellesmere Island and northeastern Greenland. The ice island had been the northern tongue of the glacier, floating on the water and riddled with cracks, when it broke off. Now it is the largest iceberg to have formed in the Arctic since 1963. Most Arctic icebergs that "calve" into the sea—somewhere between ten and forty thousand of them—are more on the order of hundreds of yards in length, though many much larger ones have calved over the years, an example being the Jacobshavn Isbrae glacier, part of which sank the *Titanic*. The rate of calving has picked up considerably in recent years, lending special credence to the idea that warming ocean temperatures are causing the edges of glaciers to melt more rapidly. Most estimates show the entire Greenland Ice Sheet taking centuries to melt entirely, but many such estimates of the rate of melting ice in the Arctic have been found to need revision as the actual melting rates have exceeded the estimates in so many cases. We can safely say that low-lying places such as the Outer Banks of North Carolina are not suddenly going to disappear in the waves as a result of this giant ice island, but it is an ominous reminder of things to come.

Another way altogether to look at what may lie ahead is to go far back in time to a warm period between two bouts of glaciation. This is the Eemian period, which began around 130,000 years ago and lasted some 16,000 years. An organization from the University of Copenhagen, the North Greenland Eemian Ice Drilling Project, is probing a core in the Ice Sheet that will include, at its bedrock bottom, ice from the Eemian. From that ice core they will be able to look carefully at the Eemian's warmest years, and in the process examine in great detail an analogue of what the Earth now faces in this period of global warming.

Scientists already know that the Greenland Ice Sheet shrank by some 30 percent in the Eemian, contributing 3 to 7 feet to an overall global rise in sea level of 6 to 10 feet. From the various particles and molecules in ice cores, scientists can determine local temperature, ocean surface temperature, and various other conditions, and from tiny bubbles of air trapped among the ice crystals it is possible to measure the amount of greenhouse gases such as carbon dioxide in the actual atmosphere of a distant age. During the Eemian there was a lot less carbon dioxide in the atmosphere than today. And yet the sea level was far higher than it is now. Although this suggests the possibility of something else being at work (perhaps melting ice from Antarctica or the melting of methane hydrates), it also suggests we are entering the danger zone as far as carbon dioxide level is concerned. It is now higher than it has been for millions of years.

11 ANIMALS

CHANGING THE GUARD

A polar bear stands on a fragment of her former territory, a sliver of brilliantly white ice in a darkened sea. This is an iconic photograph, almost a cliché among the many symbols and graphics of the public media signaling the oncoming changes in the planet's climate. The polar bear stands at the top of the Arctic food chain (leaving aside humans, of course). It is the ultimate predator there, one of the largest of living bears, finely tuned by thousands of years of adaptation to live almost entirely in and on two forms of water: liquid and solid, ocean and ice.

We learn with a certain sense of irony that about 150,000 years ago some brown bears living within the Arctic Circle began evolving very rapidly, adapting to the opening of new (frozen) habitats. What is ironic is that the polar bear we know came about in perhaps as little as 20,000 years, which in evolutionary terms is a mere trice. We know this thanks to a fossil jaw and tooth of a polar bear that were found on the Svalbard archipelago of Norway in 2004. Polar bear fossils are extremely rare; once a polar bear dies, its body tends to fall through the ice into the ocean depths, or to be quickly scavenged. Analyzing the fossil's DNA (specifically the mitochondrial DNA that exists in the body's cells only and that is passed on exclusively from the mother) allowed researchers at the University of Buffalo and the University of Oslo to make the evolutionary connection of polar bears to the brown bear populations living today on Alaska's Admiralty and other islands.

Early in the polar bears' career, having adapted to the extreme cold anatomically, physiologically, and behaviorally, they then had to survive an interglacial warming period. How they survived is not known, but scientists believe the changes in the Arctic today may be occurring at too rapid a pace for polar bears to adapt and survive as they did before. They are now more "evolutionarily constrained,"

Charlotte Lindqvist of Oslo's Museum of Natural History says, because they have become so highly specialized to living the icy life. For example, the females hollow out a nest in the snow where the cubs are born. But with the rains coming earlier these days in some places, those dens collapse before the cubs can be moved, and they perish.

What is probably the most reliable study of polar bear numbers was released in 2009 by the U.S. Fish and Wildlife Service, documenting the status of polar bears (and walruses) in the Southern Beaufort Sea, which is shared by the United States and Canada, and also in the Chukchi/Bering Sea shared by the United States and Russia. At least 1,397 polar bears were counted in the Beaufort Sea, but "human-caused mortality" was found to be taking the lives of 54 animals a year, well over the sustainable rate of 22 polar bears killed a year. Similarly, an unsustainable number of polar bears are lost annually in the Russian waters, up to 250 animals from a population of about 2,000.

Responding to these data, Brendan Cumming of the Center for Biological Diversity (which has an oceans program though it is located in the desert of Tucson) said they confirm what biologists have long known: "Even if the population numbers are not precise, we know that without their sea-ice habitat they are likely doomed."

On the other hand, some Southern Beaufort Sea polar bears may be getting a slight jump on the relentless messing up of their traditional habitat. This is seen in another study by bear biologist Karyn Bode of the U.S. Fish and Wildlife Service, released in January 2010. She cautions that the long-term study was primarily aimed at tracking changes in bowhead whale migration routes, and polar bear population figures were an ancillary feature. Nevertheless, they do seem to confirm that over a twenty-seven-year period, "bears that use the nearshore area are more likely to occur on land in recent years because their preferred habitat, sea ice, is unavailable." Between 1979 and 1987, only 12 percent of bear sightings were on land, not ice. Between 1997 and 2005, however, 90 percent of bear sightings were on land, not ice.

Of course, the more time polar bears spend on open land, the more likely they are to run into people. Far northern settlements are certain to become more common as the warming, increasingly ice-free Arctic hosts large-scale mining, oil and gas development, and other visitors, including tourists and adventurous yachtsmen. In confrontations that arise, the humans will almost surely prevail. These days the Canadian town of Churchill is the most reliable place to see polar bears since so many of them come into town to scavenge garbage and hunt house pets, a kind of melancholy experience for all, one assumes. Is an inland-dwelling garbage-eating polar bear really a polar bear?

Given the odds, it is not likely that polar bears will be able to evolve into something quite different to match the new environment that is on the way, changing its anatomy and physiology and behavior practically overnight.

The odds are not improved by the findings of Robert Rockwell of the American Museum of Natural History in New York and his colleagues, that more grizzly bears have been seen roaming polar bear habitat in northern Manitoba. Grizzlies were long since thought extirpated from this region, with the barren lands of Hudson Bay keeping them to the south where they could feed happily on berries and meat (caribou, moose, fish). It isn't clear yet whether the grizzlies are staying in polar bear country year-round, but if and when they do there will be considerable competition among the two populations. Rockwell says grizzlies "are a new guy on the scene, competition, and a potential predator for the polar bears that live in the area." Grizzlies, he says, would almost surely hibernate in the same area where mother polar bears den, with the grizzlies emerging from their dens at the right time to prey on the polar bear cubs. Alternatively, there is evidence in the form of several hybrids that polar bears and grizzlies can interbreed successfully, so it possible that the pure polar bear may eventually disappear into the realm of what might be called the pizzly bear. Norwegian scientists have recently found another threat that polar bears face. Along with certain gulls, they are the Arctic animals most at risk from the alphabet soup of pollutants and contaminants such as PCBs and DDT carried north from the industrialized nations in ocean currents.

For polar bears, if it isn't one thing, it's another.

Yet another large Arctic mammal could find itself the prey of northward-bound grizzly bears: musk oxen. These Pleistocene creatures live in the harsh world of the Arctic tundra and, attractively, gather into a united front—a wall—to shield their young from predators such as wolves. It has been speculated that the arrival of human hunters in their midst some twelve thousand years ago was responsible for what has been perceived as a drastic decline in their numbers. At that period, many North American animals such as mammoths, giant sloths, and wooly rhinoceroses went extinct; some scientists argue that it was humans who brought the extinctions about. Others say it was the rapidly changing environment as the glaciers melted back into Canada, bringing on a chaotic patchwork of climate conditions that foreclosed the livelihoods of this great Ice Age fauna.

Using mitochondrial DNA, Beth Shapiro of Penn State and her colleagues have been able to show that fluctuations in musk oxen population over a hundred thousand years—including the decline that began twelve thousand years ago—were brought about by climate, the result of a warming that eradicated musk oxen across much of their range, leaving most of the remaining animals in Greenland. In fact, humans and musk oxen arrived at about the same time, and both populations began to expand.

No one knows exactly what it is about warmer temperatures that cause the oxen population to plunge, but with the current acceleration of warming in the Arctic the musk ox may well be in the same boat as the polar bear.

And so, most likely, is the walrus, that enormous, bewhiskered, and slightly goofy-looking sea mammal that for some people is a caricature of a member of the British House of Lords. The male walrus weighs up to 4,400 pounds, females considerably less. Extremely social animals, they spend the summer and autumn in groups of tens of thousands on beaches. The rest of the year they live (in smaller groups) on shelf ice, diving down some 600 feet to forage on the sea floor, using their sensitive facial bristles to locate clams (their preferred food) and a host of other benthic sea creatures.

Unlike seals, walruses need to pause and rest on the ice between dives, and they need a place for the calves to stay while the mothers feed themselves. The sea ice must be thick and strong to support their weight, but it is now growing thin near shore in many places, or melting altogether. To reach strong enough ice, the walruses need to head north, often for such distances that they become separated from their calves, which are then subject to drowning or starving. One observer on a Coast Guard icebreaker reported "the calves would be swimming around us crying. We couldn't rescue them." And once the walruses find ice in the north that will support them, they may also find themselves in waters so deep they cannot reach the seabed.

In 2007, an enormous group of about forty thousand walruses hauled out of the sea and onto the Russian coast, the largest such phenomenon ever known in the Russian Arctic and considered to be the result of the loss of thick ice in the Chukchi and East Siberian seas. Forty thousand animals does not sound like an endangered species, but long before the time that summers in the Arctic are mostly free of sea-ice, the walruses may be gone for good.

It appears likely that, except for some whale species, what are sometimes called the "charismatic megafauna" of the Arctic are headed for extinction or, in some cases, extremely reduced circumstances. They include the hooded seal, the main prey of polar bears; the ringed seal, which, like the polar bear, dens in a lair under the snow and loses pups when the lair collapses with early rains; and narwhals, once thought to be maritime unicorns. Caribou and reindeer numbers have dramatically declined in the last three decades overall, plunging nearly 60 percent according to a study by the University of Alberta released in 2009. Among problems brought on for these ungulate herds by the warming are more intense insect activity in the summer, and greening of the land earlier in spring ahead of the arrival of the migrating animals, meaning mothers and calves feed on lower-quality forage. More than likely, the reindeer and caribou can avoid extinction as long as the Inuit, Lapps, and other native inhabitants of the Arctic continue to see them as important to their traditional lifeways.

Complications to this picture of declining numbers keep turning up as ecological insights into the Arctic become more sophisticated and thorough. For example, a study led by Eric Post of Penn State and reported in 2009 showed that in the Low Arctic tundra some trees and shrubs have been growing farther north as (over the past two or three decades) the ice and snow cover receded northward. At the same time, shrubs and trees actually promote deeper snow accumulation, which in turn promotes higher soil temperatures in winter, and thus more microbial activity in soil, which in turn increases the suitability of the region for shrub growth. This perhaps lengthens the season during which the tundra serves as a carbon dioxide sink, the shrubs and trees taking up carbon dioxide from the atmosphere.

Indeed, it has been something of a certainty that the planting or natural spread of trees and shrubs is one of the best ways to slow down global warming since they sequester a lot of carbon dioxide during their lifetime of growth, releasing it only when they die and decay. It is also known that trees, in the process of evapotranspiration (a plant's version of sweating water through small leaf pores called stomata), act as air conditioners, cooling the surround to some degree. But now, sorry to say, researchers at the Carnegie Institution for Science have found that when the carbon dioxide level in the atmosphere is high, the leaf pores shrink, causing less water to evaporate and the tree's cooling effect to cease.

The researchers at Carnegie say this effect, blocking evaporation, causes considerable warming itself. Averaged over the entire globe, the blockage causes 16 percent of the current warming of the land surface, while in certain parts of North America, eastern Asia, and most of the Amazon rain forest it causes more than 25 percent. These results may be challenged and quite possibly emended by future studies, as is so often the case in the scientific exploration of the world. Meanwhile, this polar study—the sort of thing that is released to the public almost daily—is a useful reminder that something as large as a planet's atmosphere and as small as a leaf's pores act in strange and yet-to-be-thoroughly-understood ways. This is another factor that probably needs to be included in the vast array of calculations in accurately modeling what we are doing to our world, in this, the greatest experiment ever run by humans.

Back to the trees and shrubs moving northward: musk oxen and reindeer browse on them, limiting their function as a carbon dioxide sink. At the same time, the grazing, trampling, and manure production of the herbivores encourages the growth of grasses, which attract geese, whose presence increases the productivity of lakes. Furthermore, with less widespread snow cover and a longer growing season in Svalbard, the wild reindeer have benefited in terms of reproductive success. But Low Arctic reindeer have apparently been unable to adjust their calving season to synchronize with the growing season, which is causing population decline. According to Eric Post, "Inuit hunters at my study site in Greenland have all but given up on caribou hunting there. What," Post wonders, "will be the next component to disappear from their traditional lifestyle, a lifestyle that has worked for thousands of years?"

Post points out that most of the scientific efforts so far to understand Arctic ecosystems have focused on the melting Arctic ice in the summers. But equally important, he says, are other results of warming temperatures. The Arctic is a summer home for thousands upon thousands of shorebirds and other migratory birds. Birds migrate to the Arctic in spring and summer from five continents, and how they fare in the north every year has effects that are worldwide. For example, in the early spring thousands of shorebirds called knots leave their wintering grounds in South America and head north, arriving on the beaches of Delaware just as a separately timed migration of horseshoe crabs arrives there as well. The female crabs (they aren't crabs but more like ancient trilobites), having traveled thousands of miles impelled by the rhythms of the moon, through the Atlantic from Africa, deposit their eggs in the Delaware sand and head back out to sea. The knots, at this waystation, feed voraciously on the buried horseshoe crab eggs, allowing the birds to continue their migration, ending up in the Arctic with time to nest and for their young to emerge, just as the warming temperatures there bring forth enormous swarms of insects to feed on. One might say that in such migrations, as in show business, everything is timing. And the timing is now off in many instances.

Some migrants to the Arctic have indirectly changed their timing, not of course because they know the warming is occurring sooner in the far north. Instead, some accidentally have earlier breeding dates, meaning that the young are born early as well. Early birth also seems to bring about earlier northward migration later on. This response to warming summers in the Arctic has been found occurring in a variety of birds—some of the change taking place in only two or three generations. But this cannot be the case for knots. With Arctic warming occurring earlier than it has during the millions of years of this precisely timed multipartner dance, the knots will have to make up all their time only in the journey from Delaware to the Arctic, or perish. It is not at all likely that the horseshoe crabs are going to hurry up on their way to Delaware.

Overall, warmer summers in the Arctic are challenging all manner of nesting seabirds. Accustomed to cold, dry summers, they now confront more storms, heavy fog, rain, freezing rain, wet snow, and stronger winds. The main causes of mortality until recently—fishery collapse, parasites, introduced rats and other predators, and storms at sea—have changed. Now these migrants encounter additional dangers: crashing into one another or cliffs during thick fogs, being slammed into the ocean by winds rushing downslope, as well as heat stress and blood loss from excessive mosquito bites. On cliffs where thousands of shorebirds nest, melting snow and chunks of ice fall more frequently, the result of more common freeze-thaw actions, and take the young birds with them to drown in the sea.

The oceans themselves are undergoing a significant sea change besides the increase in water temperature, which itself causes the water to swell in volume, adding to actual rises in sea level occurring in numerous parts of the world. An extraordinary fact is that about one-third of all the manmade carbon dioxide emissions—from such disparate sources as fossil fuel use, cement plants, deforestation, and other human activities too numerous to mention—end up in the ocean waters. The carbon dioxide that enters the oceans decreases the water's pH, creating a cascade of chemical changes that are known, in a general sense, as ocean acidification. It is also known that whether or not humans are able to curb these emissions, the ocean will continue to grow more acidic, and the long-term effects of this remain unknown but are unlikely to be beneficent. During the existence of the industrial revolution, which began around the 1830s, the average pH of the oceans deceased by what seems a very light amount. In the early 1800s, the pH was 8.2. Today it is 8.1. (The lower it is, the more acidic, as many owners of home pools have learned.) But life in the oceans has adapted over hundreds of thousands of years to an average pH of 8.2, so again we are creating a considerable change over a very small amount of time. Various computer models show a continuing decrease of two or three units by the end of this century, making the ocean more acidic than it has been for hundreds of thousands of halcyon years of marine evolution. Fairly simple experiments have shown that the most immediate near-term effects of this sudden change will be on marine organisms with calcium carbonate shells—that is, tiny shrimplike animals called copepods whose carbon-based shells dissolve in water if it is too acidic, and animals such as clams whose stages of growth are severely stunted by increased acidity, creating smaller versions.

If one could weigh all the copepods in the world, their weight, some say, would be greater than that of any other creature (though others say this record belongs to ants). In any event, copepods are a major link in the Arctic food chain, grazing on algae (the bottom of the Arctic food chain) that live on the bottom of the sea ice and in miniscule tunnels throughout. Various wormlike creatures squeeze into the tunnels and graze on the algae that also feeds the copepods. Copepods in turn (along with squid and octopus) are a major food source for skinny little fish called Arctic cod, which school in the thousands and feed everything from the Arctic's larger fish to birds, narwhals, and other marine mammals, and on up to polar bears and humans. As Alun Anderson writes, "Any change that happens down here, at the bottom of this web, may alter the shape of the whole web of life in the Arctic seas." And this includes the Bering Sea and the Barents Sea, two of the world's most productive fishing grounds.

Change, of course, is exactly what is happening throughout the Arctic, most of it unprecedented and most of it faster than anyone would have predicted only a decade ago. The details of the changes, their ramifications throughout the Arctic and the lands and waters to the south, can only be guessed at now. What large mammal will take over the exalted position in the food chain of the polar bear? What warm water copepod will take over from the one that thrives in the icy waters of the Barents Sea? Thousands of scientists from disciplines most people have never heard of are currently, almost frantically, trying to establish baselines from which the rapid alteration of the Arctic ecosystems can be measured and understood. Many others, conservation scientists, desperately seek ways to hold on to some of the ecosystems and their inhabitants, maintaining them into a future that remains ill understood. Their work is something akin to the efforts of the French doctor in the novel *The Plague*, by Albert Camus. It is work one must do simply because one can, however hopeless it may be.

The Arctic, unlike rain forests, grasslands, coral reefs, and other ecosystems, is not a hotbed of biodiversity. There are relatively few species, all beautifully adapted to a very harsh surround, one that is in itself delicately balanced. Speaking not of the Arctic specifically but of biodiversity in general, the British magazine *New Scientist* ran a brief editorial in April 2010, entitled "Let's Put an End to Biosentimentality." It spoke of the controversial topic of introduced species and concluded by saying, "With a large proportion of species set for extinction in the coming century, we cannot be choosy about future sources of diversity. If we want thriving ecosystems we may have to embrace exotic invaders. . . . This prospect may horrify many. But it is too late to be sentimental about the past."

12 WHO OWNS THE ARCTIC?

On November 28, 2008, the Canadian Broadcasting Company confirmed reports that the *Camilla Degagnes*, a commercial cargo ship strengthened against the depredations of ice on hulls, had sailed from Montreal and resupplied four of the remote western hamlets of Nunavuk. If the ghost of John Franklin were still beset somewhere near King William Island, it was now free to go wherever newly satisfied ghosts go, for this was the first transit of the Northwest Passage made without the help of an icebreaker. Indeed, the crew reported that during the entire voyage through the passage no ice was to be seen. This ice-free route through the Northwest Passage occurred some thirty to fifty years before most computer models of the changing climate of the Arctic said it was likely to come about.

Not only is this feat a signal that the centuries-old dream of finding a path from the Atlantic to the Arctic Ocean and thence to Asia (and the reverse) has now been achieved. Commercial traffic will soon be a reality, in the summer months at least—including freighters, supertankers, cruise ships, adventure-seeking yacht owners, perhaps even American aircraft carriers, all plying the Northwest Passage (at least in the summer). It served to stir up an old diplomatic problem between Canada and the United States that had been discussed over the years in Ottawa and Washington, though never with great urgency.

The issue to be decided was (and still is) whether the Northwest Passage is an internal waterway of Canada or, as the United States prefers, an international strait, part of the open ocean and governed chiefly by the freedom of the seas. One flap occurred in 1969 when the United States sent an ice-strengthened supertanker, the *Manhattan*, through the passage. It was at the time the largest commercial ship ever to sail under the Stars and Stripes. Accompanied by an icebreaker, its mission was to test the passage as a route for taking oil from Alaska's Prudhoe Bay oil fields to the Atlantic Seaboard.

Such a route would be some 4,000 miles shorter than the one through the Panama Canal, a prodigious savings in fuel, time, and other costs. Consonant with its definition of the passage, the United States made a point of not asking Canada's permission. Rather than let this pass, thereby creating a precedent, the Canadian government awarded the United States permission for the journey and even provided a Canadian icebreaker to help out as needed.

This was a semifriendly sort of diplomatic jousting between allied governments, even though much of the Canadian public was outraged. By contrast, the American public was largely unaware of any fuss, much less what it was all about. Many Canadians tend to feel that their northern lands and waters are very much part of their history and identity and are jealous of their prerogatives in the Arctic. Until recently (for example, the 1980s), the American public—outside of Alaskans—has thought of the Arctic Ocean as something barely relevant to the business of the United States, except for keeping an eye on the Soviet Union by means of the North American Aerospace Defense Command (NORAD) and the Distant Early Warning Line (DEW), in which efforts Canada was a partner, and submarines. In any event, Canadians who live in the Arctic tend to resent the ignorance and impositions of those whom they call with some derision southerners, and this includes not just Americans but Canadians in such places as Ottawa and Toronto.

In any event, the flap over the *Manhattan* was dealt with according to the intent of the UN Convention on the Law of the Sea, which was signed and ratified starting in 1982 by most maritime nations of the world. Unsurprisingly, the treaty calls for maritime disputes between nations to be settled by diplomacy, not aggression. Of the five nations bordering on the Arctic Ocean, Russia, Norway, Denmark/Greenland (the latter is still part of the Kingdom of Denmark), and Canada are signatories to this treaty. Only the United States has refused to sign and ratify it, though successive administrations have for the most part adhered to its principles.

Another American use of the Northwest Passage long preceded the *Manhattan*: nuclear attack submarines dispatched not merely to achieve the North Pole but also to explore the ocean bottom and the state of the ice above, and to be on the lookout for their equally lethal Soviet counterparts lurking off North America. Such expeditions were not public or announced by the U.S. Navy, and certainly permission from the other Arctic nations was never sought. Some of these journeys took the submarines under the ice of the Northwest Passage, and the Canadian government almost surely knew they were occurring. This would appear to be an early example of international "don't ask, don't tell."

What is at stake in this squabble over the Northwest Passage? In fact, we should think of this disputed waterway in the plural, as the Northwest Passages, since northern and southern waterways are available that, in addition, cross over into each other at three points. The passages stretch across the bottom of the pyramid-shaped archipelago of islands that the British ceded to Canada in the nineteenth century. With a couple of minor exceptions, ownership of these islands has not been in dispute since. They are part of Canada.

The American view in this dispute is that the Northwest Passages connect two large expanses of the high seas—the Atlantic and Arctic Oceans—and that they have been used for international traffic. Looked at legally, the Americans say that Canada owns the waterway but foreign ships have every right to transit through. To back off from this perspective (the Americans fear) would set an unfortunate precedent, allowing free transit of waterways such as the Strait of Malacca to be confounded by other nations.

The Canadian view is that the passages are an internal Canadian waterway subject to the full force of Canadian law and requiring permission for their use. Once the *Manhattan* had successfully navigated the Northwest Passages (albeit with the active help of the Canadian icebreaker), the Canadians realized that they were, as matters stood, in no way capable of regulating foreign ships in this internal waterway. To do so responsibly would call for enormous expenditures on search-and-rescue capabilities, recordkeeping, and other associated chores, not to mention enforcing environmental regulations as well as immigration violations (some people had in fact sneaked into Canada after slipping onto cruise ships headed from Europe into the Canadian islands in the Arctic).

As part of enforcing environmental regulations, the Canadian government would have to see to it that ill-equipped rust-bucket container ships did not run afoul of the hundreds of miles of shorelines involved. "The Arctic marine ecosystem is one of the most fragile on earth," Michael Byers, professor of international law at the University of British Columbia, has written, "with incredibly specialized species relying on a precarious ice-water interface that is kept in balance by only fractions of a degree of temperature." The Canadians knew that oil spills in Arctic waters would be far more difficult to deal with than those in warm water. In ice-cold water, spilled oil leaves a toxic residue that will endure for many decades if not centuries. In 1970, rather than go head-to-head with the United States over the issue of the passages, the Canadian parliament adopted the Arctic Waters Pollution Prevention Act, which called for strict safety and environmental features on all ships within 100 nautical miles of the Canadian coast. The United States complained (territorial waters extended only 12 miles from land at that time), but after a decade or so the matter died down. The stringent Canadian act was effectively replaced by the 1982 UN Convention on the Law of the Sea.

In the 1970s, the Canadians also began referring to the passages as "historic internal waters," pointing out that people had been using the Northwest Passages for a very long time. The Canadian historic claim (which added weight to their claim of legal ownership) depended on the long British exploration of the region, starting with Frobisher in 1576, but much more to the point was millennia of Inuit hunting and fishing there, and even living directly on the ice. The frozen waterways of the passages had long served as highways for Inuit dog teams.

In 1988, the United States and Canada signed the Arctic Cooperation Agreement, which said that American icebreakers going through the passages would need the consent of Canada but it would never be denied. It amounted to a formal agreement to disagree over the legal status of the passages. At the turn of the century, the legal issue remained unresolved. As a practical matter, with the collapse of the Soviet Union, submarine traffic carried less of an international threat, though patrols by both sides continued. At one point the European Union proposed some principles by which the Northwest Passages should be managed; the proposal went nowhere, and in Canadian diplomatic circles a joke suggested that the proper response was for Canada to instruct the Mediterranean nations how to manage their sea.

In this century, as it became clear that the Arctic Ocean is losing ice at a rapid rate, a number of new national security concerns for both Canada and the United States became pressing. Rogue states, terrorist groups, and smugglers of drugs or even weapons of mass destruction might find ways to take advantage of an ice-free Northwest Passage. The Law of the Sea permits Canada to have total control over maritime use of the lands along the passages, such as loading and unloading cargo, and illegal immigrants taking leave of cruise ships. But this is not the same thing as owning (and patrolling) the entire route. As the period of ice-free months lengthens, the two North American countries will be compelled to produce more capable search-and-rescue operations and keep this long-unusable but now increasingly convenient channel free of international crime. Presently, and for the near future, customs agents as well as immigration and other law enforcement officials are few and far between, especially compared to that other hemispheric shipping route, the highly regulated Panama Canal.

Meanwhile, the Northeast Passage (what is called the Northern Sea Route these days and consists essentially of the waters off the northern shore of Russia, which extend from Murmansk to Kamchatka) will be opening up to largely ice-free commercial traffic before long. Even now, in late summer, ships can navigate through ice-free waters north of the Russian islands offshore that form the Northern Sea Route's actual course. The United States is not about to quarrel with Russia over the legal status of the Northern Sea Route. Besides the Northwest Passage, the eastern route is the only other waterway or strait in the world for which status has not already been settled legally. The Canada–U.S. dispute over the Northwest Passages will one day probably be settled by the United States letting Canada have its internal waterway status (after all, the Northwest Passage is some 800 miles long, hardly the same sort of practical matter as, say, the Bosporus). And once that is agreed, there should be few impediments to the two nations sharing the rapidly growing chores and costs of maintaining the passages.

In August 2007, a member of the Russian Duma (or parliament) led an expedition to the North Pole during which aquanauts planted a titanium canister containing a Russian flag in the ocean-bottom muck some 2 miles down at the North Pole. This was widely interpreted as a signal that Russia, whose northern shoreline comprises about one-half of the entire circle of lands around the Arctic Ocean, was muscularly claiming sovereignty over the entire ocean, causing a serious shudder among the four other Arctic Ocean nations. Some saw presentiments of war.

It turned out that the expedition was mounted by a man running for reelection to his seat in the Duma, that the Kremlin had not approved the effort, and that it was basically a PR stunt. As Premier Vladimir Putin pointed out, it had no more territorial meaning than the American flag Neil Armstrong placed on the moon in 1969. No country is likely ever to "own" the Arctic Ocean. It is also highly unlikely that the Arctic nations will sit still for a Norwegian claim of the North Pole, Norway being the closest nation to it. But quite a bit of the lands under the Arctic Ocean have already been divvied up among the five nations that border it, and not without some lingering disputes.

Territorial seas in the Arctic, as elsewhere, extend 12 miles out to sea. Sovereignty in these waters extends upward into the air space, and down the water column to and including the seabed. Beyond this limit are what are called exclusive economic zones. They extend from 12 to 200 miles from the shoreline and provide the nation with sovereign rights to explore, exploit, conserve, and manage both living and nonliving resources in the water column and the continental shelf. If one of the five countries determines that its continental shelf extends beyond the 200-mile limit, the country must apply to the UN Commission on the Limits of the Continental Shelf to confirm the rights. All the rest of the Arctic Ocean and its seabed is considered the common heritage of mankind, managed by the International Seabed Authority.

All five of the nations bordering the Arctic Ocean have busily explored the underwater world they can claim. Just where the continental shelf ends at any given point is a complicated matter, judged by some highly technical provisions to do with thickness of sediments and the shortest distance to the foot of the slope and other calculations. But given the length of its shoreline, Russia claims an area larger than Europe. In addition, Russia, Canada, and Denmark are eyeing an underwater mountain range, the Lomonosov Ridge, that runs north of Ellesmere Island and Greenland, apparently all three making a claim that the mountains are an extension of their continental shelves. This remains controversial and awaits some Solomonic judgments by the UN commission. Meanwhile, Greenland is well along the path to becoming its own nation—a sixth Arctic nation. In June 2009, it voted for new self-governance that specified Greenland would keep half of all revenues from oil, gas, and minerals discovered on the island, and for an unspecified period of time also receive an annual grant of $600 million from Denmark. As the revenues from drilling and mining begin to come in, the grant will be lowered or discontinued. But those revenues depend on further melting of the Ice Sheet (and a potentially devastating rise in global sea level).

Beyond the issue of the Lomonosov Ridge, which an independent Greenland might lay claim to as well, the remaining difficulties are chiefly the result of overlaps between bordering claims: chunks of seabed that are highly desirable given the amount of recoverable oil and natural gas that is reported to exist everywhere on the continental shelves. (The U.S. Geological Survey published a report saying that 13 percent of the world's oil reserves are in the Arctic, as is 30 percent of the world's natural gas.)

One dispute is between the United States and Canada over just such a good-sized chunk of sea floor in the Beaufort Sea, while the Russians and Norway squabble over another such chunk, as well as disagreeing over whether Russia can use land on the titularly Norwegian Svalbard Islands and fish in the surrounding seas. The United Nations leaves these overlap disputes to the nations involved to settle by diplomacy among themselves, or judgment by an agreed-on international court, or just agreeing to disagree and not exploit the disputed areas. Leaving oil and natural gas in the ground when the prices are right is not as yet a common attitude among mankind, though finding a way to do just that would be better for the planet. Another option for dealing with overlapping claims is to share the proceeds arising from exploiting a piece of disputed continental shelf. The need for resolution of these disputes will, of course, be all the more urgent once the actual amount of seabed natural resources involved becomes clear.

Meanwhile, all the Arctic Rim states held a summit in Greenland in May 2008, which Barry Scott Zellen, the editor of *Strategic Insights*, has called "the first step in this direction toward a collaborative management regime for Arctic maritime commerce and resource development."

The next steps cannot come soon enough.

13 THE GREENLAND EXAMPLE

On the last day of August 2010, four intrepid (or crazy, depending on one's point of view) members of Greenpeace suspended themselves from tents on an oil drilling rig named *Stena Don*, which was operated by Cairn Energy of Edinburgh and located in the ocean about a hundred miles offshore from west Greenland. The Cairn operation was the first drilling for oil in a decade in this area that is sportingly called Iceberg Alley, lying between Canada and western Greenland. And Cairn was the first to claim that it had located signs of significant reservoirs of hydrocarbons. Cairn said that Greenland might sit above billions of barrels of petroleum, and with Exxon Mobil and Chevron joining in this could make western Greenland a major producing center. Similar expectations exist for the waters off east Greenland.

Alarmed at this prospect, Greenpeace sent one of its ships, the *Esperanza*, to the site to protest the drilling and perhaps even interrupt it. The Greenpeace vessel was tailed by a Danish warship carrying commandos with the job of keeping Greenpeace from interfering.

"We caught them napping," said a Greenpeace official aboard the *Esperanza*. The four people in tents had food supplies for at least four or five days. Cairn made no comment while for some reason its stock fell 0.5 percent, which was better than a widely consulted European oil and gas index that fell by 1.7 percent. Cairn Energy is active in oil exploration not only in Greenland but in Tunisia, Bangladesh, Northern India, and Nepal. Their presence in Iceberg Alley and the presence of Greenpeace alongside is typical of the forces, fears, and events that are soon to be at work in almost every part of the Arctic waters.

As for Cairn Energy, its first drilling attempt, and two subsequent efforts, turned out to be disappointing failures. Even so, Greenland awarded new exploration licenses to eight companies, including Cairn, Shell, the Norwegian Statoil, and ConocoPhillips, with the expectation that these efforts might lead to yet further attempts farther offshore. Meanwhile, a Shell plan to drill in the Chukchi sea off Alaska was held up by the U.S. Environmental Protection Agency, which demanded a more elaborate analysis of the plan's effect on nearby Alaskan communities.

The nightmare for environmentalists and native communities was rendered all the more frightening by the BP calamity that played itself out in the Gulf of Mexico, as Cairn was drilling off Greenland in the short Arctic summer. Any oil spill in the Arctic Ocean is likely to be far more devastating than the BP spill, in spite of the fact that most of the drilling in the Arctic is and will be in waters that are only a third as deep as the Gulf blowout.

To begin with, suppose the blowout occurs in the latter days of the short four- to five-month ice-free period. There would not be time to drill a relief hole, not enough time before the ice began to set in, to avail oneself with whatever booms and other equipment might control the surface oil. And most oil drilling throughout the Arctic is going to occur in hard-to-reach, remote areas. On the other hand, the ice-free period will continue to grow longer. In any event, dealing with the rapidly changing and highly unpredictable climate and weather conditions of the Arctic will challenge the finest minds, the most assiduous inspections, and the best intentions of all concerned.

Cairn, of course, claims it is more careful than BP was and uses the safety techniques and inspections the Norwegians employ in their offshore drilling. (They've never had a blowout.) The Canadian government is releasing anti-spill equipment to those towns nearest drilling or potential drilling. But even with preparation and training, the 200-mile-an-hour winds that occasionally blow across Greenland could make it impossible for assistance to reach a rig that experienced a blowout.

Most of the people who live on Greenland (which is growing closer every year to becoming a completely autonomous territory) are looking forward to being citizens of a fabulously wealthy oil-producing nation. Granted semiautonomy by the Danes in 1979, it still receives an annual $600 million stipend from Denmark. Once oil revenues pour in, the mostly Inuit population of the world's biggest island (except for Australia) will be able to do without the stipend and, some say, become a new Saudi Arabia. A potentially similar future also lies ahead for the Inuit people of the new province of Nunavut, recently carved out of Canada's Northwest Territory and the Arctic archipelago. It is not clear how much the native people will share in the industrialization of the Russian Arctic.

Ironically, what will bring extraordinary wealth to many of the people of the Arctic is exactly what is bringing about the greatest change in the nature of the Arctic for many millions of years, and thus in the nature of the entire planet. Some if not many of the native peoples of the Arctic rue the vast and rapid changes taking place in their lives as a result of the warming, the loss of sea ice, and the end of the quiet hunting way of life. They are a bit sad that all this will be replaced by noisy, dirty, frantic, wealth-producing extractive industries. But the horse has already left the barn.

ILLUSTRATION CREDITS

Figure 2:   reproduced with the permission of the Naval Institute Press

Figure 4:   reproduced with the permission of the Naval Institute Press

Figure 5:   reproduced with the permission of Dr. Claire L. Parkinson, NASA Goddard Space Flight Center

Figure 6:   reproduced with the permission of Dr. Claire L. Parkinson, NASA Goddard Space Flight Center

Figure 7:   reproduced with the permission of Dr. Claire L. Parkinson, NASA Goddard Space Flight Center

Figure 8:   reproduced with the permission of Dr. Claire L. Parkinson, NASA Goddard Space Flight Center

Figure 15:   ©Penguin Books, Ltd. Reproduced with permission

Figure 22:   Image courtesy of William W. Fitzhugh, Smithsonian Institution.

Figure 24:   From *The Arctic Grail*, by Pierre Berton, © 1988 by Pierre Berton Enterprises Ltd. Used by permission of Viking Penguin, a division of Penguin Group (USA) Inc.

Figure 25:   From *The Arctic Grail*, by Pierre Berton, © 1988 by Pierre Berton Enterprises Ltd. Used by permission of Viking Penguin, a division of Penguin Group (USA) Inc.

Figure 26:   From *The Arctic Grail*, by Pierre Berton, © 1988 by Pierre Berton Enterprises Ltd. Used by permission of Viking Penguin, a division of Penguin Group (USA) Inc.

Figure 28:   From *The Arctic Grail*, by Pierre Berton, © 1988 by Pierre Berton Enterprises Ltd. Used by permission of Viking Penguin, a division of Penguin Group (USA) Inc.

Figure 31:   From *The Arctic Grail*, by Pierre Berton, © 1988 by Pierre Berton Enterprises Ltd. Used by permission of Viking Penguin, a division of Penguin Group (USA) Inc.

Figure 33:   From *The Arctic Grail*, by Pierre Berton, © 1988 by Pierre Berton Enterprises Ltd. Used by permission of Viking Penguin, a division of Penguin Group (USA) Inc.

BIBLIOGRAPHY

Aagaard, K., et al. 1996. "U.S., Canadian researchers explore Arctic Ocean." *Eos*, 77, 209, 213.

Ackley, S. F., W. D. Hibbler III, A. Kovacs, W. F. Weeks, A. Hartwell, and W. J. Campbell. 1973. *Investigations performed on the Arctic Ice Dynamics Joint Experiment, March 1971.* U.S. Army Cold Regions Research and Engineering Laboratory, Hanover, NH, Research Report 315.

Ahrens, C. D. 1988. *Meteorology today* (3rd ed.). West, St. Paul.

Amundsen, R. 1912. *The South Pole: An account of the Norwegian Antarctic expedition in the "Fram," 1910–1912,* vols. I and II. John Murray, London.

——. 1927. *My life as an explorer.* Doubleday, Page, New York.

——, and L. Ellsworth. 1927. *First crossing of the Polar Sea.* George H. Doran, New York.

Anderson, Alun. 2009. *After the ice: Life, death, and geopolitics in the New Arctic.* Smithsonian Books, HarperCollins, New York.

Anderson, W. R. 1959. *Nautilus–90–north.* World, Cleveland.

Andrée, S. A. 1896. "A plan to reach the North Pole by balloon." *Proceedings Sixth International Geographical Congress*, 211–27.

Anonymous. 1895. "Will never see the Pole." *New York Times*, 2 October, p. 9.

——. 1899. "The Sverdrup expedition." *American Geographical Society Bulletin*, 31, 91–93.

——. 1904. "An old story of Arctic exploration." *Scottish Geographical Magazine*, 20, 415–23.

——. 1909. "Cook's claim to discovery of the North Pole rejected; outraged Denmark calls him a deliberate swindler; having no original observations, he used Loose's 'fakes.'" *New York Times*, 22 December, pp. 1–3.

——. 1909. "Dr. Cook home; no proofs yet." *New York Times*, 22 September, pp. 1–2.

——. 1909. "Fraudulent observations made for Dr. Cook before his records sent to Copenhagen; sworn testimony of the men who made them." *New York Times*, 9 December, pp. 1–3.

——. 1909. "Peary lands; refuses honors." *New York Times*, 22 September, pp. 1–2.

——. 1926. "Amundsen back from lecture tour." *New York Times*, 4 March, p. 18.

——. 1926. "Amundsen in role of Cook's defender." *New York Times*, 24 January, p. 2.

———. 1978. "4 men, in a 44-day trek, reach the North Pole in snowmobiles." *New York Times*, 20 April, p. 68.

Asher, G. M., editor. 1860. *Henry Hudson, the navigator*. Hakluyt Society, London, no. 27.

Astrup, E. 1898. *With Peary near the Pole*. C. A. Pearson, London.

Balchen, B. 1958. *Come north with me*. Dutton, New York.

Barrow, J. 1818. *A chronological history of voyages into Arctic regions; undertaken chiefly for the purpose of discovering a north-east, north-west, or polar passage between the Atlantic and Pacific*. John Murray, London.

Beechey, F. W. 1843. *A voyage of discovery toward the North Pole*. Richard Bentley, London.

Belt, D. 1997. "An Arctic breakthrough." *National Geographic*, 191, 2, 36–57.

Bent, S. 1870. "Communication from Captain Silas Bent upon the routes to be pursued by expeditions to the North Pole." *American Geographical and Statistical Society Journal*, 2, 31–40.

Berton, P. 1988. *The Arctic grail: The quest for the North West Passage and the North Pole, 1818–1909*. Viking, New York.

Best, G. 1578. *A true discourse of the late voyages of discoverie, for the finding of a passage to Cathia*. Reprinted in 1867 for the Hakluyt Society, no. 38.

Browne, B. 1913. *The conquest of Mount McKinley*. Putnam, New York.

Bruemmer, F. 1966. "Kodlunar Island's gold rush." *Canadian Geographical Journal*, 72, 2, 48–51.

Bryce, R. M. 1997. *Cook and Peary: The polar controversy, resolved*. Stackpole Books, Mechanicsburg, PA.

Byers, M. 2009. *Who owns the Arctic? Understanding sovereignty disputes in the North*. Douglas & McIntyre, Vancouver/Toronto/Berkeley.

Calvert, J. 1960. *Surface at the Pole: The extraordinary voyages of the USS Skate*. McGraw-Hill, New York.

Caswell, J. E. 1956. *Arctic frontiers: United States explorations in the far north*. University of Oklahoma Press, Norman.

Central Intelligence Agency. 1978. *Polar regions atlas*. Washington, DC: U.S. Government Printing Office (stock number 041-015-00094-2).

Childs and Peterson. 1856. *Dr. Kane's great work*. Childs and Peterson, Philadelphia.

Clark, K. 1969. *Civilization*. New York: Harper and Row.

Colony, R., and A. S. Thorndike. 1984. "An estimate of the mean field of Arctic sea ice motion." *Journal of Geophysical Research*, 89, 10, 623–629.

Cook, F. A. 1908. *To the top of the continent*. Doubleday, Page, New York.

———. 1913. *My attainment of the Pole*. Polar, Chicago.

Corner, G. W. 1972. *Doctor Kane of the Arctic seas*. Temple University Press, Philadelphia.

Cullen, Heidi. 2010. *The weather of the future*. Harper, New York.

Daly, C. P. 1870. "Annual address: Review of the events of the year and recent explorations and theories for reaching the North Pole." *American Geographical and Statistical Society Journal*, 2, LXXXIII–CXXVI.

Davies, T. D. 1990. "New evidence places Peary at the Pole." *National Geographic,* 177, I. 44–61.

Deacon, M., and A. Savours. 1976. "Sir George Strong Nares (1831–1915)." *Polar Record,* 18, 113, 127–41.

Delgado, J. P. 1999. *Across the top of the world.* Facts on File, New York.

DeLong, E., ed. 1884. *The voyage of the* Jeanette: *The ship and ice journals of George W. DeLong.* Houghton, Mifflin, New York.

De Veer, G. 1609. *Three voyages by the north-east towards Cathay and China undertaken by the Dutch in the years 1594, 1595, and 1595.* Reprinted in 1878 for the Hakluyt Society, London, no. 13.

Dumas, D., ed. 1984. *Arctic: Handbook of North American Indians,* vol. 5. Smithsonian Institution, Washington, DC.

Ellsberg, E. 1940. "The drift of the *Jeanette* in the Arctic Sea." *American Philosophical Society,* 82, 889–96.

Ellsworth, L. 1927. "At the North Pole." *Yale Review,* 16, 738–48.

Emerson, C. 2010. *The future history of the Arctic.* Public Affairs, New York.

Fisher, D. E. 1992. *Across the top of the world.* Random House, New York.

Gad, F. 1970. *The history of Greenland.* Vol. I: *Earliest times to 1700.* London: C. Hurst, London.

Golder, F. A. 1914. *Russian expansion on the Pacific, 1641–1850. An account of the earliest and later expeditions made by the Russians along the Pacific coast of Asia and North America; including some related expeditions to the Arctic regions.* Arthur H. Clark, Cleveland.

Gordon, E. C. 1986. "The fate of Sir Hugh Willoughby and his companions: A new conjecture." *Geographical Journal,* 152, 243–47.

Greely, A. W. 1909. "Polar exploration during the year 1908." *Independent,* 66, 685–89.

Grierson, J. 1960. *Sir Hubert Wilkins: Enigma of exploration.* Robert Hale, London.

Guttridge, L. F. 1986. *Icebound: The* Jeanette *expedition's quest for the North Pole.* Naval Institute Press, Annapolis.

Haberman, F. W., ed. 1972. *Peace, Nobel lectures, vol. I.* Elsevier, Amsterdam.

Hall, T. F., 1917. *Has the North Pole been discovered?* Richard G. Badger, Boston.

Hansen, J. 2009. *Storms of my grandchildren: The truth about the coming climate catastrophe and our last chance to save humanity.* Bloomsbury USA, New York.

Harrisse, H. 1896. *John Cabot the discoverer of North-America and Sebastian his son.* Benjamin Franklin Stevens, London.

Hartwig, G. 1874. *The polar and tropical worlds: A description of man and nature in the polar and equatorial regions of the globe.* C. A. Nichols & Co., Springfield, Mass.; Hugh Heron, Chicago.

Hayes, I. I. 1867. *The Open Polar Sea: A narrative of a voyage of discovery towards the North Pole.* Hurd and Houghton, New York.

Henson, M. A. 1912. *A negro explorer at the North Pole.* Frederick A. Stokes, New York.

Herbert, M. 1973. *The snow people.* Putnam, New York.

Herbert, W. 1969. *Across the top of the world: The British Trans-Arctic expedition.* Longman, London.

———. 1971. *Across the top of the world: The last great journey on earth.* Putnam, New York.

———. 1988. "Did Peary reach the pole?" *National Geographic,* 174, 3, 414–29.

———. 1989. *The noose of laurels: The discovery of the North Pole.* Hodder and Stoughton, London.

Hibler, W. D., III, S. J. Mock, and W. B. Jackson III. 1974. "Classification and variation of sea ice ridging in the western Arctic Basin." *Journal of Geophysical Research,* 79, 2735–2743.

Hogarth, D. D., and J. Loop. 1986. "Precious metals in Martin Frobisher's 'black ores' from Frobisher Bay, Northwest Territories." *Canadian Mineralogist,* 24, 259–63.

Holland, C. 1994. *Arctic exploration and development c. 500 B.C. to 1915: An encyclopedia.* New York: Garland.

Hulburt, G. C. 1894. "The North Greenland expedition of 1891–1892." *American Geographical Society Journal,* 26, 74–77.

Huntford, R. 1980. *Scott and Amundsen.* Putnam, New York.

———. 1990. "The quiet heroism of Lincoln Ellsworth." *Smithsonian,* 21, 7, 171–88.

———. 1993. "Hot on the cold trail left by Sir Martin Frobisher." *Smithsonian,* 23, 10, 119–30.

———. 1997. *Nansen: The explorer as hero.* Duckworth, London.

Jackson, D. D. 1997. "A ship's gallant attempt to solve the 'Northern mystery.'" *Smithsonian,* 27, 12, 86–98.

Jackson, L. 1988. "Ice island an ideal platform." *Canadian Geographic,* 108, 6, 38–49.

Jones, G. 1986. *The Norse Atlantic saga.* Oxford: Oxford University Press.

Kane, E. K. 1853. "Access to an open polar sea along a North American meridian." *American Geographical and Statistical Society Bulletin,* I, 85–102.

———. 1854. *The U.S. Grinnell expedition in search of Sir John Franklin: A personal narrative.* Harper and Bros., New York.

———. 1856. *Arctic explorations: The second Grinnell expedition in search of Sir John Franklin,* 1853, '54, '55, vols. 1 and 2. Childs and Peterson, Philadelphia.

Kenyon, W. A. 1975. *Tokens of possession: The northern voyages of Martin Frobisher.* Royal Ontario Museum, Toronto.

Kirwan, L. P. 1959. *A history of polar exploration.* Norton, New York.

Kish, G. 1973. *North-east passage: Adolf Erik Nordenskiöld, his life and times.* Nico Israel, Amsterdam.

Kuralt, C. 1968. *To the top of the world: The adventures and misadventures of the Plaisted polar expedition, March 28–May 4, 1967.* Holt, Rinehart and Winston, New York.

Lamb, H. H. 1982. *Climate, history and the modern world.* London: Methuen.

Leslie, A. 1879. *The Arctic voyages of Adolf Erik Nordenskiöld.* Macmillan, London.

Levi, B. G. 1998. Search and discovery. *Physics Today,* 51, 11, 17–19.

Liljequist, G. H. 1960. "Did the *Josephine Ford* reach the North Pole?" *Interavia,* 5, 589–91.

Loomis, C. C. 1971. *Weird and tragic shores: The story of Charles Francis Hall, explorer.* Knopf, New York.

Lopez, B. 1986. *Arctic dreams: Imagination and dreams in a northern landscape.* Scribner, New York.

Lucas, F. W. 1898. *The annals of the voyages of the brothers Nicolò and Antonio Zeno.* Henry Stevens and Styles, London.

Lyon, G. F. 1824. *The private journal of Captain G. F. Lyon of H.M.S. Hecla.* John Murray, London.

Magnusson, M., and H. Pálsson. 1965. *The Vinland sagas: The Norse discovery of America.* Penguin, Harmondsworth.

Maloney, E. S. 1978. *Dutton's navigation and piloting* (13th edition). Naval Institute Press, Annapolis.

Markham, A. H. 1878. *The great frozen sea: A personal narrative of the voyage of the "Alert" during the Arctic expedition of 1875–6.* Dalby, Isbister and Company, London.

———, ed. 1880. *The voyages and works of John Davis.* Hakluyt Society, London, no. 59.

———, ed. 1881. *The voyages of William Baffin.* Hakluyt Society, London, no. 63.

Maury, M. F. 1859. *The physical geography of the sea.* Harper and Brothers, New York.

McFee, W. 1928. *The life of Sir Martin Frobisher.* Harper and Brothers, New York.

Mercator, G. 1569. *Map of the world.* Reprinted in the form of an atlas by the Maritime Museum Prins Hendrik, Rotterdam, 1961.

McPhee, M. G., T. P. Stanton, J. H. Morison, and D. G. Martinson. 1998. "Freshening of the upper ocean in the Arctic: Is perennial sea ice disappearing?" *Geophysical Research Letters,* 25, 1729–32.

M'Clintock, F. L. 1859. *The voyage of the* Fox *in the Arctic seas: A narrative of the fate of Sir John Franklin and his companions.* John Murray, London.

Mill, H. R. 1951. *An autobiography.* Longman, Green, London.

Mirsky, J. 1948. *To the Arctic: The story of northern exploration from earliest times to the present.* Knopf, New York.

———. 1954. *Elisha Kent Kane and the seafaring frontier.* Little, Brown, Boston.

Momatiuk, Y., and J. Eastcott. 1999. "Nanavut: Our land." *Native Peoples,* spring issue.

Montague, R. 1971. *Oceans, poles and airmen.* Random House, New York.

Morison, S. E. 1971. *The European discovery of America: The northern voyages,* A.D. *500–1600.* Oxford University Press, New York.

Mowat, F. 1967. *The polar passion: The quest for the North Pole.* Little, Brown, New York.

Nansen, F. 1890. *First crossing of Greenland,* vols. I and II. Longmans and Company, London.

———. 1898. *Farthest north: Being the record of a voyage of exploration of the ship* Fram, *1893–96, and of a fifteen months' sleigh journey by Dr. Nansen and Lieut. Johansen,* vols. I and II. Harper and Brothers, New York.

———. 1911. *In northern mists: Arctic exploration in early times.* 2 vols. New York: Frederick A. Stokes.

Nordenskiöld, N.A.E. 1881. *The voyage of the Vega around Asia and Europe, with a historical view of previous journeys along the north coast of the old world*, vols. I and II. Macmillan, London.

Oleson, T. J. 1963. *Early voyages and northern approaches: 1000–1632*. McClelland and Stewart, Toronto.

Parkinson, C. L., J. G. Comiso, H. J. Zwally, D. J. Cavalieri, P. Gloerson, and W. J. Campell. 1987. *Arctic sea ice, 1973–1976: Satellite passive-microwave observations*. National Aeronautics and Space Administration, Washington, DC.

Parry, W. E. 1821. *Journal of a voyage for the discovery of a North-West Passage from the Atlantic to the Pacific; performed in the years 1819–20*. John Murray, London.

———. 1824. *Journal of a second voyage for the discovery of a North-West Passage from the Atlantic to the Pacific; performed in the years 1821–22–23*. John Murray, London.

Paulson, C. A., and D. L. Bell. 1975. "Meteorological observations during the AIDJEX main experiment." *AIDJEX Bulletin*, 28, 1–9.

Payne, B. 1995. "The crunch to the Pole: Cruising to the North Pole on a nuclear-powered Russian icebreaker." *Condé Nast Traveler*, January, 86–93, 173–75.

Pearce, F. 2007. *With speed and violence: Why scientists fear tipping points in climate change*. Beacon Press, Boston.

Peary, R. E. 1898. *Northward over the great ice: A narrative of life and work along the shores and upon the interior ice-cap of northern Greenland in the years 1886 and 1891–1897*, vols. I and II. Methuen, New York.

———. 1907. *Nearest the Pole: A narrative of the polar expedition of the Peary Arctic Club in the S.S. Roosevelt, 1905–1906*. Hutchinson and Company, London.

———. 1910. *The North Pole: Its discovery in 1909 under the auspices of the Peary Arctic Club*. Frederick A. Stokes, New York.

Petermann, A. 1852. *The search for Franklin: A suggestion submitted to the British public*. Longman, Brown, Green; and Longmans, London.

———. 1869. *Petermanns mittheilungen Ergänzungsheft*, no. 26.

Plaisted, R. 1968. "How I reached the North Pole on a snowmobile." *Popular Science*, September, 55–59, 200, 204–06.

Powys, L. 1928. *Henry Hudson*. Harper and Brothers, New York.

Rawlins, D. 1973. *Peary at the North Pole: Fact or fiction?* Robert B. Luce, Washington, DC.

Roberts, D. 1982. *Great exploration hoaxes*. Sierra Club Books, San Francisco.

Rodahl, K. 1953. *North: The nature and drama of the polar world*. Harper and Brothers, New York.

Ronne, F. 1979. *Antarctica, my destiny*. Hastings House, New York.

Sale, R., and E. Potopov. 2010. *The scramble for the Arctic: Ownership, exploitation and conflict in the Far North*. Frances Lincoln, London.

Schlee, S. 1973. *The edge of an unfamiliar world: A history of oceanography*. Dutton, New York.

Schneider, D. 1995. "Attached to the Pole." *Scientific American*, 273, 5, 14.

Selmer, C., ed. 1959. *Navigatio Sancti Brendanis Abbatis.* University of Notre Dame Press, South Bend, IN.

Severin, T. 1978. *The Brendan voyage.* Hutchinson, London.

Shammas, C. 1975. "The 'invisible merchant' and property rights: The misadventures of an Elizabethan joint stock company." *Business History (Great Britain),* 17, 2, 95–108.

Skeats, W. W. 1894. *The complete works of Geoffrey Chaucer.* Vol. III: *The house of fame, the legend of the good woman, and the treatise on the astrolabe.* Oxford University Press, Oxford.

Smith, D. C. 1961. *By the seat of my pants.* Little, Brown, Boston.

Sörensen, J. 1932. *The saga of Fridtjof Nansen.* Norton, New York.

Stafford, E. P. 1988. "Descendants of the expeditions." *National Geographic,* 174, 3, 414–29.

Stefansson, V. 1938. *The three voyages of Martin Frobisher in search of a passage to Cathay and India by the north-west, A.D. 1576–8.* Argonaut Press, London.

———. 1940. *Ultima Thule: Further mysteries of the Arctic.* Macmillan, New York.

Steger, W. 1987. *North to the Pole.* Times Books, New York.

Sverdrup, O. N. 1903. "The Norwegian polar expedition in the *Fram,* 1898–1902." *Geographical Journal,* 22, 38–56.

Swedish Society for Anthropology and Geography, ed. 1930. *Andrée's story: The complete record of his polar flight.* Viking Press, New York.

Sykes, E. 1969. *Nicholas of Lynn: The explorer of the Arctic, 1330 to 1390.* Markham House Press, London.

Thomas, L. 1961. *Sir Hubert Wilkins: His world of adventure.* McGraw-Hill, New York.

Thomson, K. S. 1988. "Anatomy of the extinction debate." *American Scientist,* 76, 59–61.

Tierney, J. 1998. "Explornography: The vicarious thrill of exploring when there's nothing left to explore." *New York Times Magazine,* 26 July, 18–23, 33–34, 46–49.

Tucker, W., and D. Gate. 1996. *The 1994 Arctic Ocean Section: The first major scientific crossing of the Arctic Ocean* (Special Report 96–23). U.S. Army Cold Regions Research and Engineering Laboratory, Hanover, NH.

Victor, P.-E. 1963. *Man and the conquest of the Poles.* Simon and Schuster, New York.

Vowinckel, E. S., and S. Orvig. 1970. The climate of the North Polar Basin. In E. Orvig (ed.), *Climates of the polar regions,* Elsevier, Amsterdam.

Walker, G. 1998. "On thin ice." *New Scientist,* 159, 2153, 33–37.

Washburn, B. 1958. "Doctor Cook and Mount McKinley." *American Alpine Journal,* II, 1–30.

Whitaker, I. 1982. "The problem of Pytheas' Thule." *Classical Journal,* 77, 2. 148–164.

Whitehouse, J. H. editor. 1930. *Nansen: A book of homage.* Hodder and Stoughton, London.

Wilkins, G. H. 1928. *Flying the Arctic.* Putnam, New York.

———. 1931. *Under the North Pole: The Wilkins-Ellsworth submarine expedition.* Brewer, Warren, and Putnam, New York.

Willan, T. S. 1956. *The early history of the Russia Company, 1553–1602.* Manchester University Press, Manchester.

Williamson, J. A. 1962. *The Cabot voyages and Bristol discovery under Henry VII.* Cambridge University Press, Cambridge.

Wright, J. K. 1953. "The open polar sea." *Geographical Review*, 43, 338–65.

Zellen, B. S. 2009. *Arctic doom, Arctic boom: The geopolitics of climate change in the Arctic.* ABC-Clio, Santa Barbara, Denver, Oxford.

ONLINE SOURCES

Several online sources are devoted to climate change and provide a constant stream of scientific information about the Arctic. Some of the best:

http://www.climatecentral.org/topics

http://www.climateprogress.org

http://www.realclimate.org

In addition, practically no day passes without http://www.sciencedaily.com (a general science source) describing the results of a new climate science research project. Any of the government agencies and other agencies involved, such as the National Oceanic and Atmospheric Administration (NOAA) and the U.S. Snow and Ice Data Center, can be contacted online.

INDEX

Page numbers in italics refer to illustrations.